In
Search
of
Enemies

A CIA Story

John Stockwell

Former Chief, CIA Angola Task Force

W · W · NORTON & COMPANY

New York · London

In
Search
of
Enemies

A CIA STORY

W. W. Norton & Company, Inc., 500 Fifth Avenue, New York, NY 10110
W. W. Norton & Company Ltd, 10 Coptic Street, London WC1A 1PU

Printed in the United States of America.

ISBN 0-393-00926-2

4 5 6 7 8 9 0

In memory of TUBRAXEY/I

Contents

Author's Note

In December 1976 I advised my boss in the CIA's Africa Division of my intention to resign. For his own reasons, he urged me to take several months leave to reconsider. Making it clear I would not change my mind, I accepted his offer of several more pay checks and took three months sick leave.

I did not tell anyone I planned to write a book. In fact, I had no great confidence in my ability to write. I had been an operations officer—an activist—for the past dozen years in the CIA.

What about the oath of secrecy I signed when I joined the CIA in 1964? I cannot be bound by it for four reasons: First, my oath was illegally, fraudulently obtained. My CIA recruiters lied to me about the clandestine services as they swore me in. They insisted the CIA functioned to gather intelligence. It did not kill, use drugs, or damage people's lives, they assured me. These lies were perpetuated in the following year of training courses. It was not until the disclosures of the Church and Pike Committees in 1975 that I learned the full, shocking truth about my employers.

I do not mean to suggest that I was a puritan or out of step with the moral norms of modern times; nor had I been squeamish about my CIA activities. To the contrary, I had participated in operations which stretched the boundaries of anyone's conscience. But the congressional committees disclosed CIA activities which had previously been concealed, which I could not rationalize.

The disclosures about the plot to poison Patrice Lumumba struck me personally in two ways. First, men I had worked with had been involved. Beyond that, Lumumba had been baptized into the Methodist Church in 1937, the same year I was baptized a Presbyterian. He had attended a Methodist mission school at Wembo Nyama in the Kasai Province of the Belgian Congo (Zaire), while I attended the Presbyterian school in Lubondai in the same province. The two church communities overlapped. My parents sometimes drove to Wembo Nyama to buy rice for our schools. American Methodist children were my classmates in Lubondai. Lumumba was not, in 1961, the Methodists' favorite son, but he was a member of the missionary community in which my parents had spent most of their adult lives, and in which I grew up.

There were other disclosures which appalled me: kinky, slightly depraved, drug/sex experiments involving unwitting Americans, who were secretly filmed by the CIA for later viewing by pseudo-scientists of the CIA's Technical Services Division.

For years I had defended the CIA to my parents and to our friends. "Take it from me, a CIA insider," I had always sworn, "the CIA simply does not assassinate or use drugs . . ."

But worse was to come. A few short months after the CIA's shameful performance in Vietnam, of which I was part, I was assigned to a managerial position in the CIA's covert Angola program. Under the leadership of the CIA director we lied to Congress and to the 40 Committee, which supervised the CIA's Angola program. We entered into joint activities with South Africa. And we actively propagandized the American public, with cruel results—Americans, misguided by our agents' propaganda, went to fight in Angola in suicidal circumstances. One died, leaving a widow and four children behind. Our secrecy was designed to keep the American public and press from knowing what we were doing—we fully expected an outcry should they find us out.

The CIA's oath of secrecy has been desecrated in recent years, not by authors—Philip Agee, Joe Smith, Victor Marchetti, and Frank Snepp—but by the CIA directors who led the CIA into scandalous, absurd operations. At best, the oath was used to protect those directors from exposure by their underlings, although the directors themselves freely leaked information to further their operational or political ploys.

Their cynicism about the oath, and their arrogance toward the United States' constitutional process, were exposed in 1977, when former director Richard Helms was convicted of perjury for lying to a Senate committee about an operation in Chile. Helms plea-bargained a light sentence—the prosecutors were allegedly apprehensive that in his trial many secrets would be revealed, blowing operations and embarrassing establishment figures. After receiving a suspended sentence, Helms stood with his attorney before television cameras, while the latter gloated that Helms would wear the conviction as a "badge of honor." Helms was proud of having lied to the Senate to protect a questionable CIA operation, but to protect his own person, secrets would have been exposed.

Faced with a similar choice in the Angolan program—my loyalty to the CIA or my responsibilities to the United States' Constitution —I chose the latter. The CIA's oaths and honor codes must never take precedence over allegiance to our country. That is my second reason for disregarding the oath.

Even with those two reasons, I would not have undertaken to expose the clandestine services if I felt they were essential to our national security. I am persuaded they are not. That is what this book is about.

In discussing our foreign intelligence organ, we consistently confuse two very different offices, referring to both as "CIA." The one, technically called the Central Intelligence Agency's Deputy Directorate of Information, fulfills the mission outlined in the National Security Act of 1947, of centralizing all of the raw intelligence available to our government, collating it, analyzing it for meaning and importance, and relaying finished reports to the appropriate offices. Had such an office existed in 1941 we would have been forewarned of Pearl Harbor. The DDI is overt—its employees are openly "CIA" to friends, relatives, neighbors, and creditors; it is passive; and it is benign, without aggressive activity which can harm anyone.

Otherwise, we say "CIA" meaning the clandestine services of the

Deputy Directorate of Operations. This organization of about 4,500 employees is also housed in the CIA headquarters building in Langley, Virginia. Anything but benign, its operatives have for thirty years recruited agents (spies) and engineered covert action operations in virtually every corner of the globe.

I was a field case officer of the clandestine services, and by December 1976, when I announced my resignation, I was persuaded that at the very least those services needed a major reform.

Before I decided to resign and write a book I considered the options for working within the CIA for reforms. The prospects were not encouraging. The isolation of the intelligence business provides management with extraordinary leverage over the rank and file. While the CIA benevolently protected and supported officers who had been rendered ineffective by life's tragedies, it had little tolerance of the outspoken individual, the reformist. An officer could play the game and rise, or keep his peace and have security, or he could resign. I had, through the years made positive recommendations for reform both verbally and in writing, to my Africa Division bosses and on occasion to Colby himself, without result. The inspector general's office was competent to handle petty problems, but as an instrument of the director's managerial system, it could not address matters of reform. And I had found the "club" of CIA managers arrogantly resistant to criticism of their own ranks—when I spoke out about the most flagrant mismanagement that I knew about which occurred during the evacuation of Vietnam, I was politely and gently admonished. The culprit was given a position of authority, vindicated by the support of his colleagues, and I was informed I had better keep my peace. Only in the forum of public debate, outside the CIA, could effective leverage be had to correct the agency's wrongs.

After resigning I testified for five days to Senate committees, giving them full details about such agency activities as are covered in this book. Had I been reassured that they would take effective corrective action, I would have considered abandoning my own plans to write. Unfortunately, the Senate intelligence committees in Washington are unable to dominate and discipline the agency. Some senators even seem dedicated to covering up its abuses. Once again, I concluded that only an informed American public can bring effective pressure to bear on the CIA.

Others had reached the same conclusion. Philip Agee used his book, *Inside the Company: A CIA Diary,* as a sword to slash at the agency, to put it out of business in Latin America. Deeply offended by the CIA's clandestine activities, Agee attacked individual operations and agents, publishing every name he could remember. Although he made an effort to explain how and why he became disillusioned, he did not illuminate the CIA "mind." Marchetti and Snepp contributed valuable information to the public's knowledge of the CIA. *The CIA and the Cult of Intelligence* includes a vast store of information about the agency, drawn from Marchetti's experience in the DDI and in the office of the director of central intelligence. Snepp, for six years an analyst in the CIA's Saigon station, chronicles the intelligence failure and betrayals of the CIA evacuation of South Vietnam in April 1975.

My objective in writing this book is to give the American public a candid glimpse inside the clandestine mind, behind the last veils of secrecy. The vehicle I chose is the Angola paramilitary program of 1975–1976. The anecdotes I relate all happened as described. Dates and details are drawn from the public record and from voluminous notes I took during the Angola operation. In most cases there were other witnesses and often enough secret files to corroborate them. However, for reasons of security, I was not able to interview key individuals or return to the CIA for further research as I wrote. I urge the CIA to supplement my observations by opening its Angola files—the official files as well as the abundant "soft" files we kept—so the public can have the fullest, most detailed truth.

Our libel laws restrict an author's freedom to relate much of human foible. Nevertheless I have managed to include enough anecdotes to give the reader a full taste of the things we did, the people we were. But this is not so much a story of individual eccentricities and strange behavior, though I mention some. I have no desire to expose or hurt individuals and I reject Agee's approach. As a case officer for twelve years I was both victim and villain in CIA operations. In both roles I was keenly sympathetic for the people we ensnarled in our activities. Perhaps they are responsible according to the principles of Nuremburg and Watergate—which judged lesser employees individually responsible and put them in jail—but I prefer to address the issues at a broader level. Since my resignation I have revealed no covert CIA employee or agent's name, and I stonewalled the Senate and FBI on that subject when they questioned me.

My sympathy does not extend to the CIA managers who led the CIA to such depths, but in this book I have used actual names only for such managers as had previously been declared as "CIA": Director William Colby; Deputy Director of Operations William Nelson; Bill Welles, who replaced Nelson; and Africa Division Chief James Potts. And myself. The other names of CIA personnel—Carl Bantam, Victor St. Martin, Paul Foster, et al.—are pseudonyms which I invented. (Any resemblance those names might have to the true names of individuals within and without the CIA is purely coincidental.) In the field, Holden Roberto and Jonas Savimbi were well known to be our allies. Bob Denard and Colonel Santos y Castro were also public figures, widely known to be involved on the side of Roberto, Savimbi, and the CIA. "Timothé Makala" is a name I invented (makala means "charcoal" in the Bantu dialect, Tshiluba). On occasion I used CIA cryptonyms, but in most cases they, too, have been altered to protect the individuals from any conceivable exposure.

On April 10, 1977, after my resignation was final, I published an open letter to CIA Director Stansfield Turner in the Outlook section of the *Washington Post.* It outlined the reasons for my disillusionment. (The letter is reprinted in the Appendix of this book.) Director Turner subsequently initiated a house-cleaning of the clandestine services, proposing to fire four hundred people, to make the clandestine services "lean and efficient." In December 1977 Turner admitted to David Binder of the *New York Times* that this housecleaning had been triggered by my letter.

In January 1978, President Carter announced a reorganization of the intelligence community, which in fact has the effect of strengthening the CIA; and Admiral Turner has reached an understanding with Congress (of which I am skeptical—the Congress has neither the will nor the means to control the CIA). Now Turner has intensified his campaign for tighter controls over CIA employees. He is lobbying vigorously for legislation that would jail anyone who threatens the CIA by disclosing its secrets. It makes him fighting mad, he blusters, when anyone leaks classified information. Such people are violating the "code of intelligence," he charges. It is the CIA's "unequivocal right" to censor all publications by CIA people, he claims. "Why do Americans automatically presume the worst of their public servants?" he asks—a remarkable question in the wake of Watergate, FBI, and CIA revelations.

Director Turner and President Carter have it backwards. It is the American people's *unequivocal right* to know what their leaders are doing in America's name and with our tax dollars. My third reason.

For my fourth reason, I reclaim my constitutional right of freedom of speech. The Constitution of the United States does not read that all citizens shall have freedom of speech except those that have signed CIA oaths. Until there is such an amendment of the Constitution, ratified by the appropriate number of states, the Marchetti ruling rests as bad law, an unfortunate relic of the Nixon administration's bullishness. If the CIA and its "secrets game" cannot live with our fundamental constitutional rights, there can be no question, the Constitution must prevail.

But if the present administration has its way, stories such as this one would be suppressed and covered up. And the author would be punished. I invite the reader to judge which is more important: CIA misadventures such as this one, or our fundamental right to know the truth about our public servants' activities and to keep them honest?

Acknowledgments

This was a difficult book to write, and without the encouragement and support of numerous friends, it would never have been completed. I have not been motivated by money, and I have lost contact with CIA friends and colleagues with whom I shared many adventures. On the other hand, I have made new friends—journalists, writers, editors, television executives, legislators, and concerned American citizens—and the experience has certainly been more rewarding in terms of personal growth than staying within the small, closed world of the CIA would have been.

Many who helped me would prefer to remain anonymous. Their satisfaction will derive from seeing this story in print. They already know how much I appreciate their help. My special thanks go to Saul Landau, Ralph Stavins, Haskell Wexler, Patty Stern, and Zack Krieger for their work on our film, *Whistleblower*. Peter Weiss gave generously of his time and legal advice. John Shattuck of the ACLU gave advice regarding my right to publish this book, and represented me when I testified to the Senate committees. Dr. John Marcum, America's leading authority on the Angolan revolution, was especially helpful. Several reporters and three television producers have been supportive and scrupulously honest in dealing with me. Working with the staff of W. W. Norton has been a pleasure.

Although I no longer believe in the CIA's clandestine services, I hasten to add that many of its staff are people of high integrity. Some have had different experiences and have reached different conclusions about the CIA. Others have told me that they agree with my observations, but for personal reasons cannot resign. I do not offer advice, but I do wish for all of them a wider world.

Finally, I am most grateful to my parents and children for their enthusiastic support, and to B. J. McCallum, who, literally, made the effort possible, with her indulgence and indirect financial support.

Prologue

The Kissinger Grunt

December 2, 1975.

At 2:00 P.M. there was to be a meeting of the Interagency Working Group on the third floor, "C" corridor, of the Central Intelligence Agency at Langley, Virginia. The civil war in Angola was going badly for our allies, and the CIA had formally recommended a major escalation—the introduction of American military advisors—to the secretary of state, Henry Kissinger. The working group, a subsidiary of the 40 Committee, itself a subsidiary of the National Security Council, was meeting to hear Henry Kissinger's decision.

These meetings, which were happening every week or so, required a lot of preparation. I had been at it since 7:00 A.M., conferring with my boss, Jim Potts, the Africa Division chief, drafting cables to the field, slipping in and out of meetings with logistics officers, paramilitary officers, communications and reports personnel. Lunch was a seventy-five–cent sandwich, dispensed from a machine and eaten hastily between phone calls.

At 1:45 I hurried down to the Angola operations center where the four-by-five-foot map of Angola was propped against a wall, and took notes as Pat, my intelligence assistant, briefed me on the current tactical situation inside Angola. She had the information from the SOG* situation room across the building. It would have been more efficient for the SOG officer to brief me personally but he held a grudge. I had reprimanded him in Vietnam for being drunk when we were attempting to evacuate our upcountry post during a lull in the fighting. In our small world we preferred having Pat between us.

At 1:55 I hurried back to my office to gather my notes for the briefing I would give the Working Group, and to glance at last minute cables.

Pat and a secretary took the map down to the conference room on "C" corridor. Another assistant dropped off stacks of photocopied briefing papers, and hurried downstairs to meet the working group members as they arrived from the White House, State Department, and Pentagon. All visitors, even senior ambassadors and top advisors from the White House, were given visitor's badges and escorted every moment they were inside CIA headquarters.

I overtook Jim Potts, who was moving with slow dignity on a cane, his balance more precarious than when he used his crutches. Once a college football star, Potts had been struck down by polio in middle-age. I ducked past him into the conference room, to make sure everything was ready. The others filed in, exchanging amenities: the State Department officers in their traditional dark grey, vested suits; the lieutenant general from Defense in his air force uniform; the admiral wearing an inexpensive business suit; a colonel sporting a double-knit jacket and bright red slacks. There were eleven of us in the room. Each received a copy of the memos and reports we would discuss.

Potts nodded and I stood, facing the group. Using a pointer, I started at the top of the map and talked my way down through the battlefields bringing everyone up to date since the previous week's meeting. In the north our allies, the FNLA and the elite Zairian paracommando battalions, had been routed and were now a broken rabble. Kinshasa station had reported that the FNLA headquarters at Ambriz, on the coast north of the capital, was in a "stable state of panic." Only in the south were we holding on. The South African

*SOG (Special Operations Group), the agency's paramilitary office.

armored column had not yet met its match in the gathering Cuban army, but we knew it was only a matter of time before the much larger and better equipped Cuban force became irresistible.

Two weeks earlier, on November 14, frustrated by reverses on the battlefield, the 40 Committee had asked the CIA to outline a program which could win the Angolan war. As an interim measure, it had recommended the expenditure of the last $7 million in the CIA Contingency Reserve Fund, bringing the Angola program's budget to $31.7 million. On November 24, the CIA had presented the 40 Committee with optional plans costing an additional $30, $60, or $100 million, but with the agency's reserves expended, there were no more secret funds. Without authority to approve the larger amounts of money and unwilling to order an end to the CIA covert action program, the 40 Committee was frustrated. In honored bureaucratic fashion, it adjourned, requesting another agency recommendation, one that would outline a bare-bones proposal for keeping the conflict alive.

Today's meeting concerned that paper. It recommended not only the introduction of American advisors into the Angolan battlefields, but also more sophisticated and powerful weapons. The working group had endorsed the paper and Deputy Assistant Secretary of State for African Affairs Ed Mulcahy had taken it to Secretary Kissinger. Kissinger was, as always, preoccupied with other matters of state and his rather complicated social life. Ambassador Mulcahy had had difficulty gaining an audience, but had, finally, succeeded. We would soon know with what result.

At the outset of the program Potts had confided a desire to make the working group sessions so dull that non-CIA members would be discouraged in their supervision of "our" war. He had succeeded brilliantly. Working his way laboriously down a long agenda, he generally took three hours to cover one hour's material, while his listeners struggled with fatigue, boredom, and the labor of digesting lunch in the poorly ventilated conference room. Inevitably breathing grew heavier, heads would nod, bounce up, then nod again. I myself never dared to sleep; a colonel in a room full of general officers.*

Today, at least, there ought to be enough interest to keep them

---

*In the agency's personnel system, supergrades—GS 16's and above—compare to general officers in the military. I was a GS 14.

awake for a while; after all, we were meeting to plan a major escalation of a war. I finished my presentation and sat down.

Potts turned to Mulcahy and spoke pleasantly. "Well, Ed, what did Kissinger say?"

Mulcahy tamped his pipe and sucked on it for a few moments, apparently having trouble framing an answer. Potts watched him quietly.

Finally Mulcahy spoke, "He didn't exactly *say* anything."

"Did he read the paper?"

"Oh, yes. I took it to him myself just a few minutes before he left for Peking. I insisted he read it."

"You mean he didn't make any comment? He just read it and took off?" Potts looked baffled, exasperated.

Mulcahy nodded ruefully. "He read it. Then he grunted and walked out of his office."

"Grunted?"

"Yeah, like, unnph!" Mulcahy grunted.

"He's going to be gone ten days!" Potts scowled. "What are we supposed to do in Angola in the meantime? We have to make some decisions today!"

Mulcahy shrugged helplessly. They looked at each other.

"Well, was it a positive grunt or a negative grunt?" Potts asked.

Mulcahy studied for a moment, considering. "It was just a grunt. Like, *unnph.* I mean it didn't go up or down."

This group of somber men were supervising the country's only current war. They were gathered today to discuss steps that could affect world peace. No one was smiling.

Mulcahy grunted again, emphasizing a flat sound. Down the table someone else tried it, experimenting with the sound of a positive grunt, then a negative one, his voice rising, then falling. Others attempted it while Potts and Mulcahy watched.

"Well," Potts said. "Do we proceed with the advisors?"

Mulcahy scowled and puffed on his pipe, uncomfortable in his position as Kissinger's surrogate.

"We better not," he said finally, "Kissinger just decided not to send Americans into the Sinai . . ."

Everyone nodded in agreement. Inaction was safe, and easier to correct.

The meeting proceeded and I watched, taking notes and pondering. I had been involved since the outset, as chief of the Angola task force. I had considerable knowledge of the war, and, by the time Kissinger grunted, considerable doubts. This book is about those two things: the knowledge and the doubts.

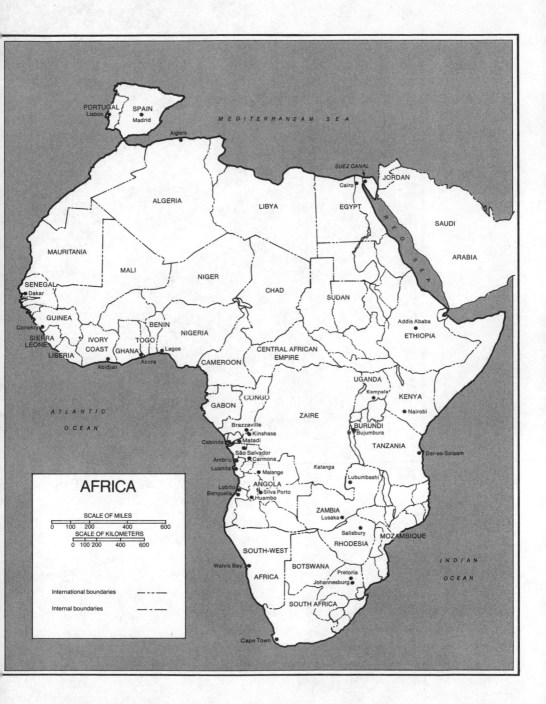

AFRICA

SCALE OF MILES

0	100 200	400	600

SCALE OF KILOMETERS

0	100 200	400	600

International boundaries — · — · —

Internal boundaries — · — · —

PORTUGAL
Lisbon
SPAIN
Madrid

MEDITERRANEAN SEA

Algiers

SUEZ CANAL

JORDAN

Cairo

ALGERIA

LIBYA

EGYPT

SAUDI

R E D   S E A

ARABIA

MAURITANIA

MALI

NIGER

CHAD

SUDAN

SENEGAL
Dakar

GUINEA
Conakry

BENIN

NIGERIA

Addis Ababa

ETHIOPIA

SIERRA
LEONE

IVORY
COAST

TOGO

GHANA

Lagos

LIBERIA

Abidjan

Accra

CAMEROON

CENTRAL AFRICAN
EMPIRE

UGANDA

Kampala

KENYA

Nairobi

ATLANTIC

OCEAN

GABON

CONGO

ZAIRE

Brazzaville
Kinshasa
Cabinda
Matadi
São Salvador
Ambriz
Carmona
Luanda
Malange

BURUNDI
Bujumbura

TANZANIA

Dar-es-Salaam

Katanga

Lubumbashi

Lobito
Benguela

ANGOLA
Silva Porto
Huambo

ZAMBIA
Lusaka

Salisbury

RHODESIA

MOZAMBIQUE

SOUTH-WEST

Walvis Bay

AFRICA

BOTSWANA

Pretoria
Johannesburg

INDIAN

OCEAN

SOUTH AFRICA

Cape Town

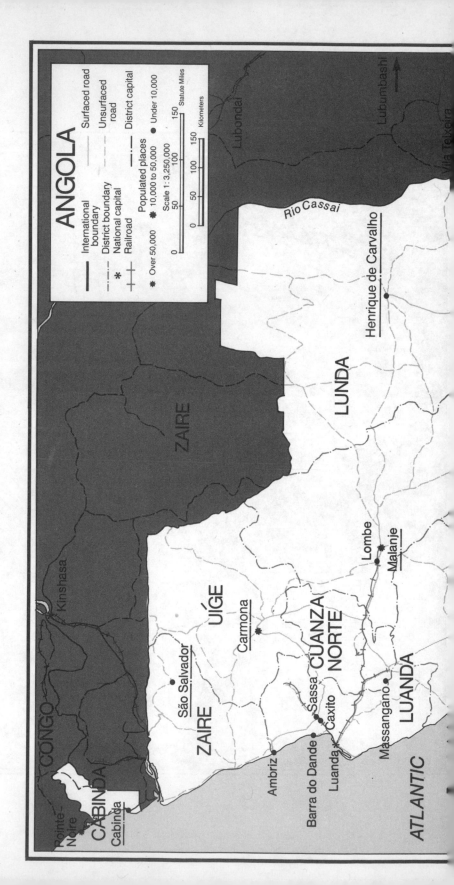

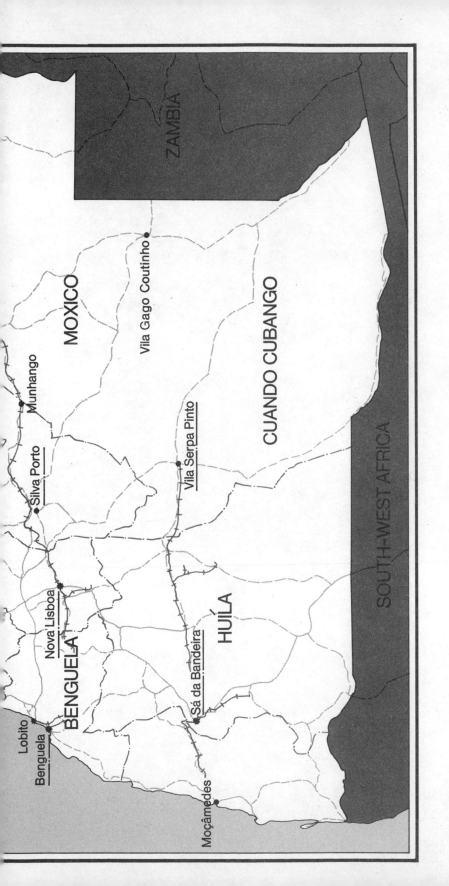

In
Search
of
Enemies

A CIA Story

1

Saigon to Washington

A Braniff jet had carried me back to Washington five months earlier, on July 30, 1975, two years to the day since my Vietnam experience had begun, when they had rushed me upcountry after a colleague's suicide. It was three months since the last helicopter had left the embassy rooftop in the final evacuation of Saigon.

My CIA dossier would show me ready for just about any assignment. I was thirty-eight years old, a GS 14 field case officer with three tours in Africa, one at headquarters, and one in Vietnam. I had been chief of the Lubumbashi base in Zaire, then chief of station in Bujumbura, the capital of Burundi on Lake Tanganyika. Back at Langley in 1972, I had served as chief of the Kenya-Uganda section, before going out to Vietnam as officer in charge of the Tay Ninh province upcountry. I had done a lot of things in the name of the CIA: recruited agents; bugged foreign embassies; run covert operations; even hired prostitutes to be used against Soviet and Chinese officials. I was, in short, an experienced, senior CIA case officer.

But where had my doubts about the CIA started? When I had

realized that my intelligence reporting during six long years in Africa had made no useful contribution? When I realized that even the "hard" target operations—the recruitment of Soviets, Chinese, and North Koreans—meant little more? In darker moments, it seemed to me that my twelve years of service had been spent in hard, sometimes nerve-racking, work that had nothing to do with the security of the United States.

But a lot of it had affected other peoples' lives. Many trusting individuals had been caught in our operational web. My first recruited agent was arrested. When I found him, "KRNEUTRON/I" was living a life of penniless indolence in a small country for which I had intelligence responsibility. His was my first recruitment, a classic, out of the training manual. He would be my eyes and ears in his country and I would solve his financial problems—we would both enjoy the camaraderie and intrigue. On my next visit I leaned on KRNEUTRON/I to produce intelligence: "Are you *sure* there is no coup plotting? If anything happens and you don't tell me *in advance* headquarters will cut my money . . . What about your cousin, the ex-president's son? Mightn't he be plotting? Maybe you'd better see him . . ."

KRNEUTRON/I saw his cousin. He and his friends *were* dissatisfied with the regime.

On my next visit the cousin was thinking of plotting something. Over six months a coup was hatched, and KRNEUTRON/I sat on the inner council.

Headquarters was delighted and authorized bonuses. We all ignored that the plotters were irresponsible youths, while the incumbent president was mature, restrained, and even pro-West. Fortunately for the country, the incumbent broke up the plot, but KRNEUTRON/I spent seven years in jail. At that time—I was twenty-nine—I sincerely believed that I was only collecting intelligence. It never occurred to me that I had fomented the plot. If it occurred to my bosses, they didn't mention it. This was the naiveté of which Graham Greene wrote in *The Quiet American,* "Innocence is a form of insanity."

Or was it in Vietnam, where CIA operations were dominated by bungling and deceit? At the end in Vietnam I had participated in an evacuation in which the CIA leaders had fled in panic, abandoning people whom we had recruited and exposed in our operations. This struck at the core of my wishful conviction that the CIA was the elite of the United States government, charged with the responsibility of protecting our country in the secret wars of a hostile world. Very little about CIA activity in Vietnam was honorable. It gnawed at my conscience. I had managed other case officers and in the end I had fled like everyone else.

But conscientious officers, whom I respected, still insisted that these experiences were misleading, that there was nothing wrong with the CIA that a good housecleaning wouldn't cure. They spoke reverently of *intelligence* and *national security* and urged me to hang on to my career and use my increasing authority to help reform the agency.

I wanted to believe them. All my life I had conformed: to a boarding school in Africa, to the Marine Corps, to the CIA. I had reveled in the challenge and sheer fun of clandestine operations, the excitement of flying off on secret missions, the thrill of finding one more way to plant a bug in a Chinese embassy, and, eventually, the gratification of supervisory authority over other case officers.

After Vietnam I had spent ten good weeks with my three teenagers, all of us starved for each other's companionship. We swam, built a canoe, camped at the beach, played tennis and chess and Monopoly and Ping-Pong, and built an addition to my parent's retirement home in the hills overlooking Lake Travis on the outskirts of Austin, Texas. In the evenings we talked, often until dawn, about their lives and mine. I hadn't known whether I wanted to go back into clandestine work. After a crunch like Vietnam. . . . Then the telephone had rung.

On the flight from Austin to Washington, I had only to flip through the newsmagazines to be reminded again of the notoriety of my employer. Two congressional committees were investigating CIA activities. During the past week alone, President Ford had apologized to the Olsson family for the death of Dr. Olsson in CIA drug experiments some years earlier; a former CIA deputy director of plans (the clandestine services) had testified that he had approved CIA contact with the Mafia to arrange the assassination of Fidel Castro; the current director, William Colby, had admitted to a twenty-year CIA practice of opening American citizens' mail. The former secretary of defense, Clark Clifford, a drafter of the National Security Act of 1947 that permitted the creation of the CIA, had recommended that covert action to be taken away from the CIA altogether. It had not been a good year for my side.

I thought back to 1964, a better year, the year I was hired. Then, the CIA had enjoyed the highest credibility, and the nation was still "continuing" President Kennedy's New Frontier. America was alive again, and I was young and restless. We would save the world from communism, the CIA and I. The agency was interested in me because I had grown up in the old Belgian Congo. My father had contracted to build a hydroelectric plant for the Presbyterian mission in the Kasai Province and my brother and I learned how to drive in the mission's five-ton truck. We were bilingual, speaking the local dialect, Tshiluba, with our African playmates. After college in the States I did a tour in a Marine Corps parachute reconnaissance company, which also interested the agency. When they first contacted me, in 1963, the CIA's paramilitary program in the Congo was in full stride.

Because of my mission background, my recruiters and I discussed the CIA's "true nature." They had been unequivocal in reassuring me—the CIA was an intelligence-gathering institution, and a benevolent one. Coups were engineered only to alter circumstances which jeopardized national security. I would be a better person through association with the CIA. My naiveté was shared by most of my forty-two classmates in our year-long training program. Our instructors hammered the message at us: the CIA was good, its mission was to make the world a better place, to save the world from communism. In 1964, I signed the secrecy agreement without hesitation, never realizing that one day it would be interpreted to mean that I had given up my freedom of speech.

My naiveté of 1964 was also shared, literally, by hundreds of journalists, publishers, university professors and administrators who succumbed to CIA recruitment, to our collective embarassment when the CIA's true nature began to surface in 1975.

One thing I thought I was sure of as I sat on the plane to Washington: the agency would not be involved in any paramilitary operations for the next decade. Not after the hard lessons of Indochina, coupled with current press disclosures. The Special Operations Group, I heard, was cutting back and transferring dozens of officers to the intelligence branches of the geographical area divisions.

It is a thirty-minute ride from Dulles Airport to the CIA head-quarters building in Langley, Virginia, ten miles from downtown Washington. Situated high over the Potomac, overlooking the George Washington Parkway, headquarters is three miles from McLean, Virginia, where CIA employees often have lunch and shop in the International Safeway. Ten minutes down the parkway is Roslyn, Virginia, where the CIA Domestic Contacts Division has its offices. The State Department, which relates closely to the CIA, is a mile beyond that, across the river.

My taxi took me through the Dolly Madison entrance, one of three gates at Langley; a guard wrote my name on a clipboard and waved us in. Dozens of employees were enjoying the sun and the campuslike grounds—walking off lunch, reading, napping on the grass. Joggers came from the basement and went into the Bureau of Public Roads grounds next door, shedding their T-shirts as they cleared the CIA gate.

It always felt good to come back. The white marble walls and columns of the gigantic foyer meant the beginnings of security, ex-clusivity. It reminded me that I was one of a small group of favored employees in the world's second largest intelligence organization,* and that while I was here I was safe from a hostile world. But how much longer? For the first time I was troubled by the CIA motto, etched boldly on the foyer wall: "Ye shall know the truth and the truth shall make you free."

The two guards who stood by a desk at the end of the foyer, waved me toward the badge office up a flight of steps on the right. I had been through this routine dozens of time; it never varied. Two women gave me my badge without asking for any identification, only glancing from my badge photograph to my face. I initialed a form.

Back in the foyer, I flashed the badge for the guards' visual inspec-tion and brushed by. They did not check the contents of my suitcase or travel bag. There were no electronic machines, codes, or recogni-tion signals. Watching 15,000 employees file in and out daily, hun-dreds every hour, each holding a badge out for inspection, had mesmerized the guards. Legend had it that people had entered the

*The KGB is by far the world's largest, the Israeli probably the best, and the Iranian and South Korean the deadliest.

building with borrowed badges, fake badges, even credit cards of the wrong color.

The 4,500 employees of the CIA clandestine services share the headquarters building with 10,000 *overt* CIA analysts and administrators. And a third of the employees of the clandestine services are also overt CIA, and come and go with the sensitive undercover officers. In fact, in numerous instances secretaries and staff employees of the clandestine services have served overseas under cover, then have been overt CIA for a tour in Washington, then returned overseas under cover. To say that this makes a mockery of the CIA's pretenses of clandestinity is an understatement.

In 1977, the CIA installed badge-checking computers which require each individual to key in an individual identification number.

The first floor of the building includes the travel offices, library, medical staff, credit union, cafeterias, and the cable secretariat. Four banks of elevators service the employees; the director has his own which runs nonstop from his penthouse offices on the seventh floor to his parking slot in the basement.

I turned left to the "blue" elevators and rode up to the third floor, where I turned right and trudged the length of "C" corridor, then left into "B" corridor, where Africa Division had its offices. The halls were bare, off-white, and the floors covered with grey green vinyl tile. Only the doors added color. They were painted bright blue, red, and yellow.

George Costello, the Africa Division chief of operations, the man who had summoned me, was in his office, an eight-by-twelve-foot cubicle with a rug, wooden desk, credenza, three chairs, and a view of the trucks and limousines in the service area of the southwest loading dock. Costello was an imposing if somewhat comical man, with a ponderous stomach, a pointed, bald head, and small round glasses. His weight was down slightly from the last time I'd seen him in May. He shook my hand warmly and I relaxed a bit. On other occasions I had known Costello to be domineering and unpleasant. He got right down to business.

"You probably guessed it has to do with Angola," he said. "Do you speak Portuguese?"

"No."

"Well, it doesn't matter. The Soviets are screwing around in Angola and the agency is supposed to stop them. We're putting together a program to support Savimbi and Roberto. This is big, the biggest thing in Africa Division since the Congo. We have $14 million, and we've already been sending some arms over by airplane. We are only sending arms to Kinshasa to replace equipment Mobutu is sending into Angola from his own stocks. The idea is to balance off the MPLA, militarily, until elections are held in October."

I listened intently, scarcely able to believe my ears. Costello was telling me we were launching another covert paramilitary operation.

He went on: "Potts and Carl Bantam are buried under stacks of IMMEDIATE cables and that's where you come in." My mind was bouncing around. Carl Bantam? He would be the new deputy division chief, the second in command. I didn't like the tie-in between myself and stacks of cables. That sounded like a paper-pushing desk job.

Costello told me the DDO* had just ordered the formation of a task force to run this program; my mind leaped ahead. I projected weeks of frenetic activity, rushing up and down the halls with IMMEDIATE and FLASH cables, with a packed suitcase behind my desk for instant travel on special missions to Africa and Europe. Or perhaps they were going to send me out to run some part of the program in the field. Over the phone Costello had mentioned travel.

The CIA's headquarters structure is geared to adjust to the world's endless crises. Overnight a sleepy little desk, perhaps occupied for years by a succession of interim junior officers from the career trainee program, becomes a bustling hub of activity for two dozen people. In 1960, a small, quiet office handling several central African countries suddenly became the Congo Task Force and then, as the Congo crisis dragged on for years, the Congo Branch. The Cuban Task Force eventually became the Cuban Operations Group. The Libyan Task Force in 1973 faded almost as quickly as it was assembled. A task force supporting a serious paramilitary program would normally have a good GS 16 at its head, with a senior GS 15 as its deputy chief, and twenty-five to one hundred people on its staff, including half a dozen senior case officers to write the cables and memos, sit in on the endless planning sessions, and undertake the numerous individual missions that inevitably arose.

*Deputy director of operations, the man in charge of all CIA covert operations; at this time Bill Nelson, who had previously been chief of East Asia.

There were two task forces, that I knew of, currently at work in the Deputy Directorate of Operations: the Portuguese, which was a major affair, responding to the continuing crisis in Portugal; and the Congo, a small unit which was coping with the Senate investigation of the CIA's paramilitary Congo operation of 1960–1965.

Obviously, I was to be one of the senior "gofers" of the Angola Task Force.

Then George sprang it on me, grinning maliciously. They were making me the *chief* of the Angola Task Force. What did I think of that?

I jerked my mind back to the conversation. Was this a joke? Now he was telling me I was going to be the chief of the task force, a GS 14 in a GS 16 job. And I was still having trouble believing the CIA would launch a paramilitary operation when it was suffering its most intense pressure from investigations and press attacks. How could the CIA get by with such a thing *now?* Were we going to lie about it? It sounded like a good way for a bunch of agency officers to go to jail! And they wanted *me* to run it?

I began pressing him with questions. What were the approvals? Was the president involved? Kissinger? The 40 Committee? Even then the CIA would be vulnerable. Other presidents had gotten us into Watergate, Vietnam, the Bay of Pigs. Even presidential approval wouldn't give the CIA much protection once Congress and the press cracked down.

Where would I stand if things went sour? Obviously, the assignment was a career breakthrough, if everything went well. If it didn't, if the operation were blown and became controversial, I could not expect to come away whole. Careers were smashed in such situations.

George developed the uncomfortable look of one who is getting in over his head. He told me that Potts, the Chief of Africa Division, was running everything, that I should check in with him and with Carl Bantam, Potts's deputy. As for himself, he, too, was troubled about the program and had decided to stay out of it as much as possible; he wasn't reading all the cable traffic. Anyway, he didn't think it would be a long assignment. All would be over by the November 11 Independence Day, when one of the three factions would inherit the country from the Portuguese. As I turned to leave, Costello came around the desk, took me by the elbow and said quietly, "John, I suggest you cover your ass. Get everything in writing, everything signed at least by Potts."

"And, congratulations, task force commander," he called after me.

2

The Angola Program

Carl Bantam, a short, greying man, sat upright at his desk working on a cable with a large black fountain pen. He didn't notice when I entered, so I reached back and rapped on the door three times. His head came up slowly. I found myself under the curious gaze of intelligent grey eyes.

"Sir, I'm John Stockwell . . . just got in from Texas . . ." My travel bag was still slung over my shoulder. I had no idea how involved Bantam was in the Angola Task Force; if he even knew I was coming.

"John!" he said pleasantly, coming around his desk to shake my hand, "Sit down." He swung the door shut without breaking eye contact. I had heard tales about Bantam two years before, when he was chief of station, Djakarta, and had had personal problems, while driving his staff hard. Now as he focused on me his eyes were clear and steady.

After a polite inquiry about my leave, he asked me for details about the fall of Vietnam. Bantam had served in Saigon as a young officer fifteen years before, and he knew all the senior officers who had been there at the end.

"Well, disgrace is too mild a word," I said. "Here's an example. In one military region the CIA chief panicked at reports that communist forces were approaching the city, and evacuated his American staff. The country had been breaking up for weeks but he had made no preparations for evacuation. He left behind secret files including the names of CIA agents, and he abandoned people, property, and personal belongings. He hadn't ordered sufficient funds to pay local employees the money which they were due and which they could have used to buy boat tickets to Saigon. One helicopter was brought in to evacuate the last six Americans. To ensure there was no difficulty boarding the chopper, he told his local employees that C-130s were arriving to pick them up on the near side of the runway. Meanwhile he and the other Americans met the chopper on the other side, firing weapons over the heads of Vietnamese case officers who had followed them, to clear the chopper for take off. *Three weeks later* the first communist troops entered the city! That's how good our intelligence was. This regional chief was given a hero's welcome in Saigon and one of the top three positions in the station, where he stayed until the final evacuation."

Such talk was dangerous, I knew. Bantam might quote me to senior East Asia Division officers. Certainly he was closer to them than to me. Perhaps one of them would be sitting on a promotion panel. I would be passed over. Some assignment I wanted would mysteriously be cancelled. A friend passing through Texas had told me that all of the senior officers from Vietnam had been given important new assignments by the director. The Saigon chief of station, Tom Polgar, was already chief of the huge Mexico City station.

Nothing could be done about the Saigon supergrades, at least not from within the CIA.* Despite the existence of an inspector general the CIA had no effective review or courts martial system. All disciplinary problems were handled within the chain of a command structure at whose top was a clique of men who had served together for a quarter of a century, insulated from outside scrutiny by the shields of clandestinity. Though the inspector general might take effective action in a clear case of malfeasance, it was virtually unheard of for an "in" supergrade to suffer anything resembling censure, no matter

*At this time, Frank Snepp was making no secret of the fact that he was writing a book about the last month in Saigon. See *Decent Interval* (New York: Random House, 1977).

how drunken, despotic, inept, or corrupt his management of a field station was. An aggressive director, brought in from outside the agency, might loosen the grip of this clique, as Admiral Turner has attempted to do, but probably not for long. The clandestinity of intelligence organizations breeds a certain arrogant softness even more than other government bureaucracies. Certainly, right after Vietnam, the incumbent CIA director, William Colby, would never disrupt the system. He was himself a charter member of the clique, having risen from the OSS, through the clandestine services in Europe and East Asia Divisions. The senior officers who had managed Saigon station were his colleagues. Any complaint to the inspector general would ultimately be delivered to the director and the other ruling supergrades would impose their subtle retribution on the whistleblower for the rest of his career.

Bantam seemed wistfully sympathetic. He kept the conversation going, giving me frank accounts of his personal experiences with Colby long before he was a public figure and with Bill Nelson, the current deputy director of operations (DDO).

One thing became clear: Carl was as frustrated over the U.S. government's losing adventures in Southeast Asia as I was. "How do you think I feel?" he asked. "Eighteen years of my life invested in losing wars in Southeast Asia." For the past two decades he had struggled in four Asian posts and three paramilitary wars, to stop the spread of communism. He had seen our nation defeated, the values of the Cold War which had guided his struggle repudiated, and the agency exposed and attacked. Rising to the level of GS 17 (equivalent to a two-star general in the military) he had been trampled by the politics, deceits, and betrayals of the United States' efforts in Southeast Asia. He had raised his family, lost his wife, conquered his personal problems, and kept his career intact. Where once his personality and energies were fired by the righteous indignations of the Cold War; now he seemed only scarred, lonesome, and pitiable.

"So now we're going to start up in Africa?" I asked him.

Once again he was candid, confessing that he too had been incredulous when he learned of the Angola program. For sure, in his view, sooner or later the Senate would put together yet another committee and tear the program apart, probably on television. And the bloody Soviets knew it. They would push us hard, and get the CIA and the United States as far out on a limb as possible.

"We may very well preside over the death of the CIA." he said bitterly.

Carl insisted that it was Kissinger who was pushing the agency into the covert operation in Angola. Kissinger saw the Angolan conflict solely in terms of global politics and was determined the Soviets should not be permitted to make a move in any remote part of the world without being confronted militarily by the United States.* Superficially, his opposition to the Soviet presence was being rationalized in terms of Angola's strategic location on the South Atlantic, near the shipping lanes of the giant tankers which bring oil from the Middle East around the horn of Africa to the United States. This argument was not profound. Soviet bases in Somalia had much better control of our shipping lanes, and any military move by the Soviets against our oil supplies would trigger a reaction so vigorous that a Soviet base in Angola would be a trivial factor. In fact, Angola had little plausible importance to American national security and little economic importance beyond the *robusta* coffee it sold to American markets and the relatively small amounts of petroleum Gulf Oil pumped from the Cabindan fields.

No. Uncomfortable with recent historic events, and frustrated by our humiliation in Vietnam, Kissinger was seeking opportunities to challenge the Soviets. Conspicuously, he had overruled his advisors and refused to seek diplomatic solutions in Angola. The question was, would the American people, so recently traumatized by Vietnam, tolerate even a modest involvement in another remote, confusing, Third World civil war? Carl Bantam and I did not think so.

The United States' troubled relations with Zaire also facilitated Kissinger's desire to act in Angola. Both Zaire and Zambia feared the prospect of a Soviet-backed government on their flanks, controlling the Benguela railroad. President Mobutu was especially afraid of the Soviets. Twice since 1960 he had broken relations with the Soviet Union, and although relations were reestablished each time, he had more recently been courting the Chinese at the expense of both the Soviets and the Americans. In the spring of 1975, Zaire's internal problems had mounted until Mobutu's regime was threatened by discontent. After fifteen years, Zairian agriculture had never

---

*This is also the rationale for the Angola operation which Colby gives in *Honorable Men* (New York: Simon and Schuster, 1978), pp. 439–40.

returned to preindependence levels although the population had doubled. Despite the investment of $700 million in Zaire by Western institutions, the economy was stagnant, in part owing to the conspicuous arrogance and corruption of the governing elite. And then, in 1975, world copper prices had plummeted, stripping the economy of essential hard income. At the same time the fighting in Angola had closed the Benguela railroad, forcing Zaire to export its copper via Zambia, Rhodesia, and South Africa.

Desperately seeking a scapegoat, Mobutu had turned on the United States, accusing its Kinshasa embassy of fomenting a coup against him. In June 1975, he expelled the American ambassador and arrested most of the CIA's Zairian agents, placing some of them under death sentences. Now, as his worries deepened with the defeat of the FNLA in Luanda, the State Department was eager to regain Mobutu's good favor by supporting his Angolan policies.

Bantam told me Colby had advised the National Security Council the CIA would have to spend $100 million to be sure of winning in Angola, and a $100-million program would be too big to keep a secret. This raised the question of the agency's own security. In the Bay of Pigs and Chile and the *Operation Mongoose* war against Castro, former U.S. presidents and their advisors had ordered the CIA into action, but the agency had taken the brunt of criticism when the operations were blown. Why didn't Colby keep the CIA out of Angola? I asked. Bantam laughed derisively, knowing Colby far better than I. Colby was the original good soldier. Whatever Kissinger or the president wanted, whether a paramilitary program in Angola or a terrorist program in Vietnam, he would do his best to oblige.

Besides, Bantam noted, the agency had some protection. According to the laws governing the CIA, President Ford had submitted his findings on Angola to the Senate, and Colby was briefing the appropriate committees.*

---

*The Central Intelligence Agency's authority to run covert operations was for twenty-seven years solely dependent on a vague phrase in the National Security Act of 1947 which read: "to perform such other functions and duties related to intelligence affecting the national security as the National Security Council may from time to time direct." In 1975 Clark Clifford testified that the drafters of this act intended only to give the president authority to undertake operations in the rare instances that the national security was truly threatened. In fact, the CIA used the vaguely

I kept expecting Bantam to withdraw into the sanctuary of his senior rank, but he seemed to feel close to me, as though we had been friends for a long time.

He looked at me absently.

"I tried to retire in June, when I came back from Djakarta," he said finally. "That's how tired I was of this sort of thing."

"What happened?"

"They turned me down."

"But at fifty you can retire whenever you want to."

"I'm only forty-seven," he said wryly.

Ouch, I thought. Open mouth and insert foot! He *looked* more like fifty-five.

"I started young," he said, letting me off the hook. We both knew that the intelligence business uses case officers harshly, burning them out at an early age.*

"What are we expected to do with the fourteen million?" I asked.

"The best we can. The 40 Committee paper reads that we are to prevent an easy victory by Soviet-backed forces in Angola."

"No win?" I enunciated each word.

---

worded charter to launch thousands of covert actions in every corner of the world. Most of them had dubious justification in terms of the United States security. (See the *Final Report of the Select Committee to Study Government Operations with Respect to Intelligence Activities* [also called the Church Committee Report], April 26, 1976.) The Hughes-Ryan Amendment to the National Assistance Act of 1974 required that no funds be expended by or on behalf of the CIA for operations abroad, other than activities designed to obtain necessary intelligence, unless two conditions are met: *(a)* the president must make a finding that such operation is important to the national security of the United States; and *(b)* the president must report in a timely fashion a description of such operation and its scope to congressional committees. Theoretically the Senate has controlled the agency budget since 1947 but CIA funds were buried in the Department of Defense budget, and without detailed knowledge of CIA activities, the Senate could make little practical use of this power.

*The CIA has a special arrangement which permits any employee who has three years of overseas duty to retire at age fifty, with as much as $20,000 per year in retirement pay. The stresses that shorten case officers' lives are not what one might guess, certainly not those of James Bond–like danger and intrigue. Most case officers work under official (State Department) cover, and circulate after hours in the world of cocktail and dinner parties. They become accustomed to a life-style of rich food, alcohol, and little exercise. At work they are subject to bureaucratic stresses comparable to a sales office or a newsroom, with publishing deadlines and competitive pressures to produce recruitments.

"Kissinger would like to win. No doubt he would like to stop the Soviets cold. But he knows that we can't get that kind of program through Congress. I guess it would take a special appropriation, probably approval of both houses. So instead we are being asked to harass the Soviets, to . . . 'prevent an easy victory by communist-backed forces in Angola'! "

I couldn't think of anything to say. Another no-win policy, harassing the Soviets as they made a major move on the world chessboard, trampling a few thousand Africans in the process. But I needed more facts and I wanted to think it over before I asked management to let me out. You don't turn down many good jobs and still get offers.

The Angola program, Bantam said, had been encrypted IAFEATURE.* Its cable distribution was *Proscribed and Limited,* i.e., IAFEATURE cables would be limited to five in number and the individuals inside headquarters who would see those cables had been carefully proscribed. It was the agency's strictest control except for *Eyes Only.*

Bantam gave me my orders. The director had approved the formation of a task force to manage the Angola program. The DDO, Nelson, had ordered that it be staffed with the best people to be found in any headquarters offices. My first job was to assemble this task force, and to locate people who could be sent to the field. I would manage the task force at headquarters and Victor St. Martin, the chief of station in Kinshasa, Zaire, would supervise operations in the field.

I pointed out that I needed to do a great deal of "reading in," familiarizing myself with recent files on Angola. True, I knew central Africa well, but I had been out of touch with Angola for years. This would be a serious handicap in a fast-moving job like the task force, until I caught up.

"Reading in," the first chore facing a CIA officer in a new job, entailed a hasty review of CIA briefing papers, biographic sketches

---

*All CIA operations and agents are identified by cryptonyms which begin with two letter digraphs designating the target country. "IA" indicated Angola; "WI," Zaire; "TU,"South Vietnam; etc. State Department principal officers (ambassadors, consul generals, chargés) all are given cryptonyms beginning with "GP." The letters of the digraph are pronounced individually, as "I, A, FEATURE." Occasionally the young women who assign cryptonyms will blend the digraph into a pronounceable word like TULIP or a phrase, WIBOTHER.

and country surveys of the target area. The objective was to acquire as rapidly as possible the common denominator of background knowledge shared by other CIA officers dealing with the same area. In addition, one was expected to have ready recall, perhaps with the help of cribsheets, of considerable detail about CIA operations in that area. Unfortunately, the CIA case officers are thus almost entirely dependent on CIA material for knowledge of their areas of operation, perpetuating CIA biases and superficial observations. It is exceedingly rare that CIA officers, including even the analysts of the Directorate of Information, will read the books and articles which the academic world publishes about their areas of interest.

Bantam told me to process through East Asia Division the next morning and hurry back to Africa Division ready to work.

As I stood there, he said, "Speaking of reading in . . . Why don't you have a look at these . . . Sit right there. No, don't take them out of my office! Just make yourself at home at that table . . . You won't bother me."

He handed me a large loose file of sensitive papers, including a presidential finding, a director of Central Intelligence memo, a 40 Committee paper, a background paper on Angola, and some rough notes, draft cables, and memos.

I glanced at the clock and noticed it was almost 7:00 P.M. although still light outside. I was uncomfortable and hungry and hadn't seen Potts yet. But I knew I had before me the charter for the nascent Angola program and I was eager to read that before doing anything else.

The Presidential Finding of July 18, 1975, was a curious document, deliberately vague and unspecific, to be fleshed out in verbal briefings by the CIA director. It said only that the president found the following operation to be important to the national security of the United States. The country wasn't even specified—only the continent, Africa. The operation was described as the provision of material, support, and advice to moderate nationalist movements for their use in creating a stable climate to allow genuine self-determination in newly emerging African states.

That was the legal justification for the CIA's Angolan paramilitary program. Behind it lay a lot of history.

After five centuries of colonial rule and fifteen years of bloody guerrilla warfare, Portugal was freeing its last African possession. In January 1975 a transition government had been established with each of three major liberation movements sharing in the preparations for independence and each campaigning throughout the country for elections in October 1975. Independence Day would be November 11, 1975. The three movements were the *Popular Movement* or MPLA (Popular Movement for the Liberation of Angola); the *National Front* or FNLA (National Front for the Liberation of Angola); and *UNITA* (National Union for the Total Independence of Angola). All three historically received help from communist countries, but the MPLA leaders had Marxist, anti-imperialist views and had once been openly critical of the United States and its support of Portugal. The newspapers spoke of the "Soviet-backed" MPLA and the "moderate" FNLA. During the spring of 1975 the transitional government had disintegrated as FNLA and MPLA forces clashed in northern Angola. In July 1975 the MPLA prevailed, evicting the FNLA and UNITA from the capital, Luanda.

I was familiar with the Portuguese colony on the South Atlantic side of Africa from childhood and adult travels. We had visited the Angolan ports, Luanda and Lobito, and had met American missionaries who told alarming tales about Portuguese administrators in the Angolan bush.

In 1961 a U.S. navy ship on which I was the Marine Corps intelligence officer put into Luanda for a brief visit. CIA assignments and temporary duty missions had placed me near Angola many times, for example, in Lubumbashi, Zaire, in 1967, when Bob Denard's squad of sixteen mercenaries invaded from the Angolan border.

My last direct experience with Angolan matters had been in February 1969, when I drove from Lubumbashi to visit an FNLA camp near the Angolan border. It had been sleepy and undisciplined, and perhaps the experience inclined me to underestimate the tenacity of the Angolan nationalist movement years later. A few leaderless soldiers in ragged uniforms and seminaked women and children, shambled between dilapidated brick buildings which were the remains of a Belgian colonial Force Publique camp. Without utilities or sanitary facilities, it differed little from a primitive African village, the small brick houses replacing thatch huts and rusty rifles substituting for more primitive weapons.

I was viewed with guarded suspicion at first, then with guarded friendliness after I shared some cigarettes and identified myself. I later wrote an intelligence report about the camp, which headquarters reports officers refused to disseminate to the intelligence users in Washington. The chief of station, Kinshasa, sent me a note in the classified pouch advising that the agency wasn't interested in Angolan revolutionary movements, and that my visit was unfortunate because it could have been misconstrued. We didn't support the black fighters and we didn't want our NATO ally, Portugal, picking up reports that we were visiting Angolan rebel base camps.

Since then I had casually monitored our Angolan policy, which was unchanged as late as 1974. It is part of the business to keep an eye on your areas of special interest. You do it casually, instinctively, over coffee with friends, or when you pass in the halls: "What's the hurry? . . . Oh? . . . What's Roberto up to these days? . . . Why hasn't anyone ever gotten us a line into the other group, the MPLA?"

For many years the Portuguese had claimed exemplary success in assimilating blacks into a colonial society which was allegedly free of racial barriers. Until 1974 they appeared to believe they enjoyed a permanent relationship with their colonies.

In the clandestine services of the CIA, we were inclined to accept the Portuguese claims of a racially open-minded society in Angola, and it was tacitly agreed that communist agitation was largely responsible for the blacks' continued resistance to Portuguese rule. The reason was basic. Essentially a conservative organization, the CIA maintains secret liaison with local security services wherever it operates. Its stations are universally part of the official communities of the host countries. Case officers live comfortable lives among the economic elite; even "outside" or "deep cover" case officers are part of that elite. They become conditioned to the mentality of the authoritarian figures, the police chiefs, with whom they work and socialize, and eventually share their resentment of revolutionaries who threaten the status quo. They are ill at ease with democracies and popular movements—too fickle and hard to predict.

Thus CIA case officers sympathized with the whites of South Africa, brushing aside evidence of oppression with shallow clichés such as, "The only reason anyone gets upset about South Africa is because whites are controlling blacks. If blacks murder blacks in Uganda, nobody cares . . ." and "The blacks in South Africa are better off than blacks anywhere else in Africa, better schools, better jobs, better hospitals . . ."

About Angola we commonly declared, "The Portuguese have

established a raceless society. They've intermarried and . . ."

In fact, the Portuguese role in Angola was historically one of exploitation and brutal suppression. Beginning in 1498 it conquered and subjugated the three dominant tribal kingdoms—the Bakongo, Mbumdu, and Ovimbundu—and exported over three million slaves, leaving vast reaches of the colony under-populated. The colonial society was segregated into six racial categories defined by the portion of white blood in each, with two categories of pure blacks at the bottom of the scale. Citizenship, economic and legal privilege accrued only to the 600,000 whites, mulattos, and *assimilados* or blacks who were legally accepted among the elite of the society. The 90 percent of the population classified as *indigenas* suffered every form of discrimination—including forced labor, beatings, arbitrary imprisonment, and execution without trial—at the hands of the colonial administrators.

In 1958 there were 203 doctors in all of Angola, statistically one for every 22,400 Angolans, although most of those two hundred served only European, mulatto, or *assimilado* patients, while a handful tended the 6,000,000 Angolan *indigenas*. Less than 1 percent of the *indigenas* had as much as three years of schooling.

John Marcum, an American scholar who visited the interior of Angola in the early 1960s, walking eight hundred miles into the FNLA guerrilla camps in northern Angola, reports that at the time rebellion erupted in 1961, 2,000,000 Angolan natives were displaced from their historic social and geographic surroundings: 800,000 were subject to rural forced labor; 350,000 faced underemployment in the slums of the urban areas; and about 1,000,000 were émigrés in the Congo, Rhodesia, and South Africa. "The disintegration of traditional society had led to widespread disorientation, despair, and preparations for violent protest." By 1961 Angola was a black powder keg with the three major ethnic groups organized for revolt.*

On March 15, 1961, FNLA guerrillas mounted a 50-pronged attack across the Congo border along a 400-mile front, killing African and Portuguese men, women, and children alike.

Portuguese air force planes immediately brought in military reinforcements using NATO arms intended for the defense of the North

*See John Marcum, *The Angolan Revolution* (Cambridge, Mass.: MIT Press, Vol. I, 1969; Vol II, 1978), for a comprehensive study of the Angolan revolution.

Atlantic area, and began striking back with indiscriminate wrath, even bombing and strafing areas that had not been affected by the nationalist uprising. Portuguese police seized nationalists, Protestants, communists, and systematically eliminated black leaders by execution and terrorism. By overreacting and flaying out indiscriminately, the Portuguese helped to insure the insurrection would not be localized or quashed.

President Kennedy made a tentative gesture of support to the revolutionaries by voting with the majority of 73 to 2 (South Africa and Spain opposing) on United Nations General Assembly Resolution 1514, April 20, 1961, which called for reforms in Angola. The United States also cut a planned military assistance program from $25 million to $3 million and imposed a ban on the commercial sale of arms to Portugal.

But the Portuguese held a very high card—the Azores air bases that refueled up to forty U.S. Air Force transports a day. We could not do without them and our agreement for their use was due to expire December 31, 1962, only eighteen months away. By renegotiating the agreement on a year-by-year basis, the Portuguese were able to stymie further pressure from Washington and obtain extensive military loans and financial credits.

Even as American bombs and napalm fell on the Angolan nationalists, and the U.S. voted the conservative line at the UN, Portugal's air force chief of staff, General Tiago Mina Delgado, was honored in Washington, receiving the American Legion of Merit from the U.S. Air Force chief of staff, Curtis Lemay, and a citation from Secretary of Defense Robert McNamara for his contribution to U.S.-Portuguese friendship. Strategic realities dominated policy.

Lisbon attributed the war in northern Angola to Congolese "invaders" and "outside agitators" acting with a rabble of hemp-smoking *indigenas* and for years thereafter, while the rebellion sputtered and flared, the United States ignored Angolan revolutionary movements. With the advent of the Nixon administration in 1969, a major review of American policy toward Southern Africa, the "tar baby" report (NSSM 39), concluded that African insurgent movements were ineffectual, not "realistic or supportable" alternatives to continued colonial rule. The interdepartmental policy review, commissioned by then White House advisor, Henry Kissinger, questioned "the depth and permanence of black resolve" and "ruled out a black victory at any stage." Events soon proved this to be a basic miscalculation.*

The April 1974 coup in Portugal caught the United States by surprise, without graceful policy alternatives and out of contact with the African revolutionaries.** The CIA had not had coverage inside Angola from the late 1960s until 1975. An official CIA station is opened only with the approval of the State Department, generally under the cover of a United States embassy or consulate. Only in rare instances is the presence of a CIA station truly unknown to the host government. Hence, in deference to Portuguese sensibilities, the subject of reopening the Luanda station was inevitably vetoed whenever it arose. Only in March 1975, when the Portuguese were disengaging and losing control, did we finally reopen the Luanda station.

Before that, most of the CIA's field intelligence about the interior of Angola had come from Holden Roberto who was the leader since 1960 of the Bakongo revolutionary movement, called the FNLA. Operating from Kinshasa (then called Leopoldville) he had established ties with the CIA.

I was less familiar with the other two factions—the MPLA and UNITA—but I knew that the latter, headed by a tough radical named Jonas Savimbi, had been supported by the North Koreans and the Chinese. I had a personal memory of Savimbi. In 1968 he had delayed the arrival of my own household effects in Lubumbashi by harassing the Benguela railroad, which was southern Zaire's vital link to the sea, bringing in all supplies and carrying the Katanga province's copper to market.

All three, Roberto and Savimbi and the MPLA, would dominate my interest until the Angolan drama was finally played out.

I picked up the memorandum to the director of central intelligence. It had been drafted in Africa Division and was designed to introduce the 40 Committee Angola options paper to the director. I read it carefully. In the second paragraph it stated that large supplies of arms to Roberto and Savimbi would not guarantee they could establish control of all Angola, but that assistance would per-

*John Marcum, "Lessons on Angola," Foreign Policy, April 1976, p. 408.
**The Pike Committee report, January 1976, analyzes the Portuguese coup as illustrative of a CIA intelligence failure.

mit them to achieve a military balance which would avoid a *cheap Neto victory* (Agostinho Neto was president of the MPLA).

I paused to reflect a moment. This memo did indeed state a no-win policy—we would be seeking from the outset only to avoid a "cheap Neto victory." I wondered what "cheap" meant. Would it be measured in dollars or in African lives?

The Soviets would certainly learn what the agency was doing and they knew very well the limitations which would be imposed on Kissinger and Ford by the American Congress and press so soon after Vietnam. Fourteen million dollars doesn't stake you to a very big war. The Congo covert action cost American taxpayers a million dollars a day for a sustained period. The CIA claimed to have won that one, although it was by no means clear ten years later what we had won—Mobutu was energetically running the country into the ground and he had turned on his American benefactors.

The fourth paragraph of the memorandum to the director stated that the CIA understood: *(a)* that Secretary Kissinger favored a $14-million commitment with emphasis on material; *(b)* that the assistant secretary of state for African affairs, Nathaniel Davis, opposed any covert program in Angola, because he doubted that such an operation could be kept secret;* and *(c)* that Ambassador Sheldon Vance (career ambassador and special assistant to the secretary of state) was interested in the operation because it would ease our relations with Mobutu.

Kissinger favors . . . I wondered if Kissinger or any of the others who were pushing us into this program were already planning its escalation. Bantam had said they got $6 million and then immediately $8 million more. Did they expect that to suffice, or were they already thinking of another ten, twenty, one hundred million once they had the American government committed?

Assistant Secretary Davis opposed the program. Bantam and I

*Davis resigned in August 1975 after Secretary Kissinger rejected his recommendation that the United States seek a diplomatic solution in Angola and play no active role in the country's civil war. Davis had argued that we must mount a diplomatic effort—a multinational effort—to get a settlement. He said we must trumpet it to the world that this is not the right kind of activity for any great power.

And he told them it wouldn't work. "Neither Savimbi nor Roberto are good fighters. It's the wrong game and the players we've got are losers" (Seymour Hersh, from officials directly involved, *New York Times,* December 14, 1975).

and Costello had reservations about it. How many others? Was there any chance for secrecy in a highly controversial program?

I turned to the 40 Committee options paper. It had been drafted by Africa Division of the CIA, on July 14, two weeks earlier, and began with a summary paragraph which concluded that Neto's forces appeared strong enough to take the Angolan capital, Luanda, and surrounding areas. Mobutu was exhausted economically and could no longer support Holden Roberto. Roberto did not have countrywide political support. It further postulated that financial and some limited material support to Roberto and Savimbi could establish a military balance and *discourage further resort to arms* in Angola. Such covert financial assistance, it continued, would prevent *the quick and cheap installation* in Angola of what Mobutu and Kaunda would regard as a pawn of Moscow on their borders.

By putting in a little money and arms we would *discourage* further resort to arms? President Johnson had called that "controlled escalation" in Vietnam. Why did the 40 Committee think it would work in Angola?

The paper went on to review the recent developments in Angola, and noted that Roberto had been given $265,000, with 40 Committee approval, since January 22, 1975, to make him competitive in the transitional government. It then listed four options for the United States in Angola: *(a)* limited financial support for political activity; *(b)* substantial financial support and covert action designed to redress the balance, costing $6 million; *(c)* larger amounts of money ($14 million) and material to give Savimbi and Roberto superiority over Neto—providing the USSR did not escalate its assistance to the MPLA; *(d)* sufficient support to sustain Roberto and Savimbi's armies for a year, costing $40 million. The latter, the paper stated, would likely match any Soviet escalation. There was no indication of how this estimate of Soviet response had been developed.

A fifth option, of staying out of the conflict altogether, was not mentioned. Clearly, the United States wanted this war. Conspicuously, we had made no move to work through the Organization of African Unity, the United Nations, or bilaterally with the Soviet Union to end the arms race.

The paper discussed the risks, concluding that the security of our program would be better protected if the Angolans got arms which had belonged to the Zairian army rather than from the USA. Officially, the United States was observing an arms embargo and should continue to do so. Broad allegations of "massive" American assistance to Mobutu and Roberto would not hurt us too badly. But a leak from an official American source would be damaging. The United States would be held to blame for spreading the civil war in Angola.

The major fear was that some American official would leak the program to the American press, the American public. From the outset, the program was being kept secret from the American people more than anyone else.

I finished with the 40 Committee paper and read several other pages of notes and draft memos. I learned that Colby had briefed the Senate Foreign Relations Committee, the Special Subcommittee on Intelligence of the House Armed Services Committee, and the Defense Subcommittee of the House Appropriations Committee, to flesh out the presidential finding, as required by the Hughes-Ryan Amendment.

The 40 Committee had met once in January 1975, once in June, and again in July to discuss the Angola program. The National Security Council had met June 27, 1975, and requested that it be presented an options paper on Angola; this was the paper I had just read.

On July 14, 1975, the 40 Committee had requested that the agency submit a covert action plan for the Angolan operation. This plan was drafted by Africa Division of the CIA and submitted July 16. It was approved the same day by President Ford, who authorized the expenditure of $6 million. On July 27, Ford had authorized the additional $8 million. On July 29 the first planeload of arms left South Carolina for Kinshasa.

It was after 9:00 P.M. when Bantam interrupted my reading to invite me to his new condominium in McLean, where we had dinner in a virtual museum of oriental art, still only half sorted out. A packing crate in one corner had "AMEMBASSY DJAKARTA" printed on one side. At 1:00 A.M. I finally stretched out in the tub of his guest bath and reflected.

While on leave I had almost convinced myself that I should get out of the clandestine services—that I did not want to travel the world living fictitious cover stories and cultivating spies all my life. Now this incredible offer had come along.

From my earliest days with the agency I had promised myself

three things: that I would always separate in my own mind the truth from the professional cover stories and lies; that I would never be afraid of the agency or any of its directors; and that I would not stay with it too long.

Vietnam had almost been too long. After that, I knew that if I did not act to resolve my conflicts with the agency I risked becoming one of the burned-out, middle-grade case officers that clog the halls of CIA headquarters. On April 23, I had flown out of Saigon in a C-130 to a refugee tent city at Clark Air Force Base exhausted and demoralized. Bitter memories crowded in while I lay for days on a cot staring at the green tent canvas overhead, waiting for a flight to the States.

A week later I was back at headquarters, wandering down the halls, sticking my head in offices, enjoying the warm greetings from old buddies and the curious stares of new officers.

In from the cold? Case officers often come back unnoticed, drained by their experiences and haunted by their consciences, by the suspicion that the things they had done were pointless as well as cruel. They rarely have the same sparkle and drive on the next assignment —or the next. In offices throughout headquarters there were those who had given up, who were walking out their years before early retirement, becoming grey fixtures like the safes and Xerox machines.

I had reached an enviable level. Senior officers were cordial and accepted me almost as an insider, and the younger officers sought out my company. I was making $32,000 a year. In twelve years I could expect to retire with a $20,000 pension. Security. The CIA almost never terminated staff officers before retirement age. Perhaps I could find a change of pace within the CIA itself, something out of operations that would keep the momentum of my career going.

Now, in one day, I had come from the sleepy hills of central Texas to learn of the CIA's latest supersecret covert action—a war that could easily escalate into a major confrontation with the Soviet Union. They were asking me to play a major role in planning and running it.

I decided to stay a few days longer, to understand this new paramilitary thing, IAFEATURE, and then face a tough decision.

3

Footsoldiers of Foreign Policy

The next morning, July 31, 1975, as I attempted to hurry through the East Asia Division processing, to get myself assigned back to Africa Division and to collect $2,000 I was due for out of pocket travel expenses, a young woman stuck her head around a partition.

"If you are John Stockwell, you'd better come to the phone," she said.

George Costello was on the line, in one of his surly moods. "Where are you? And what the hell are you doing?"

"I'm in the EA finance office, getting checked in . . . didn't Carl . . ."

"You don't seem to understand . . ." His voice was loud. I held the receiver away from my ear. "You're needed in Africa Division *now!* Screw EA! Potts has IMMEDIATE cables on his desk that should have been answered *already!* I want you back in my office *now!*"

It was Costello at his lovable best. I hurried out, not smiling as I thought of my $2,000. I needed that money. Taking the stairs from the fifth floor I hurried down "C" corridor and braced myself as I ducked into Costello's office.

He didn't look any friendlier than he had sounded. "Why weren't you in staff meeting?" he snarled.

"Didn't Carl . . ."

"No Carl didn't *anything.*"

Costello calmed himself with a visible effort and waved some cables at me. Things were happening, a lot of things. Potts was tied up for the morning assisting the director in briefing the Office of Management and Budget to get the $14 million released. People were traveling, air transports were in flight.

Costello handed me the cables and I took hasty notes, writing across their tops as he explained them. The first C-141 flight of arms' had gone out two days before. Two more C-141 flights were being put together on a high-priority basis, the arms coming from agency warehouses in Texas and the loads assembled in South Carolina. One plane would leave Sunday, August 3. The agency's Office of Logistics would handle most of the stateside coordination. Africa Division— with the help of SOG, air force liaison, and the Office of Logistics —had to plan the operation, hammer out the composition of the load, and send a formal memorandum to the Pentagon requesting the airplane. Cables had to be exchanged with Monrovia station in Liberia, where the aircraft would refuel at Robertsfield, and with Kinshasa where the cargo would be offloaded at night. The Kinshasa CIA station had its own problems: getting clearances for the flight, while keeping it secret, procuring 30,000 pounds of fuel for the plane's return, and arranging for Zairian army trucks to meet the plane precisely on time.

The CIA maintains prepackaged stocks of foreign weapons for instant shipment anywhere in the world. The transportation is normally provided by the U.S. Air Force, or by private charter if the American presence must be masked. Even tighter security can be obtained by contracting with international dealers who will purchase arms in Europe and subcontract independently to have them flown into the target area. Often, the CIA will deliver obsolete American weapons, arguing that World War II left so many scattered around the world they are no longer attributable to the U.S. In the Angola program, we obtained such obsolete weapons from the National Guard and U.S. Army Reserve stores. Initially, U.S. Air Force C-130 transports picked up weapons from the CIA warehouse in San Antonio, Texas, and delivered them to Charleston, South Carolina. U.S.

Air Force C-141 jet transports then hauled twenty-five–ton loads across the Atlantic to Kinshasa. Inevitably, the air force billed the CIA for the service, $80,000 for each flight.

Our C-141 flights were masked by regular U.S. Air Force military air charter planes which routinely delivered supplies to the U.S. Army mission in Kinshasa, and arms to the Zairian army. A U.S. Air Force plane offloading weapons in Kinshasa attracts little attention. Repeatedly during the program we would place a token amount of certain weapons, such as the M-72 light antitank rocket (LAWS) or the M-79 grenade-launcher, on an overt military air charter flight in the name of the Defense Department for delivery to the Zairian army, to lay a paper trail which would explain to auditors and prying eyes the existence of these weapons in Zaire and Angola.

A shipload of arms was being assembled at Charleston, South Carolina, to be hauled to Zaire in a U.S. Navy transport vessel, the *American Champion*.

The chief of station, Lusaka, was requesting permission to meet the UNITA leader, Jonas Savimbi, in Lusaka. Heretofore we had monitored UNITA through meetings with its other officers. This meeting was to be encouraged.

Kinshasa station was pleading for airplanes to fly military supplies to the FNLA and UNITA bases inside Angola. There was no easy answer to this one. In fact we would search the world for months for a C-130 or even several DC-3's which could support the Angola program, and never find any.

Two Zairian Air Force C-130 airplanes were being overhauled in Marietta, Georgia, by Lockheed International. Kinshasa station was urging us to expedite their completion and if necessary to foot the $600,000 bill to get them back in action—the government of Zaire itself was broke, out of credit, and unable to pay.

Six other IMMEDIATE cables required answers. One concerned the disappearance of a European journalist on the agency payroll, whom the Brussels station had sent to Luanda. Luanda station was requesting permission to have another agent attempt to find her, although this would reveal her CIA affiliation to that agent. A freelance photographer headquarters had sent to Luanda to photograph Russian arms was being indiscreet and arguing with the case officer about his allowances, claiming he couldn't survive on a $130 per diem. I drafted a cable ordering the station to send the man home, only to learn the hard way that he was a friend of George Costello. Costello had arranged his contract and was determined to keep him in Luanda at all costs.

I was getting an idea of what life would be like, running the Angolan Task Force.

As for the physical space for the task force, the desks, telephones, typewriters, safes, and the people to man it, Costello told me to see the chief of support. But as I left Costello's office, he fired a parting shot—"Don't spend a lot of time worrying about desks and people. Just keep writing answers to those cables."

I scarcely knew the chief of support, who had been brought to the division by Potts while I was in Vietnam. He was a sallow chap it turned out—a GS 15 bucking for promotion in a GS 16 job. He had spent most of his career in the Middle East, where Potts had known him for many years.

"They're not ready yet," he snapped, when I asked where my offices were to be. "We're working on it. Don't worry about it. You're going to have a beautiful vault, but it'll be a few days. These things take time." His voice became belligerent: "You just got back from a long leave so don't start bitching at me about your office space already!" He had a fat man's wheeze, compounded by the large cigar he was trying to chew while he yelled.

"No problem. But I've got to have a place to sit *now.*" I held up the cables.

"You go over to Horn and Central. They've got lots of room. They'll find a place for you." Horn and Central was the branch which handled Central Africa, including Angola.

But Horn and Central knew how to play the space game. They tried to send me back to the chief of support and when I balked, I was waved vaguely toward the outer fringes of the branch. They were overcrowded, the Horn and Central chief said, but maybe someone was on leave, or something.

I stood in the middle of the Horn and Central offices with the cables in my hand and reflected. No one was on leave. Secretaries shouldn't be displaced because of their typewriters and supplies. Reports officers tended to be surrounded by their own special files and also were nearly always overworked. In a corner was an officer I had once replaced overseas, years ago. He had never been overworked a day in his life that I knew of, but he was a section chief. Behind the next partition was a young officer who appeared to be reading a file. Probably a career trainee on interim assignment. He would be the equivalent of a second lieutenant. I was a colonel.

I closed in on him, introduced myself, explained my problem, and asked if he would be so kind as to loan me his desk for a couple of days. He leaped up and insisted it was no inconvenience at all. I slid into his chair.

A few moments later, Marvin, the deputy branch chief, loomed over the desk. We were the same grade, and friendly, but I was encroaching on his territory.

"John," he said, "we are trying to get you some working space. Now, I know you've got problems, but it would be better if we could solve them without disrupting other officers. I had Gregory working on something important . . ."

I stood, ready to insist, but a secretary hailed me with a phone call from the front office and I had to hurry off to see Carl Bantam. By the time I returned, Gregory was reinstalled at his desk with my cables neatly placed on the corner. He didn't look up as I gathered them and turned away.

Carl had given me two more cables to answer and a memo to write, all IMMEDIATE. Something had to give. My eyes focused on the floor just outside of the branch chief's offices, at the point that would bear the heaviest traffic in Horn and Central. I walked over, took off my shoes and settled into a variation of the yoga *siddhasana*, making four stacks of cables, and began to write on a yellow pad on my knee. Feet approached, hesitated, then turned towards the other door, the long way around. I ignored everything, concentrating. Marvin came to his door, turned, and went back inside his office. The branch chief himself came hurrying from his office and narrowly missed stepping on the Lusaka cables.

"You walk across my desk and I'll break your bloody leg," I said. Then I glanced up. "Oh, hi. I didn't realize it was you . . . Nobody's on vacation here at Horn and Central." His feet disappeared into Marvin's office. Leaving my work stacked on the floor I got up and hurried down the hall, responding to another summons from the front office.

When I got back almost an hour later, Marvin directed me to a desk by the window, on which my papers were already stacked. A desk by the window is one of the first small perquisites which come with mounting responsibility in the agency. Interim career trainees normally sit in the passageways along with the secretaries. Section chiefs usually have windows and get to park in the south parking lot. Deputy branch chiefs rate individual offices, branch chiefs add carpets and drapes, and division chiefs have large stuffed leather chairs and a sofa, and park in reserved slots near the main entrance. It was good to have a desk, but right then I needed something else even more—information.

There was no way I could go on answering these cables when I didn't know the players. Who was NIFIZZLE/1? IAMOLDY/1? GPSWISH? It would take hours for me to dig answers out of the files, once I learned where the files were. Clearly there would be no time for reading-in today. The most effective short-cut would be the desk officer, if she was any good.

I turned into the Angola office of Horn and Central, where the desk officer, Brenda MacElhinney, was laying out her lunch of french fries and a hamburger.

Brenda MacElhinney was very good. She produced confident, detailed answers to every question I could think to ask. MacElhinney had been on the Angola desk for a year and had recently returned from Angola where she had reopened the Luanda station.

She was typical of a number of CIA women. She had come into the agency eight years before with a solid academic background from the University of Arizona. Although she had had no problem getting into the Deputy Directorate of Operations, she wasn't given any encouragement for a field assignment and was instead stuck in one of the headquarters staffs, where her abilities were temporarily stymied. After two years of this she took leave without pay from the agency to resume work on her doctorate. She came back onboard in the hopes that she would be given a real chance in operations, in Africa Division. However, her efforts to get an overseas assignment were again frustrated. She was told, candidly, by the division chief that there were already too many women case officers in Africa Division, none of them remarkably effective. Not even the Equal Employment Office could help her get an assignment which would have been routine for a male with comparable qualifications. She eventually abandoned the fight, rationalizing that, even if it meant she was already plateaued at the GS 12 level with little chance of advancement, she had no better offers outside the agency, and she could not afford to go back to school. The mission to Luanda had been a sop to appease her anger, and perhaps it had worked. She seemed cheerful as well as knowledgable as she answered my questions.

And, as I said, she was good. "G, P, SWISH?" her laughter could be heard all over the branch. "That's Tom Killoran, the consul general in Luanda. A dear man, but he doesn't have much use for the CIA."

Brenda and I both knew that State Department principal officers often view their parasitic CIA stations as unnecessary liabilities. Generally the CIA station chief is the second or third secretary of the embassy, but he always has considerably more free funds to spend than the ambassador and all of the legitimate State Department officers together. For example, as COS in Bujumbura I had $900 per year in "representational" funds, plus an unlimited amount of "operational entertainment" funds, plus a virtually unlimited fund for agents' salaries, bribes, and gifts. Altogether I had about $30,000 cash each year to dole out or spend to enhance my effectiveness. The ambassador and three foreign service officers had a total of $2,000 between them, not enough to cover the Fourth of July reception. The extra money translates into greater social and operational activity, making the CIA man more visible and seemingly more important than the State Department officers. Often the CIA man will even establish a direct contact with the chief of state, leading him to believe that through the CIA he has the more authentic contact with the American government. At the same time, while the CIA station rarely produces significantly better or more timely intelligence than the embassy obtains through overt sources, it always represents a liability to the United States embassy as CIA officers scurry about with their semicovert operations, bribing and corrupting local officials. Since the Kennedy administration, the State Department chief of mission (the ambassador, consul general, or chargé d'affaires) is the president's official representative in a given country and all other agencies are subordinate to him. A strongly antiagency ambassador can make problems for the CIA chief of station, although any effort to evict a CIA station altogether is impossibly restricted by politics and bureaucratic inertia back in Washington.

MacElhinney predicted that GPSWISH would be greatly exasperated when he learned about the IAFEATURE program. SWISH so far had not been briefed, not even told of the 40 Committee's decision of January 1975 to fund the FNLA. He believed the MPLA was best qualified to run Angola and that its leaders sincerely wanted a peaceful relationship with the United States. SWISH had worked with all three movements and found the MPLA better organized and easier for him to see. They were the best educated up and down the line, from leaders who had taken doctorates at European universities to cadres of urban dwellers, civil servants, and technicians. By comparison the FNLA, Holden Roberto's crowd, had few educated men at the top—no intellectuals—and had spent much of its history in the cocktail parties of Kinshasa. The FNLA soldiers had been slathering animals when they came into Luanda that spring, 1975. UNITA was about the same except for Savimbi, who was a good man by any standard.

Scoffing at my notion that MPLA leaders were hostile to the United States, MacElhinney went on. It was only the CIA's historic relationship with Roberto that had us so close to the FNLA, and even he, despite many years of association, wouldn't tell us much. For example, the Chinese had publicly announced their FNLA advisor program and we knew they were at Kinkuza, Zaire, but Roberto wouldn't talk to the CIA about them. We knew even less about Savimbi—our alliance with him was based solely on his opposition to the MPLA.

The MPLA was rooted in the Mbundu people which the Portuguese had overwhelmed in the sixteenth century. The Portuguese had "transformed the Mbundu homeland in central Angola into what has been called the first black African nation to be subjected to European rule."*

Mbundu resistance erupted periodically during the next 350 years. In 1907–1910 a Mbundu leader, Cazuangongo, organized attacks on the railroads and fought a prenationalist guerrilla war from the Dembos hills.

Geographic location gave the Mbundu greater access to the Portuguese in Central Angola, and they became the domestic servants, the assistants, the black semiskilled labor force living in the *muceques* (slums) of Luanda. A handful managed to obtain advanced educations by pursuing the politically safe fields of clergy and medicine. As they studied and traveled in Europe they found that

*Marcum, *The Angolan Revolution*, Vol. I.

Marxist philosophy alone seemed to offer an alternative to Portuguese oppression; in addition to moral support, Marxism gave them organizational skills to develop a revolutionary movement. Capitalism, as espoused by the United States, firmly supported the Portuguese. Catholicism supported the Portuguese. American Protestant missionaries were at odds with the Portuguese, but in the end taught passive submission.

The modern Mbundu leaders became Marxists and organized a nationalist political movement which they eventually called the "Popular Movement," the MPLA. Their hostility to the Portuguese spilled over into criticism of the archimperialists, the United States.

The premier MPLA leader, Agostinho Neto, was born September 17, 1922 and grew up in contact with Methodist missionaries in Luanda. He was one of the few blacks to complete the Liceu Salvadore Correia, the secondary school, in Luanda. In 1947, supported by a Methodist scholarship, he went to study medicine at the University of Lisbon and Coimbra. His poems, political views, and active participation in opposition politics had him in and out of Portuguese jails from 1952–1958. He received his medical doctorate in 1958 and returned to practice medicine in Luanda. On June 8, 1960 he was once again arrested, flogged in front of his family, and taken off to jail. His intellectual ability, personal martyrdom, and prison credentials ensured his status as leader of the Popular Movement.*

CIA briefing sheets, reflecting Portuguese and FNLA biases, implied that Neto was a drunken, psychotic poet.

Two of Neto's poems follow:

Western Civilization

Tin sheets nailed to poles
fixed in the earth
make a house.
Rags complete
the landscape.
The sun penetrating cracks
awakes each occupant.
Afterwards twelve hours of slaving work
break stone
cart stone

*Ibid.

break stone
cart stone
in the sun
in the rain
break stone
cart stone!
Old age comes early.
A coarse mat in the dark night
suffices to die
grateful
and hungry.

Realization

Fear in the air!
On each street corner
vigilant sentries light incendiary glances
in each house.
Hasty replacement of the old bolts
of the doors.
In each conscience
seethes the fear of listening to itself.
History is to be told anew!
Fear in the air!
It happens that I
humble man,
still more humble in my black skin
come back to Africa,
to myself
with dry eyes.*

Arguing with MacElhinney, I took up Kissinger's simplistic line that the Soviets had to be confronted anywhere they made a move, this time in Angola. Do we just stand back and let them have a free rein with the Third World?

"You are suffering from a bad case of 'party line,' " MacElhinney informed me archly. "The Soviets did not make the first move in Angola. Other people did. The Chinese and the United States. The Soviets have been a half-step behind, countering our moves. And

*Dr. Agostinho Neto translated into English by Aaron Segal. Printed with permission, from Marcum, *The Angolan Revolution*.

don't put all the blame on Kissinger, the CIA led the United States into the Angolan mess," she added.

The Portuguese coup was April 25, 1974. But in 1973 Roberto had already begun accepting arms from the Chinese. On May 29, 1974, the first contingent of 112 Chinese military advisors, led by a major general of the Chinese army, arrived in Zaire to train the FNLA forces. The Chinese issued a press release announcing the arrival of these advisors. In July 1974 the CIA began funding Roberto without 40 Committee approval, small amounts at first, but enough for word to get around that the CIA was dealing itself into the race. In August the Communist party of the Soviet Union announced that it considered the MPLA to be the true spokesman of the Angolan people.

The Soviets began flying arms to Dar-es-Salaam designated for "African liberation movements"; the CIA could only speculate whether they were for Rhodesian and South African movements or the MPLA on the other side of the continent. On August 28 the Kinshasa press announced that the Rumanian communist party had presented a large quantity of military equipment to the FNLA. On September 10, the FNLA publicly acknowledged the receipt of 450 tons of supplies from China.

During the fall of 1974 the CIA continued to fund Roberto, still without 40 Committee approval, and its intelligence reporting on Angola was predominantly from Zairian and FNLA sources. Most important, MacElhinney emphasized, the flagrant, semiovert activities of the CIA station in Kinshasa ensured that American support of the FNLA would be widely known. There was reporting that the Soviet Union began filtering limited amounts of arms to the MPLA late in 1974.

In the Alvor agreement, January 15, 1975, the three movements agreed to compete peacefully for elections to be held in October 1975. Every indication was that UNITA and the MPLA acted in good faith, although no one could deny the likelihood of violence if one party threatened to dominate the elections.

On January 22, 1975, the 40 Committee authorized the CIA to pass $300,000 to the FNLA, which was historically the most warlike of the movements and which was thought to have the largest army. In February 1975, encouraged by Mobutu and the United States Roberto moved his well-armed forces into Angola and began attacking the MPLA in Luanda and northern Angola. In one instance in early March they gunned down fifty unarmed MPLA activists. The fate of Angola was then sealed in blood. The issue could only be decided through violence.* Again, the CIA support of the FNLA was known in Luanda and in Kinshasa where the Soviets and Cubans maintained active embassies.

Although allied with the MPLA through the early seventies, the Soviets had shut off their support in 1973. Only in March 1975 did the Soviet Union begin significant arms shipments to the MPLA. Then, in response to the Chinese and American programs, and the FNLA's successes, it launched a massive airlift. Its AN-12 and the giant AN-22 airplanes carried their loads to the Republic of Congo (Brazzaville) where short-haul air transports and small ships filtered the weapons to MPLA units near Luanda.

The Portuguese, although officially neutral, tended to favor the MPLA and did not inhibit their access to Soviet arms.

The fighting in Luanda intensified in July. With about equal force of arms, the MPLA had the significant advantage of defending the Mbundu homelands. It prevailed and evicted the FNLA and UNITA from Luanda.

MacElhinney was convinced that the CIA Angola program was a mistake which would damage and discredit the United States. We were confronting the Soviets over a country that was of little importance to either of us, at a time when the United States internal politics and public sensitivities would prevent us from following through, if the conflict escalated. The Chinese and Soviets had each made public announcements of their support of Angolan factions. The United States, under Kissinger's leadership, was publicly committed to an embargo against the delivery of arms to Angolan factions while it was secretly launching a paramilitary program. Such a program was self-limiting—too small to win, it was at the same time too large to be kept secret.

Okay, okay! I said. But what then do we do in Angola? What is our best line?

Far better would be a policy of noninvolvement. Sincerely con-

---

*Note that the original 40 Committee options paper acknowledged the United States' vulnerability to charges of escalating the Angola conflict when it stated that a leak by an American official source would be serious, that we would be charged with responsibility for the spread of civil war in Angola.

demn outside interference and prevail on all parties, including the Soviet Union and the Chinese, to work for a peaceful solution. President Senghor of Senegal had just called for United Nations initiatives to halt the fighting. We could respond. And we could establish fair ties with all three movements and welcome the eventual winner into the family of nations.

Later I took MacElhinney's arguments to Carl Bantam, unfortunately catching him in a sour mood. He brushed them aside, brusquely pointing out that we, CIA case officers, were the footsoldiers of foreign policy, professionals, paid for our special action capabilities. It was not our role to analyze policy, only to implement it. And how was I coming on the memorandum about the airplane?

There was no time for reflection. Cables kept arriving, faster than I could respond to them, and the front office maintained its clamoring pressure. By 9:00 P.M. I was wrung out. Nearly everyone was gone, a lone typewriter clattered far down the hall, an occasional phone rang. I sat for a while, appreciating the quiet. Carl had gone to a dinner with friends, leaving me a key to his place. All of the cables that I could respond to were on their way. No more IMMEDIATE cables could come to Africa Division because Registry was closed. Those marked NIACT, for "night action," would go to the twenty-four–hour DDO duty officer, who would call Jim Potts, discuss the text with him over the telephone, and send out an answer.

4

CIA People Policies

Responsibility for agency operations in Africa was centralized at the desk of the Africa Division chief, Jim Potts. Potts made all decisions about field operations and personnel assignments. The three hundred people serving in Africa Division were essentially his staff. He decided courses of action; they drafted the appropriate cables for his review before transmittal. In CIA operations, as in the State Department, the hand that signs the cables controls the action.

Potts was especially determined to involve himself in every detail of the Angola program. Crippled, a prisoner of his affliction, he compensated in full measure by throwing himself into IAFEATURE. If his body was immobilized behind his desk, his mind reached across oceans and continents. He read everything and seemed to remember it all.

Potts and I were contrasting but compatible personalities. My job as task force commander was roughly equivalent to the work of GS 16 branch chiefs, although I would defer to their senior grades. Coming in cold from an overseas assignment, I did not have at tongue tip the store of detailed knowledge I really needed for the job. That was okay with Potts. He didn't want competition in making decisions and I had what he lacked—the physical mobility to range across the building, if necessary across the world, to get things done. He was the three-star general, I the colonel. He made decisions and gave orders, and I, like the chief of staff of an army division, supervised their execution.

Potts's primary vehicle for communicating decisions was the 9:00 A.M. staff meeting, where he methodically interrogated every unit head and gave them marching orders for the day. To play the game you read every cable that had come in from your area during the night, and were ready to answer any question Potts might think to ask: "How much is IAMOGOL/1's salary?" "How many intelligence reports did he provide last month?" "Okay, draft a cable approving the onetime payment of seven hundred and fifty dollars." A normal branch might have ten cables each morning, three requiring careful study, most marked ROUTINE. (My task force received fifty or more IMMEDIATE cables daily.) Routine business consumed fifteen minutes. Potts then spent an hour on the Angola program while the rest of his staff listened, and I concentrated, taking notes.

After staff meeting Potts communicated through notes scrawled on little yellow buckslips. Known as "Pottsgrams," they often carried important decisions as well as reminders and reprimands; things like "Let's get an airplane out with some additional 4.2 mortar ammunition," or "Please find out how much the air force wants for those ten C-47's in Thailand." Potts, who had an aversion to bureaucratic structure, fired these notes at random throughout the division. The Lusaka section chief might be ordered to get out a planeload of ammunition, the Horn and Central deputy asked to draft a memorandum for Henry Kissinger, and a reports officer charged with researching the Israeli price for 120 mm. mortar ammunition. Quickly, I learned to make the rounds of all offices, collecting Pottsgrams and centralizing them at the task force.

I didn't know Potts well. He had come into Africa Division in 1972, shortly before I went to Vietnam, as deputy division chief under Larry Devlin.* In 1974 he became the division chief. His prior experi-

*Devlin was famous for running the Congo operation in early 1960 and for the Laos operation in the late sixties.

ence had been in the Middle East, Athens, where he had recently been chief of station. As an honor student and football player at Yale, graduating in 1943, Potts was a solid member of the eastern establishment which dominated the CIA.

I had heard other officers complain that he was frustrating to work with because he centralized too much control at his desk. It was said that his understanding of Africa was shallow, although he had memorized an impressive volume of facts and names.

To keep up with the task force workload I would need a staff of two dozen people, including four case officers who could answer cables and write memos; other case officers to run agents and gather intelligence about Angola; two paramilitary officers to plan the arms shipments and supervise the war; covert action specialists who would run the propaganda campaign; logistics and finance officers; reports officers to disseminate the intelligence; and secretaries and assistants.

Word spread quickly through the building that the Angolan Task Force was hiring. The day after I came back from Texas people began to seek me out. Young officers were looking for adventure and experience. Old officers hoped to work on one more operation, to hang on a while longer before retirement. After the collapse in Southeast Asia almost a thousand CIA employees had returned to headquarters. Colby had decreed that no one would be fired, not even the Vietnamese linguists who had been hired on thirty-day contracts because their educational backgrounds fell short of CIA case officer requirements. Hundreds of people were looking for jobs.

My Vietnam experience saved us from most of them. I knew too well the sloppy, low-pressure environment in which they had learned their intelligence skills. We needed speakers of Portuguese, not Vietnamese, and people who knew Africa.

At the same time, there were only a dozen genuine Portuguese linguists in the agency, and the good ones had secure jobs.

The DDO had given us a license to shanghai anyone we wanted from any office—we could have the best people in the Operations Directorate. However, having made that verbal gesture, Nelson was unwilling to back us up. No chiefs wanted to lose their best help, and we didn't have the clout to take them forcibly. Other chiefs had their own private uses for the task force, to provide for their own protegés. Rarely could I get the individual I wanted, and people were dumped on me who weren't much help.

I wanted Nick Kohler to help get the task force started, then go to Lusaka and maintain contact with Savimbi in the Angolan base camps. Nick was twenty-seven, fit, rugged, and had a military background: two combat tours as a Special Forces officer in Vietnam, a CIA tour in Vietnam, where I had known him, where he had worked sixteen hours a day and stayed out of trouble. Savimbi should take to him. Nick was a rugby enthusiast, and Savimbi had played second row while a student in Portugal.

Nick had finished his CIA Vietnam tour in November 1974. When I got back in May 1975, he had rushed up to me in the hall, his blue eyes snapping, his squared shoulders radiating physical power and drive. He was dressed in a sharp pink and grey suit with flared trousers and a hint of safari in the lapel and pockets, and three-inch wooden-heeled shoes on which he stood almost to six feet, my height. I had smiled, remembering his personnel file, which I'd read in Saigon in July 1973 on my way upcountry. Six-feet-one, the biographic sheet had said, and when I'd met him I immediately registered the exaggeration. When I got to know him better I realized he had doubtlessly seen to it that the file made him seem bigger than he was. In the same way, he bullshitted us about his investments. This thread of blarney in his character did not greatly offend me; it was a common enough trait among case officers. I had smiled again when I remembered our confrontation over his dress upcountry— when I had ordered him to stop wearing his bathing suit and shower shoes to the sweltering, upcountry office. Now he looked like a page out of *Esquire*. In short order he had told me that he was preparing for an assignment to Kinshasa, that he was juggling two girl friends, and playing around on the side, and that he had made first string on Washington's best rugby team. He had been practicing his chess and tennis, hoping to beat me, and was studying French full time, determined to make a "3" by the end of the course. We went drinking that night in Georgetown.

Potts wouldn't accept Nick Kohler and he wouldn't tell me why. In frustration I asked a branch chief and he told me, "Potts thinks Nick is too young."

The same day I bumped into Sam Hilton in the hallway in front of Potts's office. Hilton had been a staff officer of the Saigon station. He was over fifty and genial, but lazy. You got your business done in his office before five o'clock or not at all.

He collared me as I hurried down the hall; otherwise I would have nodded and walked past him.

"John, you're the head of the Angola Task Force, aren't you?" I nodded.

"Well, it looks like we'll be working together. Jim Potts just asked me if I would postpone my retirement and go into Angola to work with one of those black clowns over there."

Not the man for IAFEATURE, Hilton was a dues-paid-in-advance member of the agency's senior clique, a burned-out hero of previous wars. I tried to see Potts, then Carl. Neither was in. Finally I found George Costello. He knew Sam Hilton.

"George," I said. "Sam's not the man for the Lusaka job. He isn't fit enough and he doesn't . . ."

"Now wait a minute, John. Slow down. Sam has done some things you couldn't even touch. He parachuted into Greece when there were Nazis all over the place and single-handedly tore them a new asshole. You young people don't know what danger really is."

"How long ago was that, George?"

"Let's see . . . it was nineteen-forty-three."

"Thirty-two years ago. How old was Sam then?"

"He was in his twenties. You should have seen him. He was strong as a mule. He isn't very tall, but he could have broken someone like you in half."

"Okay," I said, "but all that was thirty years ago. I just saw him in the hall. He's fat and soft. And I knew him in Vietnam. He loafed. Drank a lot. Inhaled long black cigars."

Costello looked at me with thunder in his eyes, but I held up my hand.

"George, I hope he got medals and a hearty thanks for what he did in Greece in 1943. But this is 1975 and we're talking about Angola. Sam is over the hill physically. So are you. Right now Nick Kohler could whip all three of us at the same time. He's twenty-seven. It's his turn. You guys have to step aside and let Nick's generation have its chance."

Some pop-off valve in his mind blew and the red went out of his forehead. He was chuckling as I left his office and went to find Potts. But Potts didn't laugh. He stonily put me out of his office.

The next day I had lunch with Sam Hilton. We both took seconds of everything and then two desserts while I told him what he would find in Angola. I carefully dropped comments about Land Rovers, dust, hard beds, poor rations, and the absence of doctors, booze, and playful women. We shook hands in front of the Credit Union and I went back to work.

A few days later I heard that Sam Hilton had retired and was on his way to Florida. After some delay Nick Kohler went to Lusaka.

Andy Anderson was also interested, and he would have been a good man for Angola. But he was black. His loyalty should have been far beyond question, since he had originally been recruited to surveil and report on American black radicals as they traveled in North Africa, in one of the agency's most explosively sensitive and closely held operations against Americans. But Potts felt we had to be very careful about letting blacks into the program, because of the South African involvement.

Most minority groups in the agency are subjected to subtle but firm discriminatory barriers. It could not be otherwise. The men who control the CIA are of an older, conservative generation which has kept the agency fifteen or twenty years behind the progress of the nation at large. The Equal Employment Opportunities Office and the other standard bureaucratic mechanisms for handling complaints are ineffective against the subtle barriers of discrimination. Blacks will rarely have a specific incident to complain about, but their fitness reports will say "proficient and strong" instead of "strong and outstanding" and they have difficulty getting the good jobs, until they inevitably plateau at the GS 12 or 13 levels. The personnel management committees are exclusively white, men of the agency's older generation, and they meet behind closed doors.

In Vietnam a competent GS 13 black officer volunteered to come up to my post when we were being shelled frequently and two whites had broken under the strain. He too had a family and kids back in the States, but he ignored the danger and worked hard. When awards were given months later he received a Certificate of Distinction—a piece of paper. The rest of us got medals.

Second- and third-generation orientals are acceptable. Several have made supergrade.

One young woman was suggested for the task force with a cryptic, "If you want her." I knew Laura Holiday. In 1972 she had collaborated well with me on a special project, a test of special agent communications equipment wherein she had driven across the eastern United States alone, sending sample messages back to headquarters. But the cryptic, reserved recommendation stirred my curiosity. I took five minutes to glance at her file and read the last two fitness reports, and then I asked friends about her professional development.

After our collaboration in 1972, Laura had been assigned overseas. Her chief of station was a rising young officer with a reputation for preferring operations that included available women. Before going to the post he had persuaded the front office to give him the cover slot for a young woman officer and he had scurried about interviewing the various candidates, settling on Laura Holiday. He miscalculated. For Laura, liberation meant the freedom to say "no" as well as "yes." The COS was peevish, their working relationship was affected and he gave her a critical evaluation in her fitness report. There was nothing more to it. I accepted Laura on the task force, happy to have her.

Another agency minority has it made. Second-generation officers, generally with the sponsorship of their high-ranking fathers, have been coming into the agency in increasing numbers. Eileen Ranklin was such a person. She was twenty-four and had already been onboard for three years, although the normal age for hiring case officers is about twenty-five. An exception had been made for her because she spoke good French, and also because her father was a GS 18 division chief. Another former division chief's daughter of the same age was already serving in West Africa as a case officer, under cover as a State Department stenographer. Eileen Ranklin and four other second-generation officers were considered for the task force. Ranklin turned us down but three joined us. A fourth person, the young widow of an agency paramilitary officer, was also hired, as the agency family took care of its own.

While the task force was shaping up, arms and supplies were of course flowing steadily to Angola. Early on in these logistical doings, I had a nasty surprise—the CIA did not have a competent office to plan and arrange arms shipments. The office existed on paper in the Special Operations Group, but it was not staffed with people truly qualified for the work. Its staff of retired army, air force, and navy personnel, plus a sprinkling of younger one-tour military officers, who were originally hired on contract by the agency for paramilitary assignments in Southeast Asia, was surpisingly inept at the hard, detailed planning required for a war effort.

SOG sent us two men to plan the IAFEATURE arms flights; one, a Marine Corps major, who was doing a rotational tour of duty with CIA, helped us greatly until he was sent on another priority mission to Southeast Asia. The other, an old colleague of mine, Arnie Hall, had primary expertise as a lecturer about guerrilla patroling. He had served one tour upcountry in Laos and a few months in Vietnam, where he had helped with the final evacuation. None of which qualified him for the job of planning our arms shipments.

Arnie Hall was popular in SOG, the image of a paramilitary expert. Six inches shorter than I, his shoulders sloped three inches on either side of mine and dropped straight down to a barrel girth that bespoke of enormous physical power. A small round head sat neckless on square shoulders, cropped with hair that was never more than a quarter-inch long and mounted with a tiny, expressionless face. I first met him in 1972 in the mid-career course at the "Farm,"* when he often came to class playing his paramilitary role to the hilt, wearing combat boots and an eighteen-inch jungle knife which he would whet on a handstone during the lectures. We car-pooled together and I soon learned it was all a splendid put-on; he had in fact grown up in Philadelphia and had never even served in the infantry. He had a humorously strange mind and spontaneously flipped out in-character one-liners: "Gimme some C-4 and I'll get that truck out of the way"; or "Next time that long-winded bastard lectures us I'm going to slip some copper sulphate in his drawers." At other times he would come out with something like "Nimium ne crede colori— there's pimples under that mascara," and walk away, leaving you wondering just what intellectual interests might be hiding behind the knuckle-dragger facade.

After the marine major left on his mission, Arnie worked as a team with an African Division logistics officer—Price and Pride, we called them—to plan the arms flights. Neither had ever been to Africa. Even so, Price and Pride eventually became quite good at tailoring loads of ammunition to fit the stream of C-141s we kept launching.

There is something about an upcoming weekend that excites the decision maker. Inevitably it was late Friday before we made the decision to send another flight. Price and Pride paid the price, grous-

*Camp Perry, Virginia, the CIA training base.

ing and doodling with their notes and calculators until their figures were checked and double-checked, and the Office of Logistics could take over and deliver the required material to the air force.

"Why don't we throw in some forty-five caliber pistols?" one of them would quip, "They're worthless in combat but we can get them cheap. And how about a million rounds of thirty caliber ammunition? How much does it weigh? Somebody look up how much thirty caliber ammo weighs."

Potts had even less knowledge of infantry weapons and ammunitions. His modus operandi consisted of a quick look at *Jane's Weapons Systems* and a lengthy argument about the advantages of one rocket over another.

The results reflected our amateurism. We delivered into Angola 622 crew-served mortars, rockets, and machine guns; 4,210 antitank rockets, and 20,986 rifles,* even though UNITA and the FNLA combined never fielded more than 10,000 soldiers. Most of the rifles were obsolete World War II semiautomatics, no match for the AK's the MPLA was getting.

All of these guns cost a lot of money. While we knew that the 40 Committee had authorized sufficient funds, it took us many months to obtain a full-time financial expert who could tell us just where our money was. Until then, whenever money problems arose, Potts would take out his pen and a scratch pad and begin adding and subtracting, recalling a figure from the week before, rummaging the papers on his desk to confirm a detail. If he wasn't there, Bantam or I or someone else would fill in.

Theoretically, financial matters would be handled by the Africa Division finance officers in the support section, but they were overloaded with routine work and distracted with temporary duty missions. Whenever we pressed for better financial support, the chief of support would wave his hands expansively and say, "Don't worry about the money. You need some money, I'll find you some money," which didn't help us much in precise planning for an arms flight or budgeting for a mercenary program.

---

*In addition, the Chinese, South Africans, and Mobutu supplied several thousand rifles. See Appendix for a complete list of all arms shipped from the United States into Angola under IAFEATURE. Other countries contributed armored cars, anti-tank missiles, 120 mm. mortar ammunition, cannon and light tanks.

Carl Bantam developed into our best amateur financial expert; when something had to be gotten out in a hurry we would go to him. The price for this assistance was listening to his opinions of Africa Division's inability to handle things more professionally.

Otherwise, Bantam was frustrated and out of step. With strong reservations about our intervention in Angola, he also disagreed with Jim Potts about how we should go about it. Uncomfortable in his role as deputy chief, he attempted to make decisions, only to have Potts countermand them; he wrote cables which Potts rewrote as he would for a junior officer.

In a truculent mood, Bantam set about to devise schemes which would short-circuit our program by quickly and efficiently *winning* the Angolan war. One plan, which he outlined in a memo to the DDO suggested that we introduce one of the flying gun platforms which had been so effective in breaking up massed communist attacks in Vietnam. These were C-47's, originally called "Puff the Magic Dragon" in Vietnam, rigged with half a dozen Gatling guns programmed to aim and fire simultaneously, raining eight thousand rounds a minute into an area the size of a football field, driving a bullet into every six inches of ground. As this lumbering weapons system circles a battlefield, the stream of lead is played back and forth like a murderous garden hose; all exposed living creatures die. A more sophisticated version operates from the C-130, but at $15 million its cost was prohibitive for the IAFEATURE program. The C-47 gunship cost about $200,000, well within our budget at that time. There was no doubt whatever that in August, September, and October 1975 a pair of these gunships would have completely broken the MPLA. But in August Carl's suggestion was rejected by Potts and the CIA director, who were still working under the original 40 Committee charter which did not encourage the CIA to seek ways of winning.

Bantam had another scheme for easy victory. Called IASALA-CIOUS, it was a plan to recruit a few key Portuguese commanders in Luanda and pay them, perhaps a million dollars, to execute a coup d'état using selected Portuguese troops. These Portuguese would then issue a unilateral declaration of independence and hold the MPLA at bay until relieved by Roberto's forces. Presto, an FNLA victory. The file, assembled on an *Eyes Only* basis, contained all information the agency had on Portuguese commanders in Angola and a plan to dispatch an agent to Luanda to find one to engineer the coup.

Under other circumstances, with aggressive case officering and luck, IASALACIOUS might have worked. Certainly, the agency has engineered similar coups. But IASALACIOUS's first flaw was that the agency wasn't entrenched in Luanda. When successful, such coups are generally engineered by agency operatives who have been in the country for long periods and have developed an infrastructure of good contacts in the military establishment. Its second weakness was that not enough CIA personnel, including the Luanda chief of station, believed in it. Such a coup would put Portuguese troops in armed confrontation with the MPLA armies, whites fighting blacks, touching the fuse of racial violence. IASALACIOUS never got off the ground.

The propaganda of the Angola civil war was to be as important as the fighting. For that effort, Bubba Sanders was chosen, a senior GS 15, a short, cherubic, and energetic officer whose mission in life was to apply his irrepressible mind toward the harassment of the Soviets throughout Africa. Unfortunately, Bubba, while a fountain of schemes and plots, was not blessed with infallible judgement. His presence on the task force would be a mixed blessing, I thought, remembering a mailing other CIA propagandists had made to Burundi while I was there in 1970.

As COS, I had had approval of that operation, and I gave it, when I received the proposal from headquarters for a propaganda mailing designed to embarrass the Soviets. I assumed the mailing would be subtle and that I would see the suggested format before anything was posted. But neither I nor any other knowledgeable operations officer saw anything until posters began appearing in people's mail boxes in the capital, Bujumbura. They were about twelve by eighteen inches, printed in stark black and red, portraying a sharp military boot heel crushing hundreds of small figures. Across the top in bold French was printed, "A BAS MICOMBERO DICTATEUR!"—Down with Micombero, Dictator! Written across the bottom, as sponsor of the poster, was the cachet of a world youth congress, well known to be supported by the Soviets. The mailing worked so well that the Soviet ambassador was subsequently asked not to return from home leave in the Soviet Union.

But there was a large hitch. The propagandists had correctly sensed that Micombero ran a bitterly unpopular minority government. What they had missed, or chosen to ignore, was that the schism between Micombero and the masses was purely racial. Micombero and his government were elite Watutsi, sensitive to the threat of the suppressed Hutu masses and terrified at the possibility of a Hutu uprising. The Watutsi could only interpret the poster as encouragement for Hutu activists, who were known to be seeking support for a revolution. Periodically the Watutsi were accustomed to take preemptive measures by killing a lot of Hutus. And, lo, two years later, in 1972, in a paroxym of genocide that ranked with modern history's most brutal, the Watutsi did kill dozens of thousands of Hutus, while the United States and the rest of the world turned its back. How much of a role our ill-advised mailing played in the matter is open to conjecture.

Now three years after the massacre, I found Bubba in the Covert Action branch, already working hard on propaganda ploys to publicize the Soviet support of the MPLA in Angola. The Russians seemed to him delightfully vulnerable as they dumped arms into the civil war. He was scheduled to leave shortly for Rome, Kinshasa, and Lusaka where he would get the propaganda machine in gear.

"The key is a fourth force in Angola," he told me in his office in the Covert Action branch in "D" corridor. "We need to organize a fourth liberation front which can call for a coalition of all the forces, and denounce the Soviet arms shipments."

"Where will we get people for this front?"

"Angolan exiles—stranded students. There are some right here in the States. We'll call them the Angolan People's Front."

"Bubba, if you use Angolans who've been studying here in America, everyone will know it's *our* front. They won't be listened to by anyone but our friends."

"Well, we'll find some in Europe. They won't know the United States is involved. They'll think they are being funded by rich Portuguese refugees. We'll get Angolans who really believe in a peaceful solution, and they can operate maybe from Spain or Brazil. Can you get me the names of some Portuguese who would help?"

I promised to query the Lisbon station and the Portuguese Task Force.

"No matter," he said, "we can use Rodriguez or Jimmy Manus.

They're sitting out in McLean with nothing to do. Also, there's Bryan Cassidy up in New York; he was outstanding when we were working on the Kurds in Iraq. And we'll have to get Ray Chiles from Rome . . . at least for a couple of months. He is beautiful at this sort of thing." Rodriguez, Manus, and Cassidy were writers who supplemented their incomes by doing part-time contract work for the CIA. Ray Chiles was a GS 14 staffer with experience in covert action projects.

"All for the fourth force?"

"No, no! We've got to get the FNLA talking to the press in Kinshasa, and UNITA working with the newspaper in Lusaka. We've got reporters in our pockets in both these places and Mobutu and Kaunda aren't likely to complain when we plant articles in their newspapers. Then, we can take articles from those newspapers and have our agents in Europe pick them up and put them in the world press. We'll need officers in Kinshasa, Lusaka, London, Portugal, New York . . ."

He leaned back and smiled. "This is one PSYCH operation I'm going to enjoy! We'll call it IAPHOENIX. You know, the bird that keeps burning itself and rising up from the ashes—like the FNLA coming back from its defeats . . . IAPHOENIX, I like that!"

I stared at him in disbelief. PHOENIX had been the cryptonym for the agency's terrorist program in Vietnam. Even the agency claimed PHOENIX had killed over twenty thousand people; the Vietnamese government claimed twice as many. Colby himself had designed and managed this program, before he became director. During the spring of 1975 he had tried to explain it to Congress, and the press had worked it over.

Bubba seemed not to have heard of the PHOENIX program. He looked momentarily confused, then brightened. "Well, we'll call it IACADENCE," he said as I left.

On Saturday afternoon, August 2, Carl Bantam called to say they had gotten someone else for the task force. He seemed pleased. "It's Paul Foster," he said. "Foster is really outstanding! A GS 13 and thirty-four years old, but outstanding! He was on the Laos Task Force with me and spent five years upcountry in Laos. He can really get things done. We tried to get him to run this task force originally but East Asia Division wouldn't let him go. Nelson backed down, but now he's changed his mind again and we're getting Foster!"

This was normal internal agency politics. Obviously Nelson had reversed himself just to make it clear that he wrote the EA division chief's fitness report and not vice versa.

Carl regarded me for a moment. "Foster will be a co-chief with you. We'll rotate you back and forth to the field. In fact, you know Kinshasa so well, and he's married, maybe we'll just transfer you to Kinshasa and he can run the task force back here. That might work out pretty good. Excuse me . . ." He took a call on his phone while I tried to absorb all this.

It is common policy in the agency for senior officers to bring people with them when they transfer from other divisions and to put them in choice slots. Inevitably this means that the division's own officers are shunted aside. I had seen it happen often, although this was the first time it had struck me personally. I decided right away that under no circumstances would I work for Foster; if they wanted him to run the task force I would request another assignment. Given my reservations about the Angola program, I rationalized it would be a relief to be forced out of it. But two chiefs? That was inefficient, impractical, and to my knowledge unprecedented. I watched Carl talking into the phone, and waited to explain my views. But when he hung up he hurried out of the office and down the hall, mumbling that something had come up.

Sunday, I read cable traffic and files until 2:00 P.M., then went jogging into Great Falls Park to an isolated rock formation which projected over a ravine a few hundred yards from the Potomac River. I wanted to think about the program, perhaps even decide to bow out. The job was shaping up, but the reservations were still there. The agency, it seemed to me, had embarked on a careless, no-win intervention in another Third World morass. The Angola program seemed doomed to fail and, moreover, was fraught with liabilities for the United States, the CIA, and for John Stockwell, the task force chief.

I remembered what had happened to a friend of mine on the Cuban desk when a technical operation in Havana was wrapped up by the Cuban police. He wound up with a letter in his file, compliments of the Miami station chief, prohibiting any promotions for several years. Since such a letter would haunt him the rest of his career, he opted for early retirement and left the agency.

On the other hand, I was afflicted with bureaucratic function lust. Angola Task Force chief was what I had been prepared for in fifteen years of government service. And, I rationalized, I was being offered a unique human experience. Like most of the rest of the world, I had only read other people's accounts of Vietnam and the Bay of Pigs. Except in certain narrow areas, I had been dependent on other peoples' reporting of what had happened, and as a CIA case officer I knew well how news gets distorted. I did not know how things got done at the policy level in Washington. I had been upcountry in Vietnam, not involved in headquarters activity. Even during the ouster of Nkrumah in Ghana, I was one country away, in the Ivory Coast. The inside story came to me from an egotistical friend, who had been chief of station in Accra at the time. Now it would be different. In the Angola program I was involved from the outset. I would have access to the inner secrets and most accurate intelligence about the war. I could evaluate what was being done on the basis of personal experience in Central Africa which dated back thirty years.

After it was over, I could continue my career or resign, confident that I had really known the clandestine services, that I was not quitting just before promotion to a level where I would suddenly *understand.*

Tomorrow I would put Foster in his place and keep working on the organization of the task force. I jogged back along the trail, sprinting up hills in the fading light.

At seven-thirty Monday morning I took the IAFEATURE cables from the Horn and Central slot in Registry. In an hour I had read and sorted them into piles according to importance. Those requiring an early answer or discussion in staff meeting I read a second time, making notes of key cryptonyms, names, figures, and details.

At eight-thirty I interrupted my reading to catch Potts in his office. It was imperative that I nip the Paul Foster challenge in the bud, before Bantam could maneuver me off to Kinshasa, and take away my ringside seat in this little war. The key to my counterattack would be Potts's pride. If he felt his authority was being challenged, he would keep Carl in line. I also had the advantage that Carl was suggesting an unorthodox arrangement to favor his protegé, Foster. Potts tended to opt for standard solutions to personnel problems.

Leaning against his office door, I asked Potts about Foster's position on the task force. Apparently Carl hadn't gotten to him yet and

Potts quickly assured me that Foster would be the deputy chief. He was looking thoughtful as I left, however, and I knew I had better not slip even half a step in running the task force. My African experience was too strong a temptation if they developed problems in Kinshasa.

Then I braced Carl Bantam. When he began to repeat his plan to make us co-chiefs I quickly interrupted. I reminded him that I had extensive experience in Africa and was senior to Foster. If he and Potts wanted me to run the program, I was interested. Otherwise I could move on to another assignment. Bantam stood before me, reflecting. Most of his career had been spent as officer-in-charge. He hadn't recently served as anyone's deputy and he was realizing for the first time the limitations of his present position. He didn't have the authority to make the final decision. Reluctantly he acquiesced. I would be the chief and Foster the deputy. Bantam smiled and we headed out for staff meeting together. Of course, he would keep trying and I would be under constant pressure from the ambitious Foster, who had a strong supporter in the front office. But I could handle that. Carl and I went into the conference room together, talking about tennis.

After staff meeting I stopped in George Costello's office to drive the last nail into Foster's position. George hadn't settled down to work yet.

"George, I understand you're bringing a young hotshot in from EA Division to run the task force for us." George was an old Africa hand and would be inclined to resent Foster's intrusion.

"Well, Potts and Carl are in a little bit of a bind . . . apparently they had offered this fellow the job, but there was some mix-up."

"No problem." I said. "It's a bucket of worms anyway. I don't know how much experience Potts and Carl and the man in Kinshasa have in Africa. Or Foster. He makes it a new team. Anyway, he can run the task force and I'll go back to Texas and do some more fishing."

George Costello was a huge man. Standing, he towered over me, and jammed a thick finger against my chest.

"You aren't going anywhere. You are the task force chief. They need you more than they realize. Potts doesn't have any experience in Africa. Carl never set foot on the continent. St. Martin hasn't been in Kinshasa long. And Foster doesn't even know where it is on the map. Now you get your ass out of here and get to work."

5

Our Little-Known Allies

During the next week, August 3–9, IAFEATURE grew into a full-fledged covert action program. The principal allies, Mobutu of Zaire, Kaunda of Zambia, Roberto of the FNLA, and Savimbi of UNITA were briefed, and their cooperation assured. Paramilitary and organizational specialists flew to Kinshasa, and the task force took form.

The third C-141 flight was launched. And in long working sessions of CIA paramilitary and logistics officers, the composition of the shipload of arms was carefully formulated: twelve M-113 tracked amphibious vehicles; sixty trucks, twenty trailers; five thousand M-16 rifles; forty thousand rifles* of different caliber; millions of rounds of ammunition; rockets, mortars, recoilless rifles, etc. The U. S. Navy would bill the CIA $500,000 for the use of the *American Champion*.

Strategic and tactical radio networks were devised for use by the

---

*Some of these were diverted to Mobutu's army in Zaire. See Appendix for complete summary of the ships' cargo.

FNLA inside Angola. Mobutu's army and air force hauled enough arms for two infantry battalions and nine Panhard armored cars to the FNLA base at Ambriz, seventy miles north of Luanda.

Senator Dick Clark, chairman of the Senate Foreign Relations Committee, and his staff aide, Dick Moose, were briefed by Colby on the eve of their departure for Central Africa on a fact-finding mission. The CIA continued briefing congressional committees about the Angola program. Another 40 Committee meeting was held on August 8.

The situation in Angola was deteriorating rapidly. The MPLA controlled twelve of fifteen provinces and was gaining momentum. A radio station in Luanda boomed MPLA propaganda. The FNLA was trying to mount an offensive. Roberto and President Mobutu were pressuring the Kinshasa station. The Kinshasa, Lusaka, and Luanda stations bombarded headquarters with requirements and reports.

Every CIA activity, no matter how trivial, eventually crystalizes onto paper in the form of a cable or memorandum. In the Angola program the flow of paper was staggering. None of us had ever seen so many high-priority cables, or memoranda to the director, the State Department, the Department of Defense, and the 40 Committee. One cable would arrive from the field urgently requiring an answer, only to be superceded by another more critical, and that by yet another. The cable system worked much faster than wc did, which frustrated me at times, but also renewed my appreciation for the CIA's worldwide communications system, its heartbeat.

Cabled messages arrive at the CIA headquarters building, from radio relay stations around the world. While in the air, these messages are protected by a code which the agency hopes the Soviets cannot read. Machines at the transmitting field station automatically encode the messages, and computers on the first floor of headquarters decode them. Operators sit before the coding machines and guide them by typing signals into a keyboard. On receipt, incoming cables are reproduced automatically—some with several hundred copies, others with as few as one or two, depending on the classification and controls. Inside headquarters the cables travel by pneumatic tube to the registry section in each division, where the designating "slugs" are hastily read to determine which branch has action responsibility for each cable. The cables are then sorted into vertical trays for pick-up by secretaries from each branch. Inside the branches they are distributed to the appropriate desks and one copy is put on the reading boards for general interest within the branch.

The speed with which the system operates is breathtaking. For a FLASH or CRITIC cable the appropriate computers and lines are held open while all other traffic stops until the message comes through. A chief of station in any corner of the world can report a crisis or disaster to the division chief in seven minutes, no more time than it takes him to draft the text. IMMEDIATE cables are generally delivered within one or two hours, PRIORITY within six hours, and ROUTINE within twelve to twenty-four, depending on the volume of other traffic.

For all the technical marvels of the cable system, it is still run by fallible human beings. CIA officers know that security liabilities lie in the human activities on each end—the disposal of classified trash, the guarding of offices and safes, and the care and discretion of those who know about the cables and the operations they represent.

The reading boards can be a weak spot in the cable system's security if the branch's senior secretary is sloppy. In my first branch where I sat as an interim junior officer trainee, IMMEDIATE cables and dispatches were arriving daily from an African post that was trying to recruit a Soviet. The chief of station had managed to persuade a young American couple (representatives of a large American corporation) to encourage an alcoholic, fifty-year-old KGB officer in his amorous pursuit of the wife. The COS, who had a flair for writing and a sense of drama, reported in detail the Soviet's advances, the wife's ambivalent reactions, and the husband's confused hostility. For a period of weeks this made good reading; the branch chief's secretary gossiped with a stream of jolly voyeurs who came from all over the building, to read the latest episodes. The branch chief, a jovial GS 15 who had never served an operational tour overseas enjoyed the publicity his branch was getting. He would stand in his door and beam at his visitors as if holding a reception.

Eventually, KGB security became aware of the affair, conceivably from a leak at CIA headquarters, but more likely because such liaisons inevitably become conspicuous in a little African post. The KGB officer was last seen being escorted aboard a Moscow-bound commercial jet by two KGB security officers. Some months later, the American couple was reported to be in marital discord. By then no one at CIA headquarters outside the desk itself was reading the traffic. Or cared.

Over the years the CIA devised a special language, "cabalese," for use in cables. Originally this was done in the interests of brevity, when field operators had to decode each letter from a One Time Pad. The modern machinery is computer fast and charges no more for additional words, but "cabalese" still must be learned by newcomers to the clandestine services, who also face a strange vocabulary of cryptonyms and cable slugs.

All cables are read and edited by a succession of supervisors until they reach the division chief, who releases them. In the CIA one's cable writing is anonymous, as all cables go out from the "director."

One especially significant operational cable was the IMMEDIATE we sent the CIA station chief in Luanda on August 7. It instructed him to brief the consul general, GPSWISH, on the IAFEATURE program. Simultaneously the State Department sent a message through a special channel, called the ROGER channel, which it used exclusively for sensitive messages about the CIA, advising GPSWISH that he would receive an important briefing from the CIA station chief. This would make it clear to SWISH that the State Department endorsed the Angola program; yet it would not expose any details to the State Department communicators in Washington or in Luanda.

Potts and Bantam repeatedly massaged the cable, until they were satisfied. The briefing would inform GPSWISH of the fact that a paramilitary program was being undertaken in Angola with the approval of the 40 Committee and the highest levels of the United States government, and that it was highly sensitive. Ambassador Sheldon Vance, (temporarily) in Kinshasa, and Ambassador Wilkowski in Lusaka were the only officials outside of Washington who had been briefed. The presidents of Zaire and Zambia, Mobutu and Kaunda, were involved. This much was true, but the cable then proceeded to describe the program in less than candid terms, designed to soften the blow on GPSWISH.

It admitted that the program would support Roberto and Savimbi but claimed that it was designed to promote a peaceful solution in Angola. Funds were being provided for Roberto, Savimbi, and Mobutu, but there was to be no direct provision of materiel to the Angolan groups by the CIA. It was a resupply operation to Mobutu's army, which had been selling arms to Roberto, and there was an understanding with Mobutu that no CIA arms would go directly into Angola.

In sum it illustrated the CIA's willingness to deceive a State Department principal officer in a war-torn post that was controlled by our enemy, in this case the MPLA. Obviously our arms would not promote a peaceful solution, they added fuel to the bloody conflict. And it was more than a resupply operation. From the first airplane loads in July, throughout the war, CIA officers supervised the trans-shipment of CIA arms directly into Angola.

By the end of the second week, ten days after I had come up from Texas, the task force was lodged in a small office which was "vaulted," i.e., protected by a combination of tumbler locks and electronic sensors. Once the vault was secured at night, any unauthorized entry and even a movement as slight as a falling piece of paper would trigger alarms in the office of security. I had been joined by seven case officers, two assistants, and two secretaries. Among the officers were three of Bantam's protegés: one spoke Korean as a second language, another Japanese, and none was familiar with Africa. One of them advertised his special status by establishing bankers' hours, coming to work as late as 10:00 A.M. and leaving around 5:00—making it clear that he had "protection." The second spent hours filling, tamping, and lighting his pipe, while visiting with anyone that walked past. The third joined Laura and others by plunging into task-force activities, arriving early, staying late, and turning out good work. Thanks to their efforts the task force was functional, and in time would even achieve a certain frantic efficiency.

As I began to learn my way around Angolan matters I became aware of a major problem. The glaring weakness of the program was a lack of information about our allies and about the interior of Angola. We were mounting a major covert action to support two Angolan liberation movements about which we had little reliable intelligence. Most of what we knew about the FNLA came from Roberto, the chief recipient of our largesse, and it was obvious that he was exaggerating and distorting facts in order to keep our support. We knew even less about Savimbi and UNITA. I planned to fill this intelligence gap by sending someone into the guerrilla base camps inside Angola. My first candidate for that mission was myself.

On Friday, August 8, the 40 Committee met to discuss Angola; we had spent the day before scrambling to get ready, preparing elaborate charts for Colby's use in explaining the progress of the program. We had worked for hours in Potts's office devising a simplified, yet upbeat presentation, laced with carefully chosen phrases to achieve a positive tone. The format for each chart was initially handwritten on scratch paper by Potts himself; then we filled in the blanks with appropriate figures and details.

The charts were to be typed onto 8-by-11 1/2-inch sheets of paper and delivered to Graphics, where a layout would be perfected and a 30-by-40-inch chart produced either by hand or by photographic enlargement, and mounted on a professional poster board. It was a laborious, maddening process. Every time a chart neared final form Potts would rewrite it or change the format and we would start all over again.

This routine had continued all day and until 10:00 P.M., with Potts making major changes in his own originals five or six times. When he finally relented, I felt that the presentation made a strong case for what we had done so far. One chart showed, in contrasting colors, the estimated troop strengths of the three movements: MPLA 20,-000; FNLA 15,000, with 2,500 attacking Caxito; UNITA 4,000; white Angolans with the FNLA, 20. Roberto had repeatedly claimed to have 30,000 troops, but we had arbitrarily halved that figure because none of us believed him. Anyway, it would sound better, in view of Roberto's recent defeats, to keep the figure lower. Colby was to explain that we did not have accurate figures for the MPLA troop strengths. The "Accomplishments" board was broken into "Military" and "Political" sections, and included such things as "Mobutu persuaded to send FNLA nine Panhards and arms for two battalions"; and "Three plane-loads of arms delivered to Kinshasa"—Colby would mention the size of these C-141 transports for emphasis. Under "Political" there were items like "World sensitized to Soviet arms shipments"; and "Mobutu and Kuanda brought onboard." Another chart laid out our budget for the $14 million. We threw in an attractive little map of Angola, so Colby could show the committee members where Luanda and Caxito and Ambriz were. We also included a briefing sheet of pertinent details for Colby's use. He ought to do well in front of a sympathetic committee. Potts would be there to back him up.

Potts was in early the day of the meeting. I soon had the charts propped against the coffee table and chairs so he could see them. Potts looked them over slowly. I admired them as he went. Then it happened. Potts decided to change one of the lines on the "Accomplishments" board. And he spotted a typographical error. "We can't say that," he declared. "It doesn't look right. I thought I told you . . ."

"Well, sir, there is nothing we can do now. The meeting is at nine-thirty. Colby's car leaves at nine and it's eight-fifteen now."

"But we can't use them like that! . . . Take them back down to Graphics . . . See what they can do."

"Sir they *can't* change them now. There isn't time . . . It took them eight hours to get these done . . ."

"They always find a way. Go on. Hurry."

A director of CIA briefing of the 40 Committee was a historic event; decisions would be made, armies moved, people would die, and Colby would be calm and effective, appearing completely knowledgable on Angola and Central Africa. He could not turn and point to a chart that had a typographical error. Of all its activities, the agency is the most conscientious and professional when preparing memoranda, papers, charts, or briefings for the White House or Congress. No agent operation will ever galvanize a headquarters office into such feverish activity as the announcement that it has to prepare a paper for the director or the 40 Committee. The papers which flow up through the chain of command are letter perfect, immaculately typed, and in the crispest form of Washington's bureaucratic English.

I rounded the turn into "G" corridor, past the northeast entrance, and heard a police whistle shrill and a voice shouting "Sir . . . Sir . . . Stop . . . STOP!"

I jerked to a halt. A woman guard rushed up to me, her hand on her pistol.

"Where are you going?" she demanded.

"Officer, I have to get these to the director and damn quick!"

"That's not the way to the director's office."

"I know, but I have to go to Graphics first."

"You come to my desk, I'm going to have to get your name and badge number and check you out. You can't run in this building."

"Officer, my name is John Stockwell, my badge is HW469. You

call the Africa Division chief if you like but *I'm on my way!*"

I turned and bolted, ignoring her calls after me. It gave me a funny feeling to run from an armed officer, even a CIA guard. I wondered if she would summon help and track me down.

Of course Potts was right. Graphics did the impossible. At nine o'clock the charts were corrected and I delivered them to the director's office on the seventh floor, just as Colby walked out to meet Potts by the waiting elevator. Two of Colby's special guards, dressed in civilian clothes, turned quickly as I rushed up and watched as I handed the carrying case to Potts. One of the guards got into the elevator with Colby and Potts. They would ride nonstop to the basement where another guard was posted, and then travel in an inconspicuous brown, chauffeur-driven Plymouth sedan to the White House. I went back to Africa Division and the morning cable traffic.

Almost immediately Bantam called me in. He was beside himself, fuming and snatching at papers on his desk. I closed the door.

"Look at this! Have you seen this?"

It was a cable from Kinshasa proposing that we put fifteen agency observer teams, Americans, at key locations in the interior of Angola. It argued that this was the only way we would get the intelligence and control we needed for a successful program. It outlined the airplanes, radios, and logistical support we would need to back up the teams.

"Here we go! It's Vietnam, Laos, and Cambodia all over again! Fifty Americans now, five hundred next month. Fifty thousand next year!"

I looked at him helplessly. What could I say?

"That's just like St. Martin!" Carl exploded. "Charging a-head . . ."

St. Martin was an old East Asia hand who had been brought into Africa Division by Larry Devlin after they had worked together in the Laos program. "St. Martin has always been that way," Carl went on. "He damn near closed down my branch in Saigon in 'sixty-two. What happened was, we had approval to spend eight thousand dollars on a Montagnard program and St. Martin was supposed to deliver the money. I gave him the cash and he took off in his car. But somewhere around Dalat he gave the money to a Vietnamese colonel for a different operation. All of it! Then he turned around, came back to Saigon, got into the cash box, took the rest of our U.S. dollars, every penny we had, and gave it to the Montagnards. My branch was closed down for two weeks while the accountants came in and did an audit."

"So what happened?"

Bantam looked thoughtful. "He convinced us the Vietnamese colonel's activity was justified and there wasn't time for approvals."

Bantam shrugged. His anger was passing. "St. Martin worked for me for five tours. We made a good team. With me keeping his feet on the ground, he ran some good operations. In some ways St. Martin is the best operator in the business. A couple of times in Laos, when we were overrun and everyone was ready to quit, he literally led the way back in. He and I and Colby and Nelson . . . we all sort of grew up together in EA Division . . ."

Carl looked down at the cable again. "The terrifying thing is that Colby and Nelson might approve this . . . I'm going to draft a cable myself telling St. Martin to back off . . . and I'm going to see that they send it out."

At ten minutes before two o'clock, Potts and Carl and I walked down the hall and rode the elevators up to the seventh floor to brief the DDO. On the way, Potts told us the 40 Committee had ordered the formation of an interagency working group to monitor the Angolan program. Senior representatives of the State Department, the Pentagon, and the White House would meet as often as necessary to supervise the CIA while it ran the program. Potts clearly resented this.

"At least the CIA will chair it," he said. "We'll have all the meetings here . . . won't have to be running downtown. Maybe if I make them dull enough, they won't come too often."

Carl was silent. I knew from his earlier comments that his frustration over the agency's intervention in Angola was reaching a boiling point.

In Nelson's office we sat on orange-padded, wooden-framed chairs at one end of the large room. Nelson came around his desk and joined us, to establish closer contact. He spoke quietly, but any stranger watching the meeting would have sensed his relative importance. He was a medium-sized man, about Colby's build, with bushy eyebrows and tinted glasses, through which he looked at me with sparkling, friendly eyes. His seventh-floor penthouse office was walled on the east by floor-to-ceiling glass which provided too much bright sunshine for comfortable paperwork, and a view of the stately trees which line the George Washington Parkway.

Potts briefed him on the program, while Carl listened morosely and I took notes. He reviewed the approvals, the projected budget (still $14 million), the flights of arms, and the relative troop strengths. He also summarized the meeting of the 40 Committee, which had approved the forwarding of arms to Savimbi and had ordered the formation of the interagency working group. The 40 Committee had also discussed the need for foreign advisors to bolster the African troops of our allies. Potts mentioned the decision to send one of the agency's prepackaged units of foreign weapons.

Nelson listened, his eyes focused on the coffee table. When Potts finished, Carl took the floor. "Now would be a good time for us to decide just how involved we want to get. We're sending some arms . . . we can let them do the rest for themselves . . ."

Nelson was still silent. Potts looked argumentatively at Carl. I watched all three.

Nelson spoke. "Gentlemen, we've been given a job to do. Let's not sit around wringing our hands." He paused and looked at each of us sharply from under his thick eyebrows.

"What is our next step?" he asked.

Potts was silent, thinking. Carl was out of it.

"Sir," I said, "we've got to have a look inside Angola. We don't know enough about our allies."

"What do you suggest?"

"We should have a first-hand report from Ambriz and Savimbi's base at Silva Porto."

Potts gave me a reproachful look. Carl's face clouded even darker. I tried to ignore them, although their stares made me nervous. I knew Potts resented any subordinate taking the initiative. Since Carl had heard me expressing reservations about the program only a week before, my enthusiasm in front of the DDO must have sounded self-serving, almost hypocritical. But I was determined to be the one to survey the situation inside Angola and this was my opportunity to sell myself to the DDO.

"We would want someone with an adequate military background," Nelson said.

"Yes, sir. But also someone who knows Africa and can help us run the program back here."

"I understand you grew up in that part of Africa . . . Weren't you in the marines?"

"Yes, sir, infantry. Reconnaissance. And Vietnam, upcountry."

He looked at me thoughtfully and then at the coffee table again. I could see that he was keenly aware of everyone in the room.

"I suggest you proceed immediately to Kinshasa and then go to Ambriz and Silva Porto. When you come back, be prepared to brief whomever is interested downtown." It was an order.

My mind was already ticking off passport, shots, visas, reservations, cash. I should cable Kinshasa and Lusaka to let them know I'm coming. The Zaire embassy would be closed until Monday. The earliest I could get my visas and leave would be next Tuesday on Pan Am 151, the "Red-eye Special" from Kennedy.

Potts took me into his office to work out the details. I would take a two-man team of communicators and keep twenty-four–hour radio contact with Kinshasa. He was worried about me or any other case officer visiting an Angolan combat zone, fearful of the secrets I could reveal if I were captured and interrogated. Hence the requirement for communicators and twenty-four–hour radio contact.

On Monday morning, shortly before noon, Bill Avery came into my office. He had flown into Washington the night before from Kinshasa, where he had been helping the station receive the first shipments of arms. He spoke softly, but his voice had a hard impersonal ring. I knew him only by reputation as a senior SOG paramilitary expert.

"I just briefed Potts and Carl," he began. "I thought you should also have my report."

He and St. Martin had seen Mobutu five days before and spelled out the program to him. "Mobutu was pleased," he said. "It seemed to be about what he had hoped to get from the U.S., although he kept asking for more."

"Mobutu is screwing up Zaire pretty good, you know, "Avery continued. "He simply has no idea how to run a country."

The program needed everything. All kinds of basic equipment: Trucks, jeeps, artillery, mortars, antitank weapons, airplanes. This wasn't a very big war yet, but everyone was underestimating what we were getting into. Ambriz was seven hundred kilometers from Kinshasa over bad roads. There wasn't enough fuel, even if they had trucks. So far, Mobutu's air force was doing most of the hauling, but he couldn't be expected to risk his C-130s in Angola for long. And his DC-4 couldn't handle it all. Mobutu expected us to get some C-130s over there fast.

And some boats. Potts had just given Avery permission to add a couple of the agency's high performance Swift patrol boats* to the shipload of arms, to patrol the lower Congo River and attack coastal shipping between Luanda and Cabinda.

I had been up and down the lower Congo River several times on ocean freighters before there was regular commercial air traffic between the United States and Central Africa, and once on a U.S. Navy ship I steamed two hundred kilometers upriver to Matadi where the channel was broken by falls. From there you rode electric trains through the mountains to Kinshasa. All surface freight goes in by this same route today. Near its mouth the river flows along the Zaire/Angola border, with the shipping channel actually in the Angolan half, making this vital link with the outside world, like the Benguela railroad, subject to Angolan control. Boats and coastal steamers ply a lazy trade up and down the Atlantic coast, and agents were reporting that the MPLA was constantly shipping arms from the Congo (Brazzaville) to Luanda.**

"And one more thing," Avery said, choosing his words carefully. "The Kinshasa station has some problems. St. Martin is energetic and imaginative. But sometimes he gets carried away with enthusiasm. Headquarters should make its cables to Kinshasa crystal clear to avoid misunderstandings. If possible, you should keep St. Martin on a short leash. Jimmy Bartlett, the deputy COS, is steady as a rock. That will help." Avery went on to suggest we keep the other members of the Kinshasa station out of it; run it with temporary officers

---

*The Swift is a favorite CIA patrol craft of about fifteen meters, which the agency used on Lake Tanganyika during the Congo operation of the 1960s, and also in Southeast Asia.
**The French Congo and Belgian Congo both assumed the title, Republic of Congo, at independence in the early 1960s. In 1971 Mobutu changed the name of the Congo (Kinshasa) to "Zaire."

who could be yanked out when it was over. And Kinshasa needed help right away: air operations officers, ground, maritime, logistics, and finance officers. They desperately needed infantry training officers because no one in the area knew how to handle the weapons we were sending.

"How about you," I said. "Would you be willing to go back?"

He looked morose. "I suppose I would. This is the only war we've got right now."

Next morning I took my suitcase with me to work, ready to travel. At 1:00 P.M. a secretary drove me to Dulles in her Nova. On the way she handed me my worn black diplomatic passport, my tickets, and fifteen hundred dollars.

"How did you get the money," I asked, counting it.

"I signed your name, over at State."

"Forgery?"

"Just be glad I didn't sign for three thousand and keep the rest."

She also handed me a slender notebook which looked at first like an ordinary checkbook. Inside was a pad of edible, water-soluble rice paper which, supposedly, I could gobble down if I were captured. I asked her what my Angolan hosts were supposed to think when I consulted my checkbook in the Angolan hinterlands. For her benefit I tore out a page and masticated laboriously until I could finally swallow it. Like many OTS (Office of Technical Services) gimmicks, this was a classroom toy which had little use in the field. A case officer hardly wants to make irreplaceable notes on paper that dissolves at the slightest touch of sweat or rain. And I had little confidence in the ability of this paper to fulfill its intended purpose. I had once presented an agent in training with a similar pad. By way of demonstration, I had torn out a page and dropped it in my gin and tonic. For the rest of the meeting it had floated buoyantly, unaffected by the liquid.

Attached to the pad was an ordinary looking Bic ballpoint, impregnated with esoteric writing chemicals. With the point retracted I could write secret messages which the Kinshasa station could develop by spraying on certain chemicals. I clipped it in my jacket —at least it was a functional ballpoint.

I got on the Eastern flight to New York broke—no one had made arrangements to pay the $2,300 air freight charges for our sixteen boxes of radio gear, and we all chipped in from our travel allowances. Even so, I had the same peaceful feeling you get after you leave the plane on a tactical parachute jump. Behind are hours of tedious preparation. Shortly will begin another exhausting ordeal. But for the moment your chute is open, you're safe, it's quiet, and you've nothing to worry about. The task force was looking good, and this trip was going to be bloody interesting.

I dozed all the way to New York.

6

Kinshasa

Good case officering requires intense concentration. As the semi-literate sergeant told us in Marine Corps basic school: "Proper prior preparation prevents piss-poor performance, sir." Prior *mental* preparation minimizes the case officer's risks. I spent the fifteen-hour flight from Kennedy International to Ndjili Airport at Kinshasa doing mental exercises in my conversational French; I hadn't been in a French-speaking country for five years and it wouldn't do to go up against Roberto fumbling for words like a tourist with a phrase-book. I then set my mind on Kinshasa and Angola and tried to relive every experience I'd had in both, seeing the people again, remembering names, incidents, walking through airports, restaurants, offices, judo clubs.

This mission was important and I knew it could easily attract the attention of the Soviets, Cubans, Chinese, North Koreans, or French, although none of them would be likely to do anything dramatic to obstruct it. The press was an obvious liability.* Probably most worrisome was the knowledge that every step I took would be watched by jealous colleagues. St. Martin and some officers in Kinshasa station would be especially critical. To them I would be a headquarters staff officer intruding in their territory.

CIA lore is full of incidents which have happened to case officers while they traveled the world. Case officers are subject to the same embarassments any tourist suffers—snarled schedules, lost passports, lost money and luggage, and getting off the plane at the wrong destination. In addition, case officers have been known to lose secret notebooks or be recognized by agents from their operational past and blow their new covers and missions. More often than one would believe, they have chatted indiscreetly with total strangers and had the conversation reported to other CIA officers. Professional reputations, if not careers, are seriously damaged by such incidents.

Airports are especially hazardous to case officers. Customs and immigration officials are trained to detect the unusual. In some countries they are especially alert to CIA officers. They can arrest, search, and detain anyone they choose under the pretext of suspected smuggling. I once watched an angry Zairian official very nearly strip and search the person of a CIA GS 17 who had forgotten to speak politely.

During a four-hour lay-over at Kennedy I had briefed the communicators on our mission. They had been "volunteered" so abrupty they scarcely had time to assemble the necessary gear, much less think of where they were going. Neither had ever been to Africa or knew much about Angola. Once in Kinshasa they would disappear into the closed world of the embassy communications center, while I was busy with St. Martin, the FNLA, and UNITA. And inside Angola I would be immersed in my mission while they monitored the radios. In the privacy of a crowded restaurant we had talked about Angola and then gossiped, establishing the bonds of under-

---

*Actually, at least in more routine operations, case officers most fear the U.S. ambassador and his staff, then restrictive headquarters cables, then curious, gossipy neighbors in the local community, as potential threats to operations. Next would come the local police, then the press. Last of all is the KGB—in my twelve years of case officering I never saw or heard of a situation in which the KGB attacked or obstructed a CIA operation.

standing and confidence that would make us a team when we hit the field.

Just before we boarded Pan Am 151 I had telephoned headquarters. Things sometimes happen quickly in the intelligence business. More than once case officers have had their missions changed after their seat belts were buckled. Paul Foster came on the line and we chatted for a few minutes. When we hung up I stood reflecting on CIA telephone security. We had mentioned the FNLA, Angola, and some communications equipment that was being procured. Any intelligent person eavesdropping on the conversation would know that I was on my way to Kinshasa on an important mission relating to the war in Angola.

We banked over the Congo River and the mountains, descending to Ndjili Airport, twenty miles from Kinshasa. Landing heavily, we taxied to the nondescript white terminal. A half-mile on our left, were several rough-looking corrugated iron hangers, two C-130s, a DC-4, a couple of C-47s, and several single-engine planes—Mobutu's air force. Strewn about the grass between runways was a graveyard of stripped airframes, relics of the CIA Congo program of the 1960s.

It was just after 4:00 P.M. local time. Inside there would be the usual forty-minute wait for our luggage, perhaps longer, considering our sixteen boxes of radio equipment. My cable had made it clear we were bringing in a large quantity of gear that could not be opened by customs officials in a public air terminal. CIA procedure in such cases called for the local station to process the papers in advance of our arrival, getting help from the embassy administrative officer, and for a case officer to meet us at the airport to insure that there were no snags.

Someone was waving at us, a young man in a sports shirt, not an American. He would be the embassy's administrative assistant, a local, no doubt a displaced European whose primary responsibility was to meet and guide all official American visitors through the pitfalls of Zairian customs. He introduced himself as "Monsieur Albert," took our passports and began processing us into the country.

No one from the station was in sight, a bad sign. While waiting for Monsieur Albert to work his magic, I turned and walked to a souvenir counter and began bargaining with the salesclerk, practicing my French. Some time later one of the communicators called to me.

"Hey, John!" he said, "You'd better get over here."

At the baggage claim counter it was pretty clear that things had come unstuck; we were in danger of going public on the spot. A customs officer had a firm grip on one of our boxes, tugging at the tape. The other communicator was just as firmly holding the top of the box down. They were glaring at each other. Three other customs officers were hurrying up, looking aggressive.

Since the first days of independence Zairian customs officials have struggled to assert their authority over arrogant white travelers, especially those who insist on diplomatic privilege or other special treatment. After independence, the airport was one of the first places to be Africanized and the colonial whites, while contemptuous of the blacks' ability to officiate, were anxious—airports were their sole link with the security of their motherlands. Whites sneered and the blacks responded with harassment and delays. In recent years the tension had subsided. Now Zairian officials process most passengers with little comment, but incidents still occur.

Monsieur Albert was standing several feet back, obviously intimidated. The other passengers had long since cleared through the area and left.

I stopped a polite yard short of the official and addressed him, citing the privileges of my diplomatic passport. He was unimpressed with protocol, and snapped an order in Lingala. Two guards pounced on the boxes and disappeared into the restricted area. I followed the customs official into his office, realizing that he was in charge of the airport. At least, I insisted, he could grant me the courtesy of a call to the embassy. St. Martin eventually came on the line and wanted to talk to the customs officer. I listened in. St. Martin was pulling out all the stops, threatening to call President Mobutu himself. The customs official was still unimpressed. He hung up after St. Martin told me to wait where I was.

I sat down and began to work on the customs officer and his assistant. The customs chief of Ndjili Airport could be valuable when IAFEATURE personnel and equipment began pouring into Kinshasa. His assistant was from my old province, the Kasai, and we both spoke Tshiluba fluently. They began to thaw.

To the case officer intelligence is people, not information. Recruiting agents is the name of the game. A case officer who recruits gets promoted, and good officers are *always* assessing people for recruitment, nearly everyone they meet. DDO studies have shown that 10 percent of the case officers make 90 percent of all recruitments, comparable to the ratio of submarine commanders in World War II who sank ships. Most case officers never recruit an agent in their careers and must accept the lesser role of maintaining operations others have created. Recruited airport officials, taxi drivers, and police officers are considered part of the "plumbing" of a CIA station —with little access to intelligence themselves, they facilitate the case officer's other activities.

When the phone rang an hour later, we were having our second beer, the two Ndjili officials and I. I would probably never see them again, but talking to them, "establishing rapport" as we said in the CIA, gave me confidence. After a four-year absence from Africa I had not lost my touch.

Our beer-fueled rapport made it easy for the two officials to back down. "Mon ami," the Kasaian said. "Why didn't you tell us these boxes have special radio equipment for the president to use in Angola?"

Our embassy limousine pulled onto the crowded highway, Monsieur Albert braking and swerving defensively around other vehicles but plunging directly into the potholes. If Kinshasa had been spruced up and the roads repaired for the Ali-Foreman fight the year before, you couldn't tell it now. Bracing the rice paper notebook on my knee I jotted down biographical details about the customs officials. Someone from the station might follow up.

The station administrative officer helped us unload our boxes in front of the embassy. I thanked Albert and was almost through the door when he called out, "M'sieu' John, I think you're missing a box."

He was right. There were only fifteen.

"Welcome to Kinshasa," I muttered, continuing up the stairs.

I was not a stranger here, and I had worked with four of the regular officers in the Kinshasa station in previous assignments. The deputy chief of station, Jimmy Bartlett, had been under business cover when I was in the Ivory Coast. I had been his inside man, his only direct contact with the CIA. Another case officer, Roger Mueller, was a chess buddy from my previous headquarters tour. He was handling some of the Kinshasa station's unilateral operations (most of Kinshasa station operations have always been bilateral, i.e., declared to the Zairian security service) and hoped to stay out of the Angolan program. Jerry Jacobson had an elaborately backstopped cover position in the consular section that led him to avoid the station offices altogether. He had been an interim career trainee when I was chief of the Kenya/Uganda section in 1972.

The clandestine services is a small clubbish unit of 4,500 people compartmented into geographic divisions. Africa Division itself had less than 400 staffers and after ten years I knew nearly all of them. Our assignments and operational travels overlapped and crisscrossed like the trails of migrating wildebeest on an East African plain. A night on the town in Paris, a three-day course in lock-picking at headquarters, lunch in a Nairobi restaurant, all years apart, can be enough for a kind of understanding rare in other lines of work.

A man I felt I understood, despite our differences, was an officer who had addressed my training class at the "Farm" in 1965. Afterwards, he had opened up a surprisingly long way, referring to an adventure in Lubumbashi, driving about town after curfew with Patrice Lumumba's body in the trunk of his car, trying to decide what to do with it.* Five years later I found this man in an Asian post, the chief of station, sitting at a desk mounted on a platform a foot higher than the rest of the room. His chair was a tall, straight-backed Victorian antique, behind it was a background of flags and drapes. He was glisteningly bald, and stared down at me through half-closed, puffy eyes, as I tried to brief him about my mission. And in 1974 I found him again, in a European station, still playing at "Goldfinger" in his antique chair, the same one as far as I could tell. We dined in the palatial "safehouse" apartment which the U.S. taxpayer maintained for him in the city. (His other home was a residence thirty miles away.) Twice during dinner he went to the tiled lavatory where he spent fifteen minutes scrubbing and drying his hands, cleaning his fingernails, and staring at himself in the mirror. Such eccentricities and trademarks become part of CIA lore.

The CIA's clubbishness is in a good part responsible for many of the CIA's current problems. How does one discipline a colleague

*He presented this story in a benign light, as though he had been trying to help. It was not until 1975 that I learned the CIA had plotted Lumumba's death.

who twenty years before spent sweltering nights with you in a Chinese embassy installing "bugs"? Or who was the godfather of your children twenty-five years ago in Rome? Or whose wife was now your wife, the exchange having taken place long ago in Bangkok? In an open, competitive environment one might do the necessary thing, but in the closed fraternity of the CIA it was impossible.

Jerry Jacobson's cover as the ambassador's assistant was about as well protected as the agency is able to manage as he was more fully integrated into the State Department personnel system. Nevertheless, any State employee in Washington could ascertain the truth with a simple inquiry in the right place, and at least every American in the Kinshasa embassy would be fully aware of Jerry's real work. Inside the State Department, a separate personnel office handles CIA paperwork and travel arrangements. The dozens of various forms in each file bear special indicators which ensure segregation. The CIA has never been as successful in putting officers in deep cover as the Russian GRU and KGB. Deep cover requires patience and Americans are not patient. After a couple of years in one place they begin to demand promotions, reassignments. No one wants to be a career private, or even a career captain. They want to be in the mainstream, to advance up the chain of command. Recognizing this, when the agency finds someone with deep cover potential, it makes them *contract* or *career agents*. The connotation is ominous—agents are not insiders; agents are to be used, and discarded when their usefulness is finished.*

The agency has attempted to cope with this disability in many ways over the years, initiating and dropping one deep-cover program after the other. The latest strategy is a parallel recruitment and training program. Young officer candidates are kept outside the headquarters building and away from the historic training and processing centers in the Commerce building on Glebe Road in Arlington Virginia** and the "Farm" at Camp Perry. Some of these deep-cover officers will take State Department Foreign Service Institute courses in Washington and then go to the field as embassy economic or

---

*CIA staff officers are called case officers and their sources or spies are called "agents." This is the opposite of the FBI where "agents" are the inside officers.
**Formerly this was the "blue building," across the street from the present Commerce building. CIA shuttle buses and limousines make hourly runs between all the principle CIA buildings in the Washington area.

consular officers; others will be businessmen, professors, students, or tourists. But they will still be conspicuously "CIA" to all who work with or near them, in the embassies, in Washington, or in the local communities overseas.

Few experienced CIA case officers will ever be enthusiastic about acting as an "agent" in a dangerous situation. They know too well how agents are sometimes abused by the CIA. For example, one extremely valuable Vietnamese agent had for years reported accurately on the communist high command. He became so famous inside the agency that he was discussed openly at headquarters and in Saigon, even at social functions in front of nonagency Americans and foreigners. At headquarters he was commonly cited by lecturers in the Vietnam orientation seminar, attended by a wide variety of people outside the DDO. This insecure, unprofessional conduct was a clear threat to the agent's life as well as to his viability as a reporting asset. The case officer tried to deal with it through the chief of station, but the COS refused to take any action, claiming that an effort to quiet the gossip would only provoke more.

At the same time in the COS's office, there was another top-secret operation which was handled much differently—a friend warned me to quit asking about it lest I be ordered out of the country by the COS. Eventually, I learned about it from an officer who worked with me up country. On a previous tour my friend had helped install "bugs" in the South Vietnamese presidential palace.* The CIA was eavesdropping on President Thieu's private conversations. Security of the two operations differed as night from day, precisely because exposure of the audio operation against Thieu would be sensational news, embarrassing to the United States president, and possibly fatal to the COS's career; the agent, on the other hand, though he was providing incomparable intelligence, was not a political entity. His exposure would be an inconvenience, but not a catastrophe, except to himself.

The Kinshasa station offices on the second floor of the embassy had changed little since my last visit six years before. I found the deputy COS working at his desk, waiting for me. He offered to lock up any notes I had, but declined to stop somewhere for a drink and a chat about Kinshasa.

He would instead drive me to St. Martin's villa. On the way to the

---

*The CIA had given Thieu presents of TV sets and furniture which were bugged.

car he apologized for the problem at the airport, adding, "The bastards *are* bloody difficult."

"Why didn't you get the proper customs clearances," I asked, "and meet me at the airport?"

"St. Martin wanted to take care of it himself—show 'em he knows the president, I guess."

Had St. Martin set me up? It was a machiavellian thought, but such events in defense of CIA "territory" were common enough.

St. Martin's huge villa, twenty minutes from the embassy, had been used by Kinshasa station chiefs dating back to Larry Devlin, when he ran the Congo program in the early sixties. I had slept in its guest rooms several times over the years.

The foyer, where Jimmy set my bag, was as large as the living room of most American homes. Beyond was a vast space with three separate clusters of furniture, rather like a hotel lobby. That was the living room. A wall of french windows opened onto the $40,000 swimming pool, which another COS had added at government expense in 1968. The right wing of the house included four or five bedrooms, each with its own bath. On the left were the dining room, kitchen, pantry, and servants' quarters. Altogether there were six bathrooms, including the one in the additional servants' quarters in the yard. The villa was cooled by a dozen air conditioners, mounted in the walls.

The rent and utility bills for all this, I had heard, came to $40,000 a year, initially paid by the embassy, reimbursed by the CIA. In the CIA view, such luxurious accomodations were necessary to give the station chief sufficient presence in the community; I had often wondered if the U.S. taxpayer would agree. Did the American public visualize its cold warriors doing their work in the back alleys of the world?

St. Martin hurried out to greet me. He was of medium height, slender, with greying hair. His eyes sparkled, but the stresses of case officering and the attendant cocktails, cigarettes, and long hours were reflected in the lines and shadows of his face.

Jerking his head back toward the living room he indicated that a meeting was in progress. I could see an African sitting on one of the sofas. St. Martin led me to the door of the hall and pointed to a bedroom. Would I please make myself at home and come out when I was refreshed.

St. Martin's living room was a busy place. Station personnel dropped by to confer with him and chat with me. Africans and Europeans, obviously agents and developmental contacts, came and went, passing each other in the foyer or sitting at different points in the living room while St. Martin hopped back and forth.

Most who entered St. Martin's villa would be aware that he was CIA. This flagrant exposure of agents to each other and to other CIA station personnel scarcely shocked me—it was normal for most CIA stations. I was a little surprised to find, in the middle of the crowded living room, an untended, wide-open briefcase—I wasn't sure which CIA officer had left it there—with sensitive IAFEATURE cables right on top.

Separate offices, housing, social habits, and the custom of inheriting the house, car, and "friends" of one's predecessor make it rare that any CIA officer is known in the official community of the host country as anything other than "Mr. CIA" or "one of *them.*"

Most case officers accept this notoriety with a perverse pleasure. Many operate as though they wore invisible badges, proclaiming, "I'm CIA, talk to me." This cavalier approach to cover became the vogue under Allen Dulles, the gentleman agent of World War II, whose superficial operations in neutral Switzerland inclined him permanently to underestimate the realities and consequences of intelligence operations. Nothing pleased Dulles more than to be known to the world as the CIA director. And he was fond of holding regional meetings overseas, rather like sales conferences, with his station chiefs. While abroad, in insecure areas, he made a great show of turning up the volume on radios or even taking conversations into the bathroom where a running shower could provide security against "bugs."* From these histrionics it was logical to conclude that while Dulles was completely indifferent to his field officers' covers, he did not fancy being quoted in police or opposition reporting.

Senior officers competed to emulate the style of the gentleman spy, and younger officers could not be expected to keep a separate discipline. In Kinshasa in the late 1960s the chief of station would hold large cocktail parties for Zairian liaison officials and members of the diplomatic community. He required every member of his CIA sta-

---

*Modern technology now easily penetrates the sound of a running shower, to record voices.

tion to attend those parties, laughing at any who protested that their covers would be blown.

Like most young officers who had learned by the book, I was rudely awakened to the operational realities of the field. My predecessor in one post had handled five clandestine agents. Three of them communicated through post office boxes; to deliver a written report and pick up money, they would call the European receptionist at the embassy, who was neither cleared for CIA activities nor completely loyal to the Americans. She would in turn relay the messages, advising the chief of station something to the effect that, "Your friend from Fada called. He has a shipment of skins and needs eight thousand bananas." The CIA station secretary would then drive to the post office and service the appropriate box. She did this so regularly that the beggars on the steps of the post office, in an effort to be helpful, would call out as she parked the car, "Non, Mademoiselle, he did not come yet," or "Oui, Mademoiselle, it is ready."

Once or twice a month, in this tiny fishbowl of a town, the case officer would meet each agent a block from the embassy in a safehouse which was "covered" as an embassy guest apartment. After parking in the lot behind, the case officer would take the back stairs to the third floor, while the agents came up the front. Three of the five agents were introduced to me in that apartment, two during the same morning. The fifth I met in the living room of the case officer's house. Later, I discovered that the servant in the apartment below the safehouse was the brother of the servant in my predecessor's house. He knew exactly what was going on and could identify all the agents. So could the Greek couple that ran a little grocery store on the ground floor. As I made friends through sports and chess, I began to receive well-meant suggestions. "M. David [my predecessor four generations before] used to live in my cousin's house. He said it was very good for his activities." Or, "M. Jacques used to pick up the Lebanese gentleman in the alley behind my store . . . It's a safe spot and no one can see, except from my balcony." Such conversations also occurred in my other posts, where other American embassy personnel and people in the official community had gossiped freely about their "spooks."

In Burundi a succession of case officers had written numerous intelligence reports from information gathered by their agents, mostly about the Congolese rebels across Lake Tanganyika. These reports repeatedly described the activities of a submarine on the lake, mercenary-piloted airplanes which flew from landing strips in the hills of Burundi, and large supplies of rifles buried near Rumonge. That all of these notions were ludicrous, entirely at odds with physical, logistical, and political possibilities, did not deter CIA headquarters. Africa Division blithely disseminated hundreds of these reports to the intelligence community.

Over the years I learned that the operational standards I had found in my first assignments, low as they were, were fairly typical of most CIA stations.

Jetlag brought me awake the next morning just as light was coming in through the window. I showered and dressed quickly, and went outside. It was nearing 7:00 A.M. The sky was heavy with clouds. Outside, away from the air conditioners, I could hear Kinshasa's morning sounds: people calling out, a car, a truck, some yellow and black weaverbirds quarreling in a palm over the back wall. In the driveway a uniformed African, doubtless St. Martin's chauffeur, was polishing a Mercedes 220. He grunted when I addressed him, but didn't seem to speak any language I knew. I wondered how St. Martin communicated with him. The Mercedes was sleek and new.

Nearly all case officers in the field are authorized QP, or quasi-personal, cars which are paid for by the agency. The justification is that an automobile is as essential to a spy handler as it is to a field salesman stateside. The argument loses some force when officers insist, as they often do, on having a Mercedes or Audi rather than a less conspicuous Volkswagen or Renault.

Back inside I found St. Martin drinking coffee in his bathrobe.

"John," he said, "I've got to meet Colonel Mwamba for breakfast. Maybe you'd better go on to the office and wait for me. Take my car. Tell the driver, 'American embassy.'" He paused and poked at an empty coffee cup. Then he pushed at a buzzer on the wall. "Where is that damn 'boy'?"

To St. Martin I was an intruder, a representative from headquarters. He would keep my leash as tight as possible. Thus, I was not surprised when he showed up about eleven and gave one of his American case officers elaborate instructions on exactly where to take me, which car to use, whom we should talk to, and when to come back. While I was in Kinshasa, I was in a difficult position, having no control over my schedule, my transportation, and my lodging. On the ground here, St. Martin was god. While it would never do for me to return to headquarters with only a superficial understanding of the FNLA, it was equally important to maintain the amenities. In any contest St. Martin would win. Colby, Nelson, and Potts were sure to support their station chief.

The FNLA headquarters occupied a block-sized compound not far from the embassy. It was surrounded by a high, bare brick wall. In front of a sheet-iron gate stood a solitary guard in a shapeless uniform. He held an old-looking FAL automatic rifle. Only after considerable name-dropping were we permitted inside.

The inner compound was crowded with small brick buildings, their screenless wooden doors and windows unpainted and in many cases splintered and broken. Between the buildings ran narrow dirt drives and walkways. The compound, I guessed had once been used by a small trucking company or perhaps a produce wholesaler. Dozens of people bustled from building to building, some wearing the grey green uniforms of war, others in civvies and barefoot. For every soldier there seemed to be several women and children. The sultry air carried the smell of cassava root and open sewage. A truck laden with people growled slowly through the gate, followed by a jeep filled with soldiers.

The FNLA was rooted in the Kongo tribe. Once the greatest tribe of the west African flank, when the Congo was splintered in the nineteenth-century partitioning of Africa, the Kongo gave its name to the Belgian Congo, the French Congo, and the mighty Congo River. Portuguese slave traders conquered the tribe, and hundreds of thousands of its sons and daughters were part of the flow of slaves to Europe, Brazil, and North America. Despite subjugation by the Portuguese, the Bakongo migrated freely across the superimposed colonial borders, following economic opportunities and fleeing oppression.

In 1878 the Baptist Missionary Society (BMS) of London was received in São Salvadore, the historic capital of the Kongo nation, by the Kongo king, Dom Pedro V. Thirty years later a BMS interpreter, Miguel Necaça, became the father of the modern Kongo liberation movement. He was followed by other mission-educated Kongo activists, who struggled to gain control of the Kongo chieftainship, only to be thwarted as the Portuguese succeeded in maintaining a succession of puppets on the traditional throne. By 1942, however, the activists had settled in the Belgian Congo under the leadership of Miguel Necaça's son, Manuel Barros Necaça. This exile group, first called the Matadi and Leopoldville groups, evolved into the UPA (União das Populacoes de Angola) in 1958, and became the FNLA in 1961. With the departure of the Belgian colonialists from Zaire in 1960 and the ascendancy of a government friendly to the Angolan rebels, the FNLA at last had a secure base of operations.

In March 1961, years of careful planning culminated in the massive invasion across the Zairian border. The violence of this revolt appalled even FNLA leaders in Kinshasa, who had underestimated the repressed hatred and frustration of the Kongo tribesmen. Although the revolt was partially checked by the brutal reaction of the Portuguese army, guerrilla fighting continued in northern Angola until 1974 when Portugal lost its will to keep its African colonies.*

Now, fifteen months later, I commented to my escort officer that all the faces we saw in the FNLA compound in Kinshasa were somber. "Yeah, well," he said, "they've taken some losses in Angola, you know."

Eventually we found a well-fed young man named Timothé Makala, who was supposed to escort me to Ambriz the next day. Makala, it seemed, had just returned from university studies in the United States and seemed nervous and flustered about our mission. Eventually he admitted, with some embarrassment, that he had never in his life set foot in Angola.

We had scarcely settled down to talk, when my CIA escort officer attempted to drag me away, announcing, "Well, St. Martin said we should come directly back to the office."

I took his arm and steered him to his car.

"Listen, you go ahead. Tell St. Martin I'll be along before lunch. I want to browse around, get a feeling for these people."

"I'd better stick with you. St. Martin said . . ."

"You just go on."

He started the motor, then cut it, attempting to get out again. "How will you get back to the embassy? I'd better stick around. This place isn't too safe, you know." He rolled his eyes around the compound.

I held the door firmly shut.

*Marcum, *The Angolan Revolution,* Vol. I.

"I'll *walk* back to the embassy. Or catch a cab. Or maybe one of these nice people will take me to lunch. I've got a job to do and not much time to do it. Please . . . Just go back to the office . . . Tell St. Martin everything will be fine. At the latest I will be at his house before two, to meet Roberto."

He started the motor again and drove briskly out the gate, with an I'm-going-to-tell-my-daddy look on his face.

I found Johnny Eduardo, the FNLA second in command, in an office, trapped by a dozen people who were contending loudly for his attention. Seated behind a bare table, looking hot and uncomfortable, Eduardo acknowledged my arrival with a nod, but made no effort to rise. I was barely able to squeeze forward and shake his hand. There was no chance I could make myself heard over the din. We shrugged at each other and I elbowed my way back out. Eduardo was reported to be less tolerant of the Americans even than Roberto, whose arrogance was notorious. No matter that we were bankrolling their war, Eduardo would continue to resent us.

So much for the FNLA headquarters, I thought ruefully, feeling the noontime heat as I walked out of the compound.

What would I find at the FNLA front north of Luanda? We were gambling $14 million that the FNLA fighting organization would be more impressive than its Kinshasa headquarters.

Holden Roberto arrived at St. Martin's at five. While we waited, Bubba Sanders scurried in, trailed by Raymond Chiles. They had slipped into Kinshasa that morning to launch the FNLA propaganda effort, using Kinshasa newspapers. Filled with ideas, they already seemed to know their way around. They dropped names and spoke in half-sentences, as though they had worked in IAFEATURE before, and I guessed they had, many times, in other countries, with different players.

Holden Roberto was trailed by four aides and staffers. We rose to meet them. Taller than the others and wearing an exquisitely tailored Zairian bush jacket, Roberto was a dominant but rebarbative figure. His mouth turned slightly down in an expression of permanent disapproval. His negative impact was compounded by small, darkly tinted glasses which he never took off. I could sense no warmth, although he addressed me politely enough. Bubba and Ray would have some difficulty producing a sympathetic propaganda photo.

Born in São Salvadore, Angola, on January 12, 1923, Roberto was named after a missionary who baptized him Holden Carson Graham. His mother was the eldest child of the revolutionary patriarch, Miguel Necaça, and his father worked for the Baptist mission. In 1925 he was taken to Kinshasa where he attended the Baptist mission school until graduation in 1940. In 1940–1941 he attended school in São Salvadore to discover his Angolan roots. Thereafter he worked for eight years as an accountant for the Belgian colonial administration and played soccer on local clubs where he established lasting friendships with future Congolese politicians. During a visit to Angola in 1951 he witnessed the brutalization of an old man by a callous Portuguese *chefe de posto* and was shocked into political activism.

In 1958 he was elected to represent the UPA at the All-African Peoples Conference in Accra, Ghana. Since blacks in the Belgian and Portuguese colonies could not obtain international travel papers, he was obliged to make his way clandestinely via the French Congo, the Cameroons, and Nigeria. It was worth the trouble. In Accra, Roberto met the cream of the African revolution—Patrice Lumumba, Kenneth Kaunda, Tom Mboya, Franz Fanon, and many others. He was well launched. He rejected Marxist advances, but did espouse Maoist lines, writing friends that "without bloodshed revolution is impossible."

Before returning home he obtained a Guinean passport and visited the United Nations General Assembly in New York where he managed to foment a debate about Angola. He also visited Tunisia, where he gained the sympathy of President Habib Bourguiba. Back in Kinshasa in 1959, he established control of Bakongo revolutionary activities and took credit for the March 1961 offensive in Angola.

Thereafter he formed the Exile Revolutionary Government of Angola (GRAE), drawing in the Ovimbundu activist, Jonas Savimbi, as his foreign minister. His alliance with the Zairians held fast, transcending several upheavals and changes of government. Roberto's relationship with the ultimate Zairian strongman, Joseph Désiré Mobutu* was sealed when he dropped his Mukongo wife and married Mobutu's sister-in-law.

Roberto had continuously resisted a standing MPLA petition for

*Mobutu later changed his name to Mobutu Sese Seko.

a union of all Angolan liberation movements. Agostinho Neto had even followed Roberto to the United States in 1963, calling for a meeting with him and for a sympathetic hearing from the American establishment. Neto was rebuffed on both accounts. The Americans would not hear Neto out, since he was tainted with the Marxist brush. Roberto ducked him, allegedly fearing that the better organized MPLA leaders threatened his dominance. Perhaps, also, Roberto was wise enough to know that competition between his "conservative" movement and the ominously Marxist MPLA would gain him sympathy in the United States. To guarantee the breach between the two movements, Roberto's forces repeatedly captured MPLA activists in northern Angola and transported them to its base at Kinkuza, Zaire, and killed them.

In fact, Roberto was only "conservative" insofar as the word applies to East-West competition. Apart from ideological trappings, he and Neto preached the same things for Angola: national independence, democratic government, agrarian reform, economic development, pan-African unity, and the total destruction of colonial culture.* And Roberto and his FNLA fighters were the more violent.

At any rate, in Kinshasa, Roberto was our man. St. Martin scurried about serving drinks, after arranging the seating so that he and Roberto were on the couch together.

I was placed across the diameter of a pretty large circle, virtually out of the proceedings. Occasionally St. Martin moved a hand in my direction and Roberto glanced at me. God knows what yarn St. Martin was spinning.

"Monsieur le president," I interrupted, rising. "You will be traveling with me tomorrow?" I walked over and sat on the edge of the coffee table in front of Roberto.

"No, I will meet you in Ambriz. First you will go to Carmona to meet my command there."

"Thank you. In Ambriz we will have an opportunity to discuss my mission. Will you permit me to take photographs to show our experts in Washington what the terrain and weapons and FNLA fighters look like?"

"Of course, of course."

"Good. Now I understand that you and M. St. Martin have a lot

*See Marcum, *The Angolan Revolution.*

of other matters to discuss and also you will want to hear the proposals of my colleagues, M. Bubba and M. Raymond, who have come from Washington . . . please excuse me."

If I accomplished anything on this trip it would begin tomorrow in Ambriz.

7

Roberto

Twenty-one hours later I was in the thick of it. A roly-poly Portuguese colonel, Santos Castro, sat before me in the bare servants' quarters of an abandoned house in Ambriz and told me he was surrounded by ambitious fools. His face was shadowed by the light of a candle, whose flame danced in the ocean breeze. His muted, conspiratorial voice was difficult to hear above the crashing surf.

"They all want Angola," he said, "but I have the key. Without me they have nothing."

Castro was one of the people I had come to see, but it hadn't been easy to reach him. It had in fact been a long and wearing day.

To begin with, Makala had arrived late for our departure, and the FNLA truck that was to take us to the airport never showed up. We had to ride in a CIA carryall, with U.S. embassy plates, and that upset the guards at the military gate of Ndjili Airport. Eventually bribes and phone calls got us in, and two of Mobutu's mercenary pilots, a Dane and a Belgian, flew us to Carmona in a thirty-year-old DC-4. As we flew I leaned over their shoulders in the cockpit,

watching the forest below and listening to their grumbling about
their Zairian employers, "They are monkeys, I tell you, monkeys."*
The pilots had not been paid for five months and they were about
to quit.

We had been given a hasty tour of Carmona, the capital of the
northern province of Angola, by three young FNLA politicians who
coldly refused to answer questions and soon dropped us back at the
airport, thirsty and unfed. I wondered if we were putting our best
foot forward. St. Martin had insisted that I play a journalist cover
role, at least until Roberto joined us the next day.

Carmona, on the other hand, only merited a hasty tour. It was a
ghost town, its shops and houses locked and chained shut, waiting
as a prize for the winners of the Angolan civil war. At the airport
Carmona's last hundred Portuguese awaited evacuation to Luanda.
Their faces showed the despair of all refugees, whether the Belgians
I had seen fleeing the Congo in 1960, or, more recently, the frantic
mobs leaving Vietnam.

Eventually a small plane ferried us to Ambriz, a smaller abandoned town on the coast. Our arrival at the tiny dirt airstrip was
something of a diplomatic failure. The FNLA command had not
been told we were coming, and was skeptical of my journalistic
credentials. Perhaps the fifteen boxes of radio equipment threw them
off. Or my camera may have threatened them.

An African commander in new utilities, with a web belt, a new
Browning 9 mm. pistol, and canvas ammunition pouches, drove up
in a jeep and marched directly to me. He was flanked by two Portuguese commandos whose machine guns were held level, the big
muzzles pointing at my empty stomach.

The black spoke to me harshly in Portuguese.

"I beg your pardon?" I said in English.

"You are under arrest," one of the Portuguese said. "Give him
your camera."

"I beg your pardon?" I repeated

"This is a war zone! We do not allow photographs. We do not
allow reporters. You are under arrest. You will give him your camera

*This term, *"macaque"* in French, was commonly used by the whites in colonial
Africa. Since independence it is tabu. Had Makala, sitting behind me in the plane,
heard and reported the two pilots, they might have been expelled from Zaire.

and come with us." So much for the reporter story. Those were real guns pointed at my gut, loaded and cocked, and the faces behind them weren't smiling. I drew myself up.

"I am not a reporter. I am not a tourist, and I am not a missionary, either. I am a colonel in the American service and a personal representative of Dr. Kissinger. President Roberto invited me to come to Ambriz and to take any pictures necessary for my mission. He will be here tomorrow to show me your camps and your forces."

The black commander did not understand English. He reached impatiently for my camera. Obviously, a nonverbal gesture was required of me to establish authority.

"This camera has no importance," I said. Swinging the three-hundred-dollar Pentax by its strap, I hurled it thirty feet into some trash.

That seemed to impress them. At least, I hoped it had. I wanted nothing more to do with low-level political hacks. I wanted my identity, my status, and my mission understood. I wanted to see the military installations, meet the commanders, talk operations, and have the prime players seek me out. And now, unless I had miscalculated, they would. I was not eager to get back into that plane, with nowhere to go but MPLA-held Luanda. Following a few moments of silence, there was a murmur of discussion as someone translated my remarks, then the sound of machine guns being dropped in the back of the jeep. One of the African soldiers retrieved my camera. Wiping it off with his shirt, he draped it around my neck.

They guided me to the jeep, mumbling apologies, and we drove into town. My communicators followed in a Volkswagen bus with the gear. I sat stiffly in the copilot seat of the jeep, not speaking. I was still very thirsty.

The airstrip was directly on the edge of town. Our jeep took us around a small traffic circle and six blocks down the principal street to a nondescript house near the end. I had already seen, from the plane window, that two blocks away, on my left, was the Atlantic Ocean. Two blocks on my right were bluffs which dropped off into the broad marsh. In front were rocky cliffs descending to a small river which opened to the sea. It was a lovely promontory for a sleepy tropical town, but a potential trap for an army's central command post.

Moments later I had settled into a cane chair on the veranda of a small colonial house to the indescribable pleasure of the first beer. The communicators and their fifteen boxes had disappeared into the communications center down the street.

Portuguese commandos in camouflage uniforms came and went through the house. Two Africans who seemed important disappeared inside. At the end of a long hall three drab Portuguese women were preparing food.

This was the new central command post, to which the FNLA had fled three weeks before when the MPLA pushed them out of Luanda. Seventy miles north of the capital, it was safe from raids and surprise attack, but still close enough to support a counteroffensive. Though not really a port, Ambriz provided a haven for small boats which could carry messages and even raid down the coast.

One of the Portuguese commandos joined me, a Captain Bento, as he introduced himself. He was forming a "commando unit" with white officers and black troops; according to him, the Africans were "too stupid to *lead* anything," although they could be shaped into fair soldiers. All this was said in a loud voice, and without concern that African commanders were listening nearby.

When Bento went back inside the command post, as if on cue another white appeared, one who had been among the machine-gun wielders at the airport. Introducing himself as "Falstaff," he too seemed eager to talk. Ten days later, back at headquarters, I would trace Falstaff in the CIA computer and learn that he was a Brazilian journalist who had been on the CIA payroll years before. He had not lost the habit of reporting. Captain Bento was, according to Falstaff, a "famous antiguerrilla fighter" from Mozambique, but I should beware of him, for he and a Colonel Santos Castro were rivals in the FNLA command. Each would attempt to draw me into his web.

According to Falstaff, forty Portuguese army veterans had cast their lot with the FNLA. In reality they were Angolans, white Angolans, who had never lived in Portugal. In any case they were not mercenaries; they received no money from the FNLA, but rather were fighting for their homes and their businesses, for the only life they knew. This was a familiar refrain for colonials who had fallen on hard times.

Bento was an exception, a seasoned fighter who had followed the crest of conflict from Mozambique to Angola, to indulge his passion —anti-Marxist wars.

"Why was I treated so harshly at the airport?" I asked. Falstaff explained: These white soldiers had families still under MPLA control in Luanda. All were using aliases and taking precautions to keep their association with the FNLA secret. They did not want to be photographed by an unknown journalist.

As we sat down to a skimpy meal of dried salt-fish cooked in palm oil, with a healthy sprinkling of ground red peppers, and some boiled potatoes, I was introduced with little formality to Colonel Castro, Bento's rival, and to an African, Hendrick Vaal Neto, who I recognized as IACASTLE/4, the FNLA politician who had been minister of interior in the transitional government in Luanda. Bento and Falstaff sat at the far end of the table with others who were not introduced to me. Holden Roberto had not arrived.

We ate in virtual silence. Either they were cooling it until Roberto showed up and confirmed my story, or there was too much rivalry and mistrust among these FNLA leaders. When I tried to converse, Colonel Castro gave me a "Sorry, I no speak English." Neto looked at me blankly and mumbled brusque answers to my questions. Bento gave me one hard look and concentrated on his food. Only Falstaff, perhaps eager to get back on the payroll, responded, smiling and nodding. It didn't catch on. Silence reigned. Of these men, Castro was the most consequential, and I looked him over as we ate. He was small and bald, but somehow managed to look urbane, even in a sportshirt in this rustic, middle-class, colonial dining room. After the meal he called forth enough English to bemoan his inability to offer me a good whiskey, then disappeared into the night.

Returning to the veranda alone, I settled into a chair, discouraging the communicators from joining me. I wanted no inhibition on my freedom to mix with Africans and Portuguese.

The lights went out abruptly and silence engulfed the sleepy tropical town as a big diesel somewhere in the background stopped its muffled roar. Neto brought me a candle and some matches. Diesel fuel had to be conserved, he apologized. He would not join me. I left the candle unlit and relaxed into my chair knowing from experience that everyone would bed down early—nothing so curtails a community's social life as darkness.

Rubber-soled boots scraped quietly on the dirt walk. I became aware of a man's shadowy form mounting the steps of the veranda. He paused a moment, then moved toward me. My muscles began to tighten. It was pitch black on the veranda and I was in the darkest corner near some climbing honeysuckle. How did he know where I was sitting? Had he been watching me from across the street before the lights went out? I waited silently while he approached, unable to suppress the melodramatic thought that I was in the middle of a bloody civil war. Did the FNLA command include infiltrators who would be only too happy to embarrass Roberto by having Dr. Kissinger's representative turn up missing, or dead? My visitor stopped two feet away and reached towards me, both hands close together. As I drew back, my muscles quivering with adrenalin, a dim flashlight snapped on in one hand, its light directed at a bit of paper in the other, which he pushed down into my lap, where they couldn't be seen from inside the house.

On the paper was scrawled in pencil, "Please come and see me. This man will show you the way. Castro."

The light clicked off and the man receded. I rose, picking up my travel bag, and followed him out the gate, thinking that in the spook business one takes a lot on faith. He led me silently two blocks toward the circle, a block toward the sea, and down an alley into what appeared to be servants' quarters behind a small house.

Seated at a small wooden table was Colonel Castro, his round face and grey hair caught in a candle's flickering light. He motioned to a second chair. My guide disappeared as quietly as he had come.

"Good evening," he said. "Thank you for coming to see me. It is important that you and I talk seriously, here. Those others," he waved his hand, throwing a broad shadow against the wall, "They are idiots. They want Angola, but they don't know how to get Angola. I know how. I have the key . . . I am sorry I cannot offer you a drink. We have nothing here."

I thrust a hand deep into my bag and pulled out a flask of Scotch that I carried for such occasions. Castro smiled as I set it on the table, "Your Dr. Kissinger provides well." I produced two small tumblers and poured. Santos Castro was a third-generation white Angolan, whose grandfather had established himself in northern Angola before the turn of the century, when there were only ten thousand whites in the entire country. Educated in Luanda and in Lisbon, he had done twenty years in the Portuguese colonial army, rising to the rank of colonel. For years he had been governor of the northern Uige province, among those responsible for the Portuguese army's harsh reprisals against the FNLA guerrillas. As times had changed, so had Castro's loyalties. Now he worked for his lifetime enemy, Holden Roberto, as chief of staff in the FNLA army.

Castro's "key" to Angola turned out to be a little shopworn. Six hundred Portuguese army veterans, he claimed, were poised in South Africa, awaiting his call. All were white Angolans, experienced in dealing with black guerrillas. They lacked only plane tickets and the means to fight. With them, Castro would have no trouble retaking Luanda, for Roberto, or for Dr. Kissinger.

It was a typical white colonial solution to a black African problem. "Give me a company of commandos and I'll straighten this place out in two weeks flat!"

I suppressed an urge to argue with him. He was after all the best source of information I had found. Instead, I asked him about Luanda, and other Portuguese still on the scene who might influence the course of the war.

Castro wanted what all such adventurers want—money—in this case money to field his six hundred men, even though they were not mercenaries, he proclaimed earnestly. Nevertheless, they had families to support. How much? He was grandly vague. Perhaps $1,000 each; $600,000 would get them started. Plus some airplanes and arms. Oh, yes. There was another requirement—an exclusive agreement which would eliminate rival Portuguese adventurers such as Bento. Roberto could be the figurehead, although we should deal with Castro on substantive matters.

When I was confident I knew everything he was going to tell me that night I rose to leave. We worked out future communications; he gave me addresses where he could be contacted in South Africa and Madrid, as well as Ambriz. In turn I passed him a discreet identification phrase which would get a message to me through the Kinshasa embassy telephone.

Gesturing for him to keep the Scotch, I stepped outside.

The other effect of having no electricity is that everyone is up at dawn. I joined them and spent the morning walking about, seeking answers to the obvious questions. We knew almost nothing about the war front in northern Angola. How big was Ambriz? Small, 1,000 whites and 10,000 Africans before it became a ghost town. How important? Vital, it was the FNLA's forward command post and airstrip. Our tons of arms would come in here. How many FNLA troops? In Ambriz I counted 25 soldiers, plus a few dozen uniformed hangers-on; Roberto had claimed 1,500. Equipment? There were more rifles and mortars than soldiers. Our shipments were arriving. Foreign advisors? Twenty Portuguese and two Brazilians. Chinese advisors? I couldn't find a trace of anything oriental; the Chinese weren't crossing the border into Angola. Leaders and fighting capability? I withheld judgment. I would have to get closer to the fighting front to answer all my questions.

On the cliffs near the river's mouth I stood for several minutes looking at the surf. Huge waves were cresting far out to sea, rolling majestically in to break and surge up the beach. This was world-class surf, but Ambriz was a long way from being known as a surfing resort. The waters of the Atlantic are dark and ominous off the West African coast and have bred fear in African and European minds for centuries, sparking tales of sea monsters and mysterious currents. No one was completely immune to that superstition, myself included.

Early 1961, as reconnaissance officer on a navy cruise, which President Kennedy called SOLANT AMITY, I had run covert hydrographic surveys of beach gradients and sand composition up and down the western coast of Africa, in Monrovia, Lome, Conakry, Pointe Noire, and Bathurst. My men and I would take a "Peter"* boat and fake a beer party while we dived and took soundings. None of us, though highly trained reconnaissance marines, had much stomach for the murky depths a hundred yards from the beach.

By habit I noted the Ambriz beach gradient. It was steep, the sand coarse and bottomless—it would handle amphibious landing craft badly.

Downtown Ambriz, like Carmona, was deserted and buttoned up. There were only a few African men in civilian clothes wandering about aimlessly. After a breakfast of fruit, cheese, and rather good coffee, I examined the FNLA communications center. My communicators were well established, their radios set up and in good contact with Kinshasa via the relay station in Monrovia. There was no message from headquarters and I sent a simple "all's well." Given more time I might have tried to understand why radio waves would reach fifteen hundred kilometers to Monrovia but not five hundred direct to Kinshasa.

I walked back across town to a broad field overlooking the ocean

*A Peter boat is an ancient navy landing craft.

and watched Captain Bento hold muster on his commandos. There were seven whites and fifteen blacks. Later they formed into a large squad and practiced very basic infantry maneuvers, attacking an imaginary enemy position near the beach. At least the blacks did, running a few yards and diving into prone positions at the roared commands of one of the Portuguese. The whites stood near the trucks and watched.

From previous experience I felt I could project the effectiveness and shortcomings of the African soldiers, but I wondered about the Portuguese. Were they fit? For commandos they were doing a lot of slouching around. And what was their military experience? Years of chasing poorly armed FNLA guerrillas through the bush wouldn't prepare them for conventional warfare, or give them the skills to handle heavy mortars, artillery, rockets, and armored vehicles. Doubtless they would learn fast and make good soldiers, if we had a year to get them ready. We had only weeks if we were going to halt the MPLA before the November independence date.

A lone Panhard armored car, slightly larger than a jeep, roared up and stopped, locking its wheels and sliding comically in a swirl of dust. A young white jumped out and stood by the building, posing. I decided that we had better not count too heavily on the Portuguese commandos saving northern Angola for us.

Roberto drove in from the airstrip and shook my hand distractedly. He had on slacks, a light jacket, and a beige golf cap. I barely had time to get a glass of water before he ushered me into one of the new Volkswagen minibuses and we drove away. With us were three whites: a tall, broad Portuguese named Chevier; a heavy-set man dressed in a uniform complete with major's insigna, parachute wings, and a red beret; and Falstaff. Falstaff later told me that Chevier had been the chief of the Portuguese intelligence service in Luanda during the years of struggle against the black nationals. Now, like Colonel Castro, he was lending his ability and knowledge of the MPLA to the FNLA cause. According to Falstaff, the one in utilities was a Brazilian army major, apparently there as an observer. And what were Falstaff and a Brazilian major doing in Ambriz? Falstaff ducked this question, changing the subject. But the answer was obvious. Brazil was not uninterested in the Angolan outcome.

There was a delay of thirty minutes at the motor pool, where Roberto inspected vehicles, counted spare parts, measured gasoline, and harassed all present, white and black alike. He did more talking than listening, and often interrupted people, leaving them frustrated. Then we were rolling down the asphalt road through the Angolan bush.

I stood with my head and shoulders through the sun roof of the minibus to photograph the terrain through which we were passing. It was open, dry, and reasonably even. Sixty percent was covered with meter-high grass over low rolling ridges and slopes, with scatterings of thorn, fig, wild olive, and cedar trees, which clustered into small forests. Occasional, paunchy, sentinel baobab trees made the terrain unforgettably African. Coastal, woody savannah, I believed it would be called; ideal for the movements of a battalion reinforced with light armor, permitting high mobility as well as good cover. Of course, this type of war would be fought mostly up and down the roads. We were on a reasonably good, narrow asphalt road designed to carry the five-ton Mercedes and Berliet trucks which had kept the Angolan coffee business and provincial economy rolling.

We crossed two small bridges over dry swales which would be easy to detour around except perhaps during a heavy rain. Another bridge spanned a deep creek bed with steep, rough sides. An abutment had been partially blown by an MPLA mine but was still solid enough for single-axle trucks and even armored vehicles no larger than the small Panhards. Such streams could pose serious problems if a span were completely blown. True, a U.S. Army engineer company could bridge it in two hours, but the FNLA would have no such capacity, nor would it be within the scope of our program to ship them adequate materials.

All road junctions and small bridges were manned by two or three soldiers carrying rifles, who peered at the vehicle vacantly and then brought up something resembling a salute when they saw Roberto inside. On one occasion he got out of the VW to give a befuddled young man a lecture and demonstration of the proper position of attention and salute.

As we drove on, Roberto gave me a shopping list of things they needed. He kept returning to uniforms and boots for fifteen thousand men.

"I must have uniforms to make them feel like soldiers," he said. "And boots. If I can give them boots they will fight for me."

No one in Roberto's army was receiving regular pay or allow-

ances. They subsisted on sparse rations foraged in local villages and
were supplied with such weapons, ammunition, and medicines as
were available. They were recruited on the basis of loyalty to family
and tribe and, although many would flee combat, others were drawn
by the historic motivations of war: aggression, camaraderie, excitement, and the promise of wealth when their side won.

Thirty kilometers out of Ambriz we turned suddenly onto a dirt
road in a grove of commercially planted palm trees. After several
kilometers this led us into a clearing on a small hill where a walled
compound encircled large warehouses and outlying buildings. A
large sign proclaimed FAZENDA LIFUNE—the Lifune plantation. It
was Roberto's forward command post. There were sixteen listless
soldiers and two 2.4 mortars. To one side a half-dozen women and
children were gathered around a cooking pot on a low fire, sitting
flat on the bare ground with their legs straight in front. I reflected
on the sobriety of the FNLA forces I had seen so far. These camp
followers were wives and family. I had seen no bars, prostitutes, or
drinking; the lovely women for which Angola had some fame were
all in Luanda.

I thought ruefully of my paramilitary colleagues who clamored
to get into the Angola program because it was the only war there
was. For most of them, tours in Vietnam had been exotic experiences, with little danger or difficult work, and a gluttony of sen-
sual pleasures. A famous unposed snapshot of one of the agency's
upcountry heroes told the story: he is draped in a lawn chair, his
feet propped against the sandbags of a bunker, reading the morning's cable traffic, holding a Heineken beer in his right hand
while a Vietnamese "dolly" manicures his left. Assignments in
Angola were going to be different.

The FNLA had been on the run two weeks before when Mobutu
and St. Martin had insisted that Roberto take personal command of
the battlefield, bringing with him weapons and armored cars from
Kinshasa. Now the MPLA was retreating and Roberto was flushed
with his successes. War was easy; they would soon be in Luanda
itself. Roberto was dominating every conversation, making every
decision, inspecting weapons, thrusting soldiers onto trucks, even
checking the gas in a Volkswagen's tank. When we got stuck in the
sand he was the first out of the car, tearing out grass clumps and
thrusting them under the tires. Falstaff repeatedly whispered to me

that Roberto didn't know what he was doing, didn't take advice, and was creating as many problems as he solved.

It was difficult from all this to judge the scope of fighting, but a picture was emerging. Roberto had claimed two thousand troops in the area. He claimed they were pushing back four thousand MPLA. He spoke of heavy fighting and shelling, especially on the Barro do Dande battlefield, where he proudly showed me a disabled Russian BDRM-2 armored car. But I counted only a couple of mortar craters and the bullet marks on buildings from a few magazines of small-arms fire. Falstaff, like a Roberto truth squad, whispered that the BDRM-2 had been abandoned before it was hit by the FNLA bazooka round. Barro do Dande was the scene of a small skirmish, not a battlefield. Roberto did not know the difference; before last week he had never put his own body on the line.

We encountered a truck which was returning from the front with a half-dozen prisoners in the back. Roberto questioned the guards while I took photographs of the grim, ashen-faced men it held. Roberto volunteered that they would be well treated, but I reflected that I could not blame them for their anxiety, considering the FNLA's tradition of butchering any MPLA it captured.

About 4:00 P.M. we broke into a clearing and the Sassalemba road junction. There were no buildings. Just a paved intersection and a concrete post which read "LUANDA, 32 KMS." A comical baobab tree loomed over the junction, one of its limbs splintered by a 106 round. There were no troops to be seen and no sound of fighting. Commandant Lukenge directed us to the left and we proceeded cautiously down the road.

After a few hundred yards we came upon the FNLA fighting force clustered together in a shallow dirt pit off to one side of the road. There were about eighty men in the dirt pit, which was large enough to shelter perhaps a tenth that many safely—one large caliber mortar round would have eliminated much of the FNLA fighting force on the Sassalemba front.

The soldiers stood on the asphalt and pointed down the road to where the MPLA had "counterattacked" that afternoon. A few MPLA soldiers, approaching from a half-mile away, had fled when the 106 leveled a round against them. That was counted as another battle. The prisoners we had encountered earlier had been taken when an errant MPLA jeep drove into an FNLA position.

Caxito, where we drove the next morning, unlike the other sites, looked like the scene of a real battle. We drove through it twice and I could see no building that hadn't suffered at least one mortar hit. The African houses on both sides of town had been razed. A small church school, which had been the MPLA headquarters, had suffered a devastating attack from the FNLA. Entire cinder-block buildings had been reduced to rubble; no wall was unmarked by mortar rounds, shrapnel, and small-arms fire. In the yard stood another shattered BDRM-2 and two jeeps, destroyed by repeated hits from 106s and bazookas. Roberto proudly recreated the battle for me, noting that the FNLA fire had been so accurate that a neutral Portuguese army garrison in barracks two blocks away had been untouched. Then Falstaff interpreted while Chevier told how the Zairian Panhards had become disoriented and taken the road to Luanda, and how Roberto had jumped in a car alone and raced after them miles behind MPLA lines to guide them back to the battle. I decided to believe the story. Roberto was now involved and there was no denying how intensely he wanted Luanda.

The battle of Caxito was a different matter. I walked carefully over the schoolyard, nervously mindful of the dangerous mines and duds which could be detonated by my foot. Studying the layout intently I formed my own picture of the action. No doubt the compound had been the object of a noisy and expensive attack, but there was no evidence of any defense. There were no bunkers or foxholes, no piles of expended rounds. The armored car and jeeps had been knocked out where they were parked against the wall. The MPLA had fled without making a serious effort at defending Caxito, and the damage had been done by rampaging FNLA forces as they swept through *unopposed.*

Most of the MPLA had fled, but two or three had been caught in the shelling. I snapped pictures of a cadaver in the ruins, wondering what Bubba Sanders would think to do with it. Roberto toed some rubble aside and retched when a shrunken, grinning corpse stared back at him. The author of the bloody revolt of 1961, who insisted that revolution without bloodshed was impossible, was himself weak-stomached.

On the scarred wall of the headquarters building there was a black and red MPLA poster, torn and shredded from bullets and shrapnel. I took it down and folded it into my travel bag. In front of the

Roberto intensely desired to take Luanda. Pictured with him are FNLA commanders, a Brazilian army observer (squatting), and the author.

Holden Roberto interrogates a Zairian armored unit, while the author observes.

A shrunken, grinning corpse in the rubble of Caxito battlefield.

Recently captured MPLA. Their FNLA captors had a reputation for brutality.

MPLA headquarters at Caxito after FNLA attack.

A CIA hardship assignment, upcountry in Vietnam.

building I stopped, my eye caught by a curious memento to the ironies of war. From the rubble of the driveway I extracted a large rosary which had been carved from sections of a rough African vine and strung on nylon cord. I coiled it into my bag beside the poster.

As we drove back to Ambriz in the early twilight everyone was silent. I was lost in my calculations, weighing the probable effect of CIA arms on the present level of combat and speculating about the eventual Soviet backlash. Given the weaknesses of the contending armies, one modern weapons system such as Puff the Magic Dragon could make a dramatic difference, completely dominating a battle-front. If we were in a race with the Soviets, the winner would be the first to get effective weapons and leadership into northern Angola. We could do it, if we did it now.

The next day, on the flight to Kinshasa we stopped at the deserted Negage air base near Carmona and inspected its facilities. It had been designed by the Portuguese to provide military support in northern Angola for antiguerrilla operations, and was capable of handling transoceanic jet aircraft. The control tower, warehouses, and even recreational facilities would be ideal for an American advance base if IAFEATURE ever became another Vietnam. I was tempted not to mention it to headquarters.

As we flew on, I drafted my report. In two pages, it was simple enough. But my conclusion troubled me. I was intrigued that the opposing forces in northern Angola, the MPLA, were poorly armed, poorly led, and disorganized, offering us the opportunity for a quick coup. It was feasible to rush weapons into Angola, which would decisively win the war. I knew that our policy was not designed to win, but I wanted Washington to know that the opportunity existed for a total victory, *if we provided abundant, immediate support.* Since there was no chance of the National Security Council taking bold action in August 1975, I might have served my nation better if I had attempted to discourage them by emphasizing the frailty of the FNLA army to which the United States had affixed its prestige.

Back in Kinshasa I handed St. Martin the draft report and went into the guest room for a long shower. When I came out he handed it back, suggesting only that it should be changed from the first person and put into cable format. Did he agree with it? He brushed the question aside. I should report whatever I wanted. He had nevertheless made several minor changes, with the compulsion of all agency managers to edit every draft that crosses their desks. His reluctance to discuss it made me wonder if he would file a separate cable, criticizing mine.

On the way back from Ambriz an ominous turmoil had begun to build in my abdomen, and by the next morning I was in the throes of the "Angolan anguish," bacillary dysentary. The medic at the embassy prescribed kaolin pectin and four or five days rest, but my plane was to leave the next morning for Savimbi's headquarters in central Angola and I would be bounced from truck to Land Rover for the next three days. I knew that only an occasional sip of paregoric would permit me to complete the mission, and there was none to be had without a prescription. A CIA medic once told me that illness, alcoholism, and emotional problems are responsible for 99 percent of the CIA's incomplete assignments.

To my enormous relief, one of the station's operations assistants found me at St. Martin's at six and handed me a dark vial of paregoric, laughing sympathetically at my predicament. "Don't ask any questions," she said, "just give me fifteen zaires."*

Meanwhile, I had lunched with Larry Devlin, my former patron and the famous éminence grise of the Congo program of the early sixties. After two long tours in the Congo, where he had shuffled new governments like cards, finally settling on Mobutu as president, Devlin had been put in charge of the agency's paramilitary program in Laos. And before Laos collapsed he had returned to Washington to become chief of African Division. One of the CIA's historic great "operators," he had dealt with younger case officers and agents like an Irish-American politician, giving out patronage to some and coming down hard on any who stood in his way.

In Addis Ababa in 1970, he and I had drunk whiskey from midnight to dawn, when I had delivered him to his plane. In 1974 he took his agency retirement pension of $22,000 per year and got a fabulous four-year contract with a New York financier, based on the fact that he alone of all Americans still had an intimate friendship with and

---

*An operations assistant is a secretary, bookkeeper, and "girl Friday" for the CIA field station. In the three dozen CIA posts in Africa there are perhaps four dozen such young women. They are generally twenty-two to thirty, although sometimes older, and make $9000–$15,000 a year, plus whatever allowances the different posts offer. In a small post the ops assistant is one of the two or three people in the country who knows everything the CIA is doing in that country. She types all cables and dispatches and reads all incoming traffic from headquarters. She keeps the station finance records and the cash box, and replenishes each case officer's revolving fund. On a specified day she closes the books and prepares the monthly accounting, which is then pouched to headquarters. After hours she is generally invited to all embassy and station social functions and, depending on her tastes and interests, may or may not participate in the social life of the official community. Her relationship with the chief of station is perforce close and often intimate. In most posts she is involved in operations, functioning as a cut-out for agents' reports or money, helping to spot and assess new agent candidates at cocktail parties, and helping with countersurveillance when any technical operations are running. If her rapport with the COS is not good, the tiny field office can be very stuffy. If she is promiscuous or indiscreet, the station can have serious problems. In one post the ops assistant fell in love with a leader of the local communist party and resigned and married him! The security implications for the station and its agents were mind-boggling. There were agents who would have been in danger if exposed; she knew them all: their names, how much they were paid, where they met the case officers. One agent who knew that she was witting of his CIA role offered to arrange for her quiet disappearance. This was given no consideration whatsoever. Wholesale changes in personnel eventually defused the threat.

ready access to President Mobutu. At stake was a half-billion-dollar investment in Zairian mineral resources. Before leaving the agency, he assigned Victor St. Martin as COS Kinshasa.

We lunched at a small businessmen's club, at his employer's expense. He was bored with his new job and nervous because he was being summoned back to Washington to testify to the Senate's Church Committee about the Congo program. He admitted his physical fitness was not up to par, and I scolded him, urging him to start jogging again. What would he tell the Senate about Lumumba? Certainly he would never perjure himself, his testimony would be consistent with any written record and provable facts. At the same time I guessed that only he and President Mobutu would ever know the complete truth of Patrice Lumumba's assassination in 1960. Over whiskey other agency supergrades had bragged to me about their careers, disclosing remarkable operational secrets. Larry would brag too, but when it got to Lumumba he never had much to say.

We shook hands and split, promising to meet a week later in Washington. Meanwhile, I would check out UNITA in central Angola.

8

Savimbi

I now had a good handle on Roberto and the FNLA, thought to be our chief hope in Angola, and so far the recipient of most of the CIA's largesse. To complete the picture we needed a look at the Angolan long shot, UNITA, and its chief, Jonas Savimbi. This I set out to have on Wednesday, August 20, 1975.

It was immediately clear that UNITA was an organization of very different caliber than the FNLA. The UNITA foreign minister, Jorges Sangumba, was prompt in picking us up. Sangumba and I rode to the airport in a UNITA sedan, with my communications team following in the CIA carryall.* We eased through the VIP section of the regular terminal, as Sangumba's aide cleared us past the immigrations officials, and boarded a small Lear executive jet. On the two-hour hop down to Silva Porto, the British copilot served coffee from a thermos.

---

*The two communicators did their job well and remained inconspicuous, as their role dictated. One would return to Washington and spend three weeks in the hospital, critically ill with falciprium malaria.

A liberation movement with its own Lear jet? We understood it was the gift of a London/Rhodesian investment company which was betting on Savimbi to win the war. Special access to Angolan minerals would be prize aplenty. An ideal gift, the little jet gave Savimbi long legs across Africa. He could drop in on African leaders near and far—Jomo Kenyatta in Nairobi, Leopold Senghor in Dakar, Julius Nyerere in Dar-es-Salaam—while maintaining close supervision of his campaigns in central Angola.

A UNITA commander was waiting for us beside the small Silva Porto terminal building, which was festooned with hundreds of political posters and painted slogans. His four-door Fiat sedan quickly carried us over the two-kilometer dirt track into town, where I was deposited in the living room of a small house. As Sangumba disappeared into the adjoining dining room, I caught sight of a stocky man in a dark green utility uniform sitting at the head of the table. His skin was very black and his beard full and shiny. His wide, prominent eyes flashed at me briefly.

A few minutes later, he came through the door and introduced himself as Jonas Savimbi.

"We will have time to talk, but I must first go to a meeting of the UNITA Party Congress," he said. "You are welcome to come."

I followed as Savimbi strode several blocks into a crowd of over one thousand people that closed around him, singing UNITA party songs. He mounted the steps of a public building and went inside. A few moments later Sangumba appeared on a balcony and began calling to the crowd and beckoning. I was shoved inside, where I found an auditorium packed with three hundred or more Africans. The crowd continued to chant "Savimbi," "UNITA," "Angola."

As Savimbi began to speak, the assembly stilled to hear a master of a speaking style once popular in our own society but now as rare as the deep-throated belly laugh and the barroom brawl. Savimbi's voice was rich and well-modulated. As he spoke his whole body turned to different parts of the audience and he leaned forward and gestured, reaching his hands to the people, then drawing them back to his chest. When he nodded the crowd agreed; his displeasure was theirs also; answers to his questions came thundering back in unison, "UNITA," "Angola," "MPLA." The performance reflected his missionary upbringing—his father had been a part-time evangelical preacher—and the crowd's reaction was spiritual, more like a prayer meeting than a political gathering. According to my interpreter, he was delivering predictable cliches: "UNITA is the hope for Angola"; "We have defeated the Portuguese; we will defeat the MPLA"; "UNITA will prevail." After his speech he sat down calmly.

Others rose to speak, representing different regions. This could go on all afternoon, I thought apprehensively. But after perhaps an hour Savimbi arose, made a brief statement, and left the room nodding to me to follow.

Savimbi was all business. First we would talk. Then we would tour the local UNITA garrisons. What was my mission, he asked, listening carefully while I told him. He had already been briefed by my colleague in Lusaka, I said, and I was here from Washington to study UNITA's strengths and catalogue his needs. Savimbi then began to speak quietly, simply, in detail. Troop strengths and dispositions? He unfolded a map and pointed out his principal bases and the current battles. He said he had about 300 men with him in Silva Porto. Later I counted a total of 323 divided in two groups, one at the garrison in town and the other in a camp a few kilometers out a rough dirt road.

Then came a walking, verbal reenactment of his force's expulsion of the MPLA from Silva Porto a week earlier. "My commander advanced his company across here, firing on those buildings there. We didn't have to waste much ammunition before they surrendered. No one was killed. I didn't want to fight them, but they fired on my jet before it landed. We sent fifty MPLA prisoners to Lobito on trucks."

Roberto would have exaggerated and called it a major victory, and the difference would have lain not so much in subeterfuge as in their relative combat experience. Since 1967 Savimbi had committed himself to the Angolan bush, personally leading the fighting and building the infrastructure of the UNITA movement. Also, sparing the lives of the fifty MPLA fighters probably reflected Savimbi's vision more than humanist sympathies. He suggested repeatedly in the next two days that the ultimate hope for Angola still lay at the conference table rather than on the battlefield.

Savimbi's strategic objectives seemed to lie in central Angola: the Ovimbundu heartland and the Benguela railroad. Luanda was far away, and less important.

We drove to the camp outside of town and found the garrison assembled in three company-sized ranks. On the way there, along the roadside, soldiers and civilians alike arose when they saw the car and ran forward, crying out *"Savimbi!"* and holding up their right index fingers, the UNITA symbol for national unity. The troops were unarmed and some of them poorly clad.

"I have rifles for them," Savimbi said, sensing my question, "and they know how to shoot. But I keep the rifles locked up. Otherwise they might be lost."

I asked what he needed most.

"Big mortars, and bazookas with a lot of ammunition. Weapons that will shoot far and make the enemy run away. My men are not afraid to fight close, but when they do I can lose too many soldiers. I cannot afford to lose them."

And uniforms?

"Yes, uniforms," he said, "and boots . . ." Then he reconsidered. ". . . Later. Other things are more important. My men can fight barefooted. Without guns and ammunition they cannot fight."

We ate that night at his conference table and then I sat in the living room and talked to two political operatives, including an earnest and attractive young woman who was a delegate from Serpa Pinto. From her comments I was able to make a chart of the UNITA political organization, including the congress, regional committees, and women's and youth councils.

Savimbi held a meeting in the next room until about 11:00 P.M., when he disappeared upstairs with the girl. One of the aides escorted me to stark guest quarters in a two-storied apartment building three blocks away. The night was clear and quite chilly; Silva Porto was on the same vast plateau that runs from southern Zaire through Zambia and Rhodesia. It was the dry season, the time of the year when we'd had crystal, frosty mornings in Lubumbashi.

Shortly after dawn Savimbi and I flew out in a single-engine plane so small the Portuguese pilot clucked and scowled as he calculated the fuel against our gross weight. In Cangomba, three hundred kilometers east, we transferred to a late-model Land Rover and drove in swirling clouds of dust for two more hours towards Luso.

The central Angolan highlands, though opened to European exploitation later than the Bakongo and Mbundu areas, eventually succumbed to Portuguese adventurers seeking slaves and mineral wealth. The Ovimbundu tribe which dominated the area developed

The popular Savimbi always drew large crowds, even in the sparsely populated Angolan provinces.

Savimbi speaking in his inimitably powerful and delicate style at Silva Porto *(top)* and in the bush *(bottom).*

Savimbi and supporters. UNITA's Ovimbundu people represented over half of the Angolan population.

Savimbi and a constituent.

a taste for wealth and entrepreneurship as the Portuguese subjugated them by playing tribal factions against each other. In 1902 the Bailundu king, Mutu wa Kwelu, led a general uprising that held out for two years against a Portuguese expeditionary force. Simultaneously the Cuanhama people further south sustained a resistance for four years before they too were suppressed. In the mid 1950s the Ovimbundu trailed the Mbundu and Bakongo in prenationalist development, not because they were less resentful of Portuguese domination, but because of their isolation in central Angola. Fewer managed to obtain European educations, and it was not until 1966 that they mounted an active resistance to the Portuguese.

Jonas Malheiro Savimbi was born August 3, 1934, to a prominent family of the Ovimbundu people at Munhango on the railroad near Luso. His father, Lot Malheiro Savimbi, was a railroad station master who had been converted to Christianity by an American evangelical mission. Lot Savimbi started and ran a grade school and church at his first small rail station, until protests by the Portuguese Catholic clergy resulted in his being transferred to another post. The local population continued nevertheless to support the little church, and Savimbi started another at his next post. Again he was transferred. And again. The end result was a string of schools and churches along the railroad in central Angola.

Jonas Savimbi inherited his father's respect for education. He attended Protestant mission schools, including the secondary high school at Silva Porto, and eventually graduated from the Liceu at Sa da Bandeira, Angola, at the top of his class.

In 1958 Jonas Savimbi was one of a pioneer group sent by the United Church of Christ to study medicine in Portugal. Badgered by the Portuguese police, he left Portugal in 1960 and continued his education in Switzerland, switching from medicine to political science.

In 1961 Savimbi committed himself to revolutionary activities, joining the FNLA as the GRAE foreign minister, and accompanying Roberto on one visit to the United Nations. However, in 1963–1964 diverging interests of the central Angolan people led him to split with the FNLA and begin organizing an Ovimbundu movement.* In 1967

CIA biographic publications reflect Holden Roberto's prejudices by claiming that in 1966 Roberto sent Savimbi to Cairo to hand-carry a $50,000 donation from the he was expelled from Zambia after he directed attacks on the Benguela railroad which carried Zambia's copper to the sea. He spent eight months in exile in Cairo before deciding to take personal command of UNITA inside Angola, first visiting the People's Republic of China to solicit support. The Chinese gave small amounts of material help, and the North Koreans provided guerrilla training for twelve fighters. With small numbers of men and limited means Savimbi became a festering thorn to the Portuguese in central Angola and a living legend among the Ovimbundu people.

"They used helicopters and horse-mounted troops and dogs but they could never catch us," Savimbi recalled. "They were never sure where we were. I would visit the faithful inside the cities at night. I once went right into Silva Porto and left only fifteen minutes before the Portuguese raided the house. Then I would walk for two days and nights and show myself one hundred kilometers away, and do it again and again, until the Portuguese and the people thought I was *everywhere.*"

I listened, fascinated. A little of that sort of action, magnified by rumor, poor communications, and natural exaggeration transforms a man into a god in the minds of a suppressed people. I knew from experiences in the Congo that some Africans could cover phenomenal distances on foot; this man was a strapping mesomorph who would translate his ambition into physical activity.

"I learned when to go away." he said. "I put Nzau Puna, my best man, in charge of Bie province and he couldn't seem to do anything. Finally I realized the people would never listen to him while *Savimbi* was there. So I went away and three months later he was one of my best commanders and Bie was the best province." Savimbi had thus organized UNITA into three regions and developed reliable leaders for each one.

Organization, leadership and the courage to delegate, I thought. The CIA's managers should understudy this man.

"How do you communicate with your forces in Bie and on the Lobito front?" I asked.

"I send written messages by Land Rover. It takes days. And you

---

United Arab Republic, but Savimbi absconded with the money to Lusaka, Zambia, where he used it to start UNITA. In fact, Savimbi had broken with Roberto in 1964.
*Marcum, *The Angolan Revolution,* Vol. I.

can never be sure the messenger will not be captured or killed. You don't know until you get an answer back one week, two weeks later. Before, we sent messages in the hands of runners on foot."

A system as old as Africa itself. A wiry runner carrying a letter wedged in the end of a split stick, detouring around lion prides and elephant herds in the very old days. Around Portuguese patrols in recent times. Now around the MPLA.

Savimbi spoke sharply to the driver and we skidded to a stop. He got out with me close on his heels and hurried to the roadside where a small group of serious-looking soldiers rose up from ambush positions in the waist-high grass. Savimbi talked animatedly with the leader, a young man of perhaps twenty-two.

He turned to me. "This is Ilunga! He is a swimmer! He saved my life when we were crossing the Cassai, when the Portuguese were chasing us."

He stood looking at Ilunga who returned his gaze with great dignity; the bond between them was almost tangible. Savimbi broke the spell by giving instructions on how to improve the ambush, kneeling beside an anthill and looking down the road, pointing his own automatic rifle.

As we drove on, Savimbi told me how Ilunga had saved him— years ago. It was a harrowing tale of encirclement and flight.

"We had been on the run for ten days," he recalled," with Portuguese troops on every side and closing in. Only three of us were still alive, Ilunga ran in front and Nzau Puna came behind. Puna was wounded and bleeding."

I pictured them running along a grassy ridgeline, like the one we were driving over. Savimbi would have been leaner, in tattered khaki shorts, instead of his splendid green uniform.

"We had run almost thirty kilometers since the day before but there was still no safety. We would have been caught but for Mama Tshela. She and her sister walked fifteen miles to feed us and stood guard while we slept. When the Portuguese came she fired her rifle the way I had taught her, so we could run away.

"The Portuguese had horses and dogs and an airplane. Every time we would slip away they would find us again. They drove us into open country and the plane watched us while a Portuguese squad chased us. Other times we could outrun the Portuguese easily, but we were already tired, and they had black scouts with them.

"Things did not look good. They would catch us before darkness came. And the river would not help because I did not know how to swim. We knew about Portuguese prisons if they caught us. I was not afraid to die, but I wanted to live, to free my people.

"I was worried about Mama Tshela, but later I learned that she pretended to be dead when they threw a grenade."

(The next day Savimbi introduced me to Mama Tshela, and deferred to her as a revolutionary matriarch; her face was disfigured with jagged scars.)

"We had tried to ambush a train, but the Portuguese had spies in UNITA, and they set a trap. And our dynamite didn't work right. My twelve men had not yet come back from North Korea.

"The plane dived at us when we got close to the river. I shot at it, but you never seem to hurt those planes with a rifle.

"Nzau Puna fell down. He seemed to be finished, but I carried him to the river. I did not want them to find our bodies to drag them in the streets of Silva Porto.

"We threw our weapons into the water and jumped after them. The water carried us away and Ilunga pulled me across. Our luck saved us from the Portuguese and from the crocodiles, and Nzau Puna got well.

"Another time we went back and blew up the railroad."

The story was full of associations for me; I had spent part of my childhood hiking and hunting on similar hills, near the same river, the Kasai we spelled it, four hundred kilometers north in the Belgian Congo.

In Chicala, a small town on the railroad, we stopped before a simple brick house on the only street in town. A number of somber people were gathered in front, two were wearing blood-spattered white smocks. In the anteroom were four soldiers, three seated on a bench and the other lying on a mat on the floor. All were patched with soggy bandages. The smell of rotting blood was strong and flies were everywhere. Savimbi spoke to them briefly and I followed him into the next room. A young man was stretched out on a table, his chest heaving, drawing air through a huge, gaping, bloody hole, where an hour before he had had a nose and mouth and jaw.

As we left Savimbi said matter-of-factly, "He will die. There is nothing we can do."

There was now only one doctor in all of central and eastern

Angola, and little medicine. It was a brutal place for the wounds of war, the kinds that shrapnel from mortars and rockets would make. Infections were immediate, and without antibiotics even small wounds could be fatal.

We stood on the Benguela railroad and stared down the visual infinity of rails and cross-ties. I projected my mind beyond the horizon, six hundred kilometers to Benguela itself and the crystal waters of the Lobito harbor. Turning a hundred and eighty degrees, I looked nine hundred kilometers to Lubumbashi, and remembered the huge mines which disgorged tons of copper ore to be transported to waiting ships by an endless string of open railroad cars.

Standing on the railroad tracks in the bare African veld I felt an almost mystical objectivity about the CIA and the things I had done, the pointlessness of my operations in Lubumbashi, the brutality and betrayals of Vietnam, the empty cynicism of the case officer's role. Savimbi was impatient to move on. For a moment I resented him, with his clear objectives and clean conscience. He was that rare coincidence of history, a throwback to the great tribal leaders of Africa—Tchaka Zulu, Msiri, and Jomo Kenyatta—a far cry from the conflicting values and goals of America, and of the CIA in its middle-aged mediocrity.

Our Land Rover left the improved dirt road and growled up a sandy track, halting in a small settlement. About fifty men were in view, most carrying weapons. We were fifteen kilometers from Luso where a bitter fight was taking place.

Savimbi introduced me to a tall, lean Angolan, General Chiwale, commanding general of UNITA's armed forces. The two of them talked earnestly in Portuguese and Ovimbundu. Savimbi, knowing I did not understand, turned and explained that Chiwale was going to commit more troops to the battle of Luso.

Outside, Chiwale gave a number of loud commands. (Nothing like "Fall in A and B companies, and the mortar section.") He stood in the back of a truck waving his hands and yelling, until men began milling closer with their rifles, a few individuals darting off to huts to drag out some forgotten piece of equipment. They were almost silent and looked determined. Chiwale continued at intervals to call out, until, with little more ado, they were loaded onto small trucks, jammed together until they became a indistinct mass of heads, arms, legs, and guns. The trucks sagged and buckled, the springs sitting heavily on the overloaded shackles and the tires folding over on themselves. Incredibly, the vehicles groaned forward, down a sandy track out the backside of the compound and onto the brushy plain. Chiwale, Savimbi, and I crowded against the driver in the cab of the lead truck.

After thirty minutes we stopped a kilometer short of Luso. Most of the soldiers remained on the trucks. Savimbi and Chiwale walked a few yards to one side, to a clearing where the grass and leaves of the short trees had been burned off. Kneeling, they drew diagrams on the ground like sandlot quarterbacks mapping out plays. A half-dozen soldiers moved smartly to points a few yards out, to provide security from attack, but turned inward to face Savimbi and Chiwale, instead of outward to the potential attacking enemy. Chiwale stood and ordered the rest of his troops off the trucks. Savimbi turned to me.

"Now we go back."

I remonstrated, wanting to see UNITA in action, but he was firm. Chiwale would run this battle. We barely had time to get safely back to Silva Porto before dark, and Savimbi was concerned the plane would leave Cangomba without us. Tomorrow he wanted to concentrate on preparations to attack Lobito.

"The MPLA is no problem to us," he said, habitually pronouncing it with an extra syllable—"M.P.L. ee ah!" "They run away. But in Luso we are fighting the gendarmes from the Katanga. They are very strong and they don't run away."

The Katangese gendarmes, "KATGENS" we called them back at headquarters, were refugees of Moise Tshombe's attempt to wrest Katanga province from Zaire in the early sixties. At President Kennedy's instigation, a United Nations force had crushed that secession and instead of yielding to Mobutu's dominion, the secessionist army had fled into Angola where they joined their Lunda tribal brothers and remained a menacing force of three to four thousand men, perennially poised against Zaire's exposed underbelly. Now they were automatically opposed to Mobutu and his allies, the FNLA and UNITA, whom they would implacably challenge throughout the duration of the war.

I had seen no whites with UNITA's troops, anywhere.

"No Portuguese!" Savimbi said with the only hostility I ever saw in him. "We need help, but not from *any* Portuguese! My men will

The Benguela railroad stretches away into the African veld. Savimbi and his soldiers controlled large parts of the railroad for much of the war.

Savimbi and General Chiwale plan strategy for assault on Luso.

work with Americans or Canadians. Maybe French. South Africans can help. But never Portuguese!!"

Roberto was choking down his resentment and working with the Portuguese while the war was hot and the FNLA desperate for advisors. Savimbi was too proud to turn to the Portuguese, but otherwise he had no prejudice. And no profound ideology. He was neither Marxist nor capitalist, nor even a black revolutionary. He was an Angolan patriot, fighting for the freedom of the Ovimbundu people. He had accepted North Korean training for his men, and Chinese money and arms. He liked Americans. If South Africa would give him the help he needed, he would accept.

Both he and Roberto were making mistakes, but of the two, Savimbi's mistake would be more costly. Once his acceptance of South African aid became known, he would be discredited as a black nationalist. He would win a few battles, but eventually lose the war.

Early the next morning Savimbi took me to a training camp a few kilometers from Silva Porto. The commanders, who knew we were coming, had assembled the garrison in a large clearing. Three companies formed on three sides of a quadrangle and a platoon of women in civilian dress squared the fourth. As we approached, singing and dancing women blocked our car, forcing us to walk the last fifty yards while they clapped, stamped and swirled around Savimbi. I recalled from the Congo that such singing and rhythm were historic, cultural things; in two tribes I had lived among, the Lulua and Bakete, the people moved readily into stirring chants on any occasion—when rowing a boat, returning from a successful hunt, or honoring a chief.

Savimbi made another speech, then showed me his meager armory, counting weapons and giving his personal opinion of each. In the two days, I had counted twelve different types of shoulder weapons, including some Portuguese G-3s, Belgian FNs, NATO FALs, Chinese AKs, and Soviet Kalashnikovs. They also had American bazookas, 81 and 60 mm. mortars, hand grenades, and 106 mm. recoilless rifles, but only a paltry number of rounds for each. There was no apparent logistical system, other than Savimbi's memory of what he had, and I shuddered to think of the confusion that would result from our delivery of tons of equipment and supplies.

On the way back I questioned him again about UNITA's troop strengths.

"It is hard to be exact," he said. "We are not organized that way."

Together he and I extrapolated four thousand UNITA troops more or less ready for combat, plus six thousand trainees. These were the figures I reported to headquarters.

Here was the most significant finding of my trip: We had understood that UNITA was the weakest militarily of the three liberation movements; in fact, Savimbi's army was several times larger than the FNLA's, better led, and supported by a political organization of some depth. This would be heartening news at headquarters, an unexpected asset in our war against the MPLA.

On the other hand, the UNITA forces, like the FNLA, had no logistical system, the poorest of internal communications, and no organization or leadership below the level of major.

Savimbi deposited me at the airport, shook my hand gravely, and left. There were no parting speeches, his mind was already on the preparations for the battle of Lobito.

We were back in Kinshasa by late afternoon. I went directly to the embassy, read the cable traffic, and then went into St. Martin's office. He greeted me indifferently, and then, as though in afterthought, handed me a cable, assuming a defiant stance, ready for a fight.

"Here, you better read this," he said.

"Oh, that?" I didn't take it from his hand. "Yeah, I already saw that on your reading board outside." It was his comment on my FNLA report, bearing the *Eyes Only Plotka* (Potts's pseudonym) slug, for Potts's exclusive attention. Without disputing the facts it cast a shadow on some points in my report. It was an effort to demonstrate his seniority, as basic as a dog sniffing another's urine and covering it with his own.

I had so far avoided an argument with St. Martin and meant to keep it that way.

"You are entitled to your own comment," I said about his cable. "Listen, Colonel Castro is over at the Intercontinental . . ." Castro had telephoned the embassy, requesting a meeting and in St. Martin's own city I was obliged to tell him of any agent meetings or covert activity.

The next morning I cleared through the station with little delay, only taking time to send out a brief message giving my estimated time of arrival in Washington.

Late that night I stood nursing a drink in a Madrid discothèque, watching young Europeans dance to the throbbing music. I had moved too quickly from Silva Porto to Madrid; from the chanting faithful of UNITA, who stamped and sang their worship of Savimbi, united in a life-and-death common cause; from the somber, scared soldiers of Luso; from the faceless, dying boy in Chicala; to the emptiness of a European night club.

Tomorrow I would land in D.C. and face headquarters, where reality was a committee meeting, corridor politics, and the turn of a phrase on a cable.

9

The Economy-Size War

My plane from Madrid landed at Dulles Airport mid-afternoon on Sunday, August 24. I had found an unoccupied row of seats and worked on my notes for the entire flight, breaking only to eat and to listen to a monologue from a USAID officer I had known in Abidjan.

Normally a case officer would never carry sensitive notes on an international flight. In fact, agency regulations strictly forbade it—too much risk of skyjacking, kidnapping, or search by an aggressive customs officer. But I had been faced with a dilemna common to case officers in high-priority operations. Pouch time from Kinshasa to headquarters was three weeks, and I would be required to report in detail the day after my return. So I did what most case officers do, I took a chance and stuffed the notes in my pocket. Once onboard the Dulles flight I worried less. Barring a skyjacking to Cuba or a mugging in Washington I was home free. My diplomatic passport would grease the way through the U.S. customs and immigration. My bags would not be opened.

Monday, August 25, I briefed Potts at the morning staff meeting, fleshing out my cabled report about the FNLA, and describing UNITA. Bantam told me to stand by to brief the director and the 40 Committee, but Potts scotched that, relaying the gist of my findings up the ladder without taking me along. This was consistent with his tendency to keep that level of activity to himself, and I probably encouraged his caution anyway when I confronted him in his office immediately after the staff meeting.

Potts and I had never analyzed the Angola program together. Now that I was confident of my knowledge of Angola, I wanted to have an airing, to hear his rationale for the program, and to make some basic suggestions. He had all along discouraged this kind of questioning in the staff meetings and I hoped to be more successful in the privacy of his office.

It didn't work. Potts refused to respond and the meeting became a Stockwell monologue which went something like this: We had two viable options in Angola. We could give the FNLA and UNITA enough support to win—by going in quickly with tactical air support and advisors we could take Luanda and put the MPLA out of business before the Soviets could react. Otherwise, if we weren't willing to do that, we would further U.S. interests by staying out of the conflict. The middle ground, feeling our way along with small amounts of aid, would only escalate the war and get the United States far out on a fragile limb. It would help neither the Angolan people nor us. To the contrary, it would jeopardize the United States' position in southern Africa.

Potts wanted none of it. In his best patronizing manner he averred that I would with more experience find "these situations" difficult. Clear solutions rarely presented themselves. Our program would no doubt be a compromise between my alternatives. He broke off the conversation. On the way into the working group session Thursday morning, August 28, however, he reinforced the point.

"Just stick to the facts about your trip," he said. "Don't make any conclusions or recommendations." Possibly Potts would have been happier without me along, but that would have been awkward. The working group knew of my trip and was eager to hear the report first hand.

Working group meetings were held in the DDO's spare conference room off "C" corridor on the third floor. Paneled and carpeted, with a huge oak conference table, this chamber was more attractive than Africa Division's utilitarian offices, though still confining. There were no windows and ventilation was poor. On a back wall hung pictures of some of the agency's previous deputy directors of operations. Potts sat at the head of the table with the former ambassador to Zaire, Sheldon Vance, representing the secretary of state's office on his right, and Hal Horan, the National Security Council senior staff member on his left. Other members ranged down the table: the under-secretary of state for political affairs (Joseph Sisco himself never attended, but was always represented by a senior staffer); the assistant secretary of state for African affairs (also represented by a senior staffer); Edward Mulcahy, the deputy assistant secretary of state for African affairs; Lieutenant General Howard Fish, director of the Defense Security Assistance Agency; the director of the Bureau of Intelligence and Research (INR) represented by Francis Detar; Colonel Clinton Granger, director of the planning staff, National Security Council; Rear Admiral Samuel Packer, assistant deputy director for political military affairs; Colonel Gene Rawlings, Office of the Joint Chiefs of Staff and director of the Office of Central African Affairs of the Defense Department; and Walt Cutler, director of the Office of Central African Affairs of the State Department. Potts was chairman, representing the CIA director. Various Africa Division senior officers, including of course myself, always attended.*

---

*The 40 Committee/National Security Council mechanism traditionally directs covert wars, assassination attempts, and coups in other countries. Because of doubts raised by Watergate and the Church Committee disclosures, the working group was appointed to provide closer supervision of the CIA. From 1969 to 1976 the National Security Council was dominated by Henry Kissinger, who often dispensed with its services altogether, giving his orders directly to the CIA.

The CIA has used 40 Committee approval to authenticate some of its more sensitive operations, but has by no means brought all of its covert actions to the attention of the 40 Committee. The Pike Committee (House Select Committee on Intelligence) made a serious error when it concluded in its January 1976 report that the CIA was remarkably responsive to the controls of the National Security Council (NSC) and that all major covert action projects had had presidential approval. William Corson concludes rather that ". . . it is important to remember that 75 to 85% of all covert operations and activities carried out during that period (1947–52) were never really reviewed by any organization or body outside of the group, agency or service which initiated them" (*Armies of Ignorance,* William R. Corson [New York: Dial, 1977], p. 350).

I stood in a corner of the crowded room beside the large map of Angola. Red, green, and blue stick-ons indicated areas held by the MPLA, FNLA, and UNITA; sweeping red and green arrows showed advances, and jagged bomb-bursts marked clashes. (Little figures had been traced from *Mad* magazine's, "Spy Versus Spy" series, cut from black plastic and stuck to the board to indicate the places I had visited.) Using a pointer I led the group through my trip, giving vignettes and describing personalities, as well as presenting facts and military assessments. I avoided mentioning agency officers by name, or any of the foreigners I had encountered who might eventually be recruited to work for the agency. Remembering Potts's admonition, I stuck to the trip and to the facts I had assembled. I made it clear that, despite disorganization and inefficiency, our allies seemed determined to fight and were apparently equal to the MPLA forces in numbers and effectiveness. I restrained myself from saying that if we gave them abundant, immediate support they had a chance of *winning* the civil war, and that otherwise I felt we should withdraw altogether. Potts appeared relaxed.

Then I nearly gummed up the works, simply by saying "we" when I reported going to Silva Porto. Potts blanched and a branch chief who was sitting near by began shaking his head at me. I muddled on and only later learned what was so wrong with "we." I had meant myself and my interpreter, a Portuguese-speaking case officer who had just completed a mission in MPLA-held Luanda, under official

---

Without true confessions from the operatives involved it would be impossible to estimate the percentage of operations throughout the years which have been run without NSC supervision, but certainly they were numerous, and some of major consequence. The Pike Committee was forced to rely on the testimony of reluctant witnesses and on documents the CIA selectively provided which doubtless indicated complete fidelity to NSC direction. However, what the Pike Committee was unable to penetrate was the gray area of CIA operations, where its operatives take action without leaving written traces of what they do. For example, the CIA station in Ghana played a major role in the overthrow of Kwame Nkrumah in 1966, in violation of a 40 Committee decision not to, but CIA cables and dispatches infer that all contacts with the plotters were undertaken solely to obtain intelligence on what they were doing. Similarly, CIA written records become mysteriously vague about the Lumumba assassination plot, the Trujillo assassination plot, and the Schneider assassination plot. In each case there are documents which place CIA officers in supportive contact with the eventual assassins but the link seems to break before the final deed.

State Department cover. The State Department would never have approved his subsequent appearance on the other side of the lines, in Silva Porto, so the CIA had lied to the working group about it. This sort of deceit was common enough, but they had forgotten to mention it to me. Unwittingly, I had nearly exposed the lie.

When I was done Frank Wisner, from the office of the under-secretary of state for political affairs, fixed me with a stare and asked bluntly what we hoped to accomplish in Angola. Although Frank was a State Department foreign service officer, his father had been CIA, rising to the position of chief of the Office of Policy Coordination which, in 1950, was the original clandestine services. By coincidence his father's picture hung the wall behind him, the resemblance clear enough, the father's bald pate exaggerating Frank's own premature acomia.

Wisner's question presented a good opportunity for me to relinquish the floor.

"Well, Frank," I said. "Mr. Potts was addressing exactly that question earlier today. If you don't mind, I would like to defer to him." I turned to Potts, "Sir?"

Potts sat forward, pleased to regain control of the meeting.

He spoke in bureaucratese, "Our assessment is that we can provide the wherewithal to prop up the FNLA and UNITA so they can hold against the MPLA at least until November eleventh. We can't really project beyond that date, but if they do go into independence on an equal footing we should have various options still open. Perhaps a negotiated settlement could be reached. Perhaps the Soviets and the MPLA will compromise when they see our determination."

It was as plausible an explanation of a no-win policy as would ever be given.

An hour later the general nodded and looked at his watch. Others stirred. It was well after twelve o'clock and Potts was hosting the ambassadors at lunch in the executive dining room. He reached for my arm and said, "John, do come with us." Such are the rewards of a good team player in the CIA.

During September and October, the CIA, with remarkable support from diverse U.S. government and military offices around the world, mounted the controversial, economy-size war with single-minded ruthlessness. The lumbering USAF C-141 jet transports continued to lift twenty-five–ton loads of obsolete U.S. or untraceable foreign weapons from Charleston, South Carolina, to Kinshasa, where smaller planes took them into Angola. The USN *American Champion* sailed from Charleston on August 30 with a cargo of arms and equipment. Any "snags" were handled by a phone call from the CIA to the White House, Pentagon, or State Department, and the problem magically disappeared.

CIA officers, eventually eighty-three altogether, were dispatched to the field, where they beefed up the Kinshasa, Luanda, Lusaka, and Pretoria stations, and managed the air, ground, maritime, and propaganda branches of the little war. An additional $10.7 million, authorized by the president on August 20, 1975, for the purchase of more arms, ammunition, and advisors for Angola, had brought our total budget to $24.7 million.

The deadline was November 11, 1975, when the Portuguese would relinquish proprietorship of the colony to whichever movement controlled the capital at that time.

The war was a seesaw of escalation. Momentum moved from side to side, as the United States and Soviet Union delivered obsolete weapons, then foreign troops, and eventually sophisticated systems such as wire-guided rockets and late-model jet fighter bombers.

In early September the MPLA committed a devastating, ageless weapon, the Russian 122 mm. rocket, and set the FNLA troops running, until the MPLA swept back through Caxito where I had been, and very nearly to Ambriz. Supplied by the Soviet Union, the 122 mm. rocket, as much as any one thing, eventually decided the outcome of the civil war in Angola.

The working group puzzled over this rocket, unable to grasp its effectiveness against the FNLA in Angola. On paper it appeared to be an inaccurate, pre–World War II rocket, only slightly larger than the 120 mm. and 4.2-inch mortars we had given the FNLA. Originally designed as a siege weapon of only general accuracy, it had been used by the Viet Cong to harass GVN-held cities in South Vietnam. Two men could carry it through the jungle, fire it from a tripod of crossed sticks, and flee empty-handed. In Angola its accuracy and volume of fire were increased by the use of truck-mounted launchers, called Stalin organs.

I interrupted the working group discussion to tell them about this weapon, remembering the months in Tay Ninh when we were shelled almost daily with 122 mm. rockets. "Think of the loudest clap of thunder you have ever heard and you won't be close to the one-twenty-two. If one lands within a hundred yards, light fixtures drop from the ceiling and doors jump open. The percussion charge will shatter a small house or penetrate an eighteen-inch reinforced concrete bunker. The antipersonnel charge fragments into fourteen thousand red-hot, razor-sharp slivers of steel." Such rockets, landing anywhere near our FNLA troops, would destroy their morale.

The 122 had a simple advantage over the weapons we had given the FNLA—namely, range. It would fire twelve kilometers; our mortars no more than eight. From a safe distance the MPLA could lob 122 mm. rockets onto FNLA troops who were unable to return fire.

Well-organized troops could endure such shelling indefinitely, by digging in or by aggressive patroling and maneuvering. The 122 could also be neutralized by coordinated artillery fire, tactical aircraft, or electronically guided rocketry, but these were not available to the FNLA.

The United States had no simple weapon comparable to the 122 to give the FNLA. Our weaponry jumped from the less effective mortars to heavy artillery and modern rockets. These, and tactical aircraft, could have neutralized the 122, but they were prohibitively expensive and required highly trained crews to operate them. They would also have been conspicuously American and the 40 Committee refused to authorize their use—until December, when it was too late.

The answer seemed to come from Zaire—and South Africa. On September 11, Mobutu committed his elite Seventh and Fourth Commando Battalions, flying them to Ambriz in his C-130s, and the tide swung back in favor of the FNLA north of Luanda. On September 17, a consolidated task force of Zairian, FNLA, and Portuguese troops retook Caxito; then they began a cautious advance on Luanda itself.

Another Zairian force joined a Cabindan* liberation force, called

*Cabinda was a curiosity—a small, 2,800 square mile area of 60,000 people—it came into being in 1898, when the Cabindan tribal chief had signed the Simbuluku treaty with the Portuguese, accepting their protection in order to escape the dread, forced-labor policies of King Leopold of Belgium. The Cabindan people related loosely to the Zairians of the lower Congo River, at least more than to the Mbundu of Central Angola.

FLEC (Front for the Liberation of the Enclave of Cabinda), and plunged across the Zairian/Cabinda border. Cabinda, separated from the rest of Angola by a narrow strip of Zairian territory, had been coveted by the expansionist Mobutu since his ascension to power in the mid-sixties. Mobutu's greed was further stimulated in the late sixties, when oil was discovered off the Cabindan coastline. Seeing his chance in October 1975 to annex the MPLA-held Cabinda, Mobutu approached the CIA. We promptly flew in a one-thousand-man arms package for use in the invasion, and CIA officers of the Kinshasa station began to visit the FLEC training camp to coordinate. On November 2, a joint invasion force launched a three-column attack against the MPLA defenders, who were reinforced with Cuban advisors. They were accompanied by a half-dozen French mercenaries, not that they made any difference.* The Cuban/MPLA force easily held Cabinda.

Meanwhile in the central regions of Angola, UNITA was having a difficult time with major action on two flanks. The Katangese checked them at Luso and a Cuban-led MPLA force turned them back short of Lobito, and then pressed inland from the coast, getting close enough to Nova Lisboa to cut off the city's water and electricity. Reeling, attacked on two sides, Savimbi accepted increasing South African military assistance. He was under enormous pressure from President Kaunda of Zambia to open the Benguela railroad before November 11—if Savimbi controlled the railroad by Independence Day Kaunda could rationalize continued support, perhaps even recognition. Otherwise, Kaunda would have to deal with the MPLA.

While Mobutu's commandos were attacking Caxito, a South African armored column crossed the border into southern Angola and began moving north. Fifty armored cars were manned by 250 South African soldiers, and supported by 750 command, artillery, and logistical troops inside Angola. Another 2,000 troops provided logistical support from the border. C-130s and trucks kept the armored cars fueled, and the commanders got about in light planes and helicopters. The armored cars linked up with

*These Frenchmen may in fact have been hired by the French intelligence service. French agents were appearing in Kinshasa and in Angola, but CIA intelligence on the subject was sketchy.

1,000 UNITA soldiers and swept rapidly through much larger Cuban and MPLA forces, even coping with rockets, tanks, light aircraft, and long-range artillery.

On October 28, the South African column captured Mocamedes on the southern coast. By November 7 they had taken Benguela and Lobito and were pressing north. Another column drove the Katangese out of Luso and moved toward Texeira da Sousa on the eastern border, the last railroad post held by the MPLA.

On November 8, three days before Independence, the FNLA/-Zairian column began its advance on Luanda itself, crossing the Quifangondo plain twenty kilometers from the outskirts of the city. They were supported by four 5.5-inch artillery pieces, which were supplied and manned by the South Africans, and by two 130 mm. long-barrel field guns, manned by Zairians, which Mobutu had gotten from North Korea. The 5.5-inch pieces were obsolete weapons with limited range, but the 130s could reach thirty kilometers and bring Luanda itself under fire.

In the last days before the November 11 independence ceremonies the Portuguese high commissioner prepared to depart. The remaining Portuguese colonial troops withdrew to the sixteenth-century San Miguel fort in Luanda; lining up to photograph each other beside the statue of Prince Henry the Navigator.

Outside of Luanda the MPLA now had control of only three of the fifteen provinces, a narrow corridor from the coast inland. All sources in Luanda were reporting that the MPLA leaders were terrified and were sending their families out of the country by any means available. The chief of station, Lusaka, cabled headquarters, predicting the MPLA's back would be broken in a few days. The American consul General in Luanda nervously insisted on closing the consulate and was permitted to do so by the State Department, which feared for any American official's safety if the battle came into Luanda itself. The American consular staff departed Luanda November 3, on one of the last of the refugee evacuation flights.*

Between Caxito and Luanda itself a few dozen Cubans and a

---

*The United States had contributed four jetliners to a $6 million Red Cross program, which evacuated approximately 300,000 Portuguese Angolan refugees in September and October 1975.

A variety of arms captured at Luso by the UNITA forces, including *(facing page, bottom left)* several Chinese rocket-launchers, an effective weapon against light tanks and trucks.

frightened MPLA force were preparing their defense and stockpiling the 122 mm. rockets, which had served them so well in September.

In Washington the CIA advised the working group that the high-water mark had been reached. Without a substantial escalation of commitment, including large amounts of money for arms, tactical aircraft, antitank weapons, antiaircraft rockets, and larger numbers of advisors, the outcome would favor the MPLA. Working group members could not understand this assessment and suggested that it was a CIA ploy to get more money.

After my return from Angola in late August, the headquarters Angola Task Force quickly reached full strength, with a paramilitary section, an intelligence-gathering section, a propaganda section, a reports section, and a supporting staff of secretaries and assistants. By working extra hours we were able to avoid going to twenty-four–hour shifts, but the workload was staggering and the pace frantic. For example, on September 4 alone, my notes refer to sixty-three activities of importance, things like: write a paper on Kissinger's meeting with the Zairian foreign minister; analyze a David Ottoway article in the *Washington Post* about American involvement in Angola; discuss UNITA representatives in New York (funded by the CIA) who were meeting with American journalists; attend a working group meeting; attend a personnel management committee meeting; and prepare instructions for a task force officer to hand-carry to Kinshasa, things too sensitive to be put in writing in the cable traffic.*

---

*Much CIA business is communicated to and from the field by the "back channel" —hand-carried notes, pouched single copy, official-informal letters, and verbal messages. This is consciously done to minimize the number of people inside the CIA who know of a given operation or situation, and to communicate ultrasensitive messages without leaving a written record.

One example: in 1972 the CIA station in Nairobi included a black communicator who would routinely see all of the station cable traffic. That traffic included highly sensitive messages about a Nairobi/Dar-es-Salaam operation in which black Americans traveling in East Africa were surveilled by outside agents and through the Kenyan security service. It was felt by the Nairobi chief of station that the black CIA communicator could not be trusted with knowledge of this operation and his urgent replacement by a white was necessary. The COS was not about to put that in writing, however, not even in an official-informal letter. Instead, he returned to headquarters on consultations and quietly arranged for the young man's transfer.

Among other messages, the officer was to instruct the chief of station, Kinshasa, to ask Larry Devlin to intercede with Mobutu to release the CIA agents (Zairian citizens) Mobutu had arrested, convicted of espionage and treason, and sentenced to death in June 1975. It was embarrassing to the CIA to have these men sitting on death row in Kinshasa while we were hustling Mobutu's Angola war.

In late September Larry Devlin returned to Washington to testify to the Church Committee about the CIA's Congo program of the 1960s and role in the plot to assassinate Lumumba. Of course, he visited CIA headquarters to confer with Potts and with the Congo task force, which was responding to the Senate investigation.

It hadn't taken me long to realize that Potts didn't want a verbatim transcript of any of the working group meetings. He was staying late after each session to write a summary of what had happened. This didn't seem appropriate, considering his grade and workload. I offered to write up my own notes. When that didn't seem to satisfy him, I suggested we get a professional stenographer who could take shorthand. He agreed, then changed his mind. I dropped it when I finally realized that he wanted to control the exact wording of the record of those meetings. He continued to write the reports and he did them in the form of "blind" memoranda, without headings or addressees, and kept them out of CIA official files. Thus the innermost records of the war would forever be immune to any Freedom of Information Act disclosures, or congressional investigation. Technically they did not exist: legally they could be destroyed at any time.

The meetings were also supplemented by a steady flow of working group papers—162 altogether—most of which Potts himself wrote, to brief the members on developments in the field or to document some plan of action. These were either presented to the working group during the meetings, or were delivered to them by courier. They too were kept in "soft files" in Potts's desk where they were safe from disclosure or investigation.

In the working group meetings Potts wanted to speak exclusively for the CIA and I generally obliged by remaining silent. However, one occasion when I felt compelled to speak out was in early October,

(Seymour Hersh of the *New York Times* exposed the CIA's operation against American blacks on March 17, 1978.)

when the arrival of a few hundred Cuban soldiers in Angola was being discussed. The working group was thinking of replying with another Zairian battalion, a few dozen mercenaries, and some Redeye missiles. So far it had been a gentleman's war, with modest escalations and no suprises. During the summer of 1975 260 Cuban advisors had joined the MPLA, but their presence had scarcely been felt. Now, however, the Cuban ship, *Vietnam Herioca* had delivered 700 uniformed, regular army, Cuban soldiers to Porto Amboim south of Luanda. The working group tended to view this as a worrisome escalation, but not one which seriously disrupted the quiet evolution of the war.

"Gentlemen," I interrupted, leaning forward, "I suggest we think in terms of ten to fifteen thousand Cuban soldiers, a squadron of MIGs, and a hundred or so tanks."

Silence fell while they considered the magnitude of such a force. It could march on Kinshasa virtually unopposed. The MIGs would have no problem strafing Mobutu's palace or knocking out the Inga dam which supplied electricity to the entire lower Zaire area. However, such a threat and the escalation that would be necessary to neutralize it were too big for this group to handle, and the discussion resumed at the level of a few mercenaries, with perhaps a dozen ground-to-air rockets thrown in for good measure.

As the meeting broke up one participant asked me if the CIA had any special information that large numbers of Cubans might be brought into the conflict. Others turned their heads, listening with interest. We didn't—it wasn't a matter of hard information, special intelligence, or a formal warning from the analysts of the Deputy Directorate of Information. But it was obvious nevertheless. We had introduced the Zairian battalions and the South Africans, and our side had momentum. But the Soviets had mounted a highly visible program in Angola, which was already larger than ours, and their prestige was at stake. And the Cubans had publicly stated their intention to intervene. It was illogical to hope that they would permit the U.S. a cheap victory. This wasn't the 1961 missile crisis in Cuba where our president could react with great bravado and domestic support. It was Angola, a mere five months after the fall of Vietnam.

Moreover, the Cuban policy in Angola was consistent with Cuba's ideology and its international stance. Our Angola program, like the previous Bay of Pigs and *Operation Mongoose* war against Castro, was a direct contradiction of our public policies, making it essential that we keep the American public from knowing the truth.*

The Cubans weren't ashamed of their program and they didn't need to hide it from their own people, or from the world press. In fact, on October 8, the Cuban ambassador the United Nations, Ricardo Alarcon De Quesada, had announced Cuba's position in a public speech before the General Assembly:

> In Angola the conspiracy of imperialism, its allies and lackeys, has found concrete expression in the brazen interference designed to frustrate true decolonialization while threatening its territorial integrity; snatching away from the people's liberation movement of Angola the fruits of its dauntless struggle against colonialism, while condemning the future state to control by transnational corporations. Cuba renews the expression of its full solidarity with the people's liberation movement in Angola—yesterday heroic in its struggle against the European colonizer; today firm in its defense of true independence.
>
> In the face of scandalous interference of imperialists, colonialists and racists [in Angola], *it is an elementary duty* [for Cuba] *to offer its* [the Angolan] *people the effective assistance that may be required for that country to ensure its true independence and full sovereignty.* In order to spur the decolonization process, a coherent strategy must be implemented with the participation of all progressive forces. This strategy is essential in order to face up to colonialists and racist machinations against the peoples of Namibia and Zimbabwe [Rhodesia] and must oppose colonialism in all its forms and manifestations in every corner of the earth. (Emphasis mine.)

---

*In an essay, " 'Intelligence:' The Constitution Betrayed" (*New York Review,* September 30, 1976), Henry Steele Commager states: "The fact is that the primary function of governmental secrecy in our time has not been to protect the nation against external enemies, but to deny to the American people information essential to the functioning of democracy, to the Congress information essential to the functioning of the legislative branch, and—at times—to the president himself information which he should have to conduct his office."

The Church Committee concluded: "Recent Presidents have justified secrecy on the basis of 'national security,' 'the requirements of national defense,' or 'the confidentiality required by sensitive, ongoing negotiations or operations.' . . . The Bay of Pigs fiasco, the secret war in Laos, the secret bombing of Cambodia, the anti-Allende activities in Chile, the Watergate affair, were all instances of the use of power cloaked in secrecy which, when revealed, provoked widespread popular disapproval" (Senate Select Committee Report, April 26, 1976, p. 12).

Alarcon's speech was more than polemics. After the war we learned that Cuba had not been ordered into action by the Soviet Union. To the contrary, the Cuban leaders felt compelled to intervene for their own ideological reasons.

We, on the other hand, were fettered by our secrecy and by the fact that our program would be judged wrong by the American people if they learned of it. When Savimbi began capturing Cuban prisoners, we interrogated then in Silva Porto, unable to take them even to Kinshasa for display to prove the Cuban presence in Angola. When the FNLA captured a Soviet-built armored car, we promptly flew it to Kinshasa for an FNLA-sponsored press conference. The Soviet chargé d'affaires angrily called on Mobutu, and he in turn ordered a halt to the press conference. He wasn't exactly afraid of the Soviets but he didn't really want to advertise Zaire's involvement in Angola, he said. By comparison, when the MPLA captured two South African soldiers, it promptly flew them to Lagos, Nigeria, and then to Addis Ababa for display before the Organization of African Unity.

All during the fall months our secret little drama of Angola was played before a splashy backdrop of disclosures made by the Church Committee. The former deputy director of plans (operations), Richard Bissell, testified that feasibility studies of how to assassinate Patrice Lumumba had been made in 1961. Sid Gottlieb, the CIA chief of the Office of Technical Services had hand-carried poison to Kinshasa for the Lumumba operation. Gottlieb himself testified that, years later, the CIA director, Richard Helms, had ordered him to destroy all records of the tests he had run of specific poisons to be used in killing Lumumba. The CIA's Chile operation was further exposed; its relationship with the Chileans who killed General Schneider was admitted. Under intense pressure, Colby disclosed CIA control of large supplies of deadly poison gases, which President Nixon had ordered destroyed some months earlier. Director Colby also testified about the CIA's development of exotic weapons, the press was permitted to photograph Colby showing the committee an electric pistol which fired dissolving poison pellets. The agency also admitted, in a more bizarre vein, that it had conducted drug experiments on hundreds of unwitting American citizens by hiring prostitutes to lure them into apartments, feed them drugs and seduce them, so their activities could be filmed secretly for later viewing by pseudoscientists of the CIA's Office of Technical Services.

We inside the agency reacted to these disclosures differently. The hard core was untroubled by their substance: "Are you kidding?" they would say. "Maybe we could straighten things out if the director had the balls to let us do more of that . . . After all, the other side . . ." Others felt betrayed, by the CIA directors who had led the CIA into such activities, and by the changing rules which in one decade had us as superpatriots and in another suggested we were enemies of the people. But, as the CIA's public image slipped, even the hardest cases felt insecure. If we were still the good guys, the elite of the American foreign service, we ourselves seemed to be the only ones who appreciated the fact. We drew closer into our little world, working with agency people, playing tennis with agency people, socializing with agency people. It was not a happy time to conduct a clandestine war.

Director Colby, always the good soldier, nevertheless continued to hammer away at the Senate and Congress with a barrage of secret briefings about the Angola program. Our function was to keep him supplied with charts, maps, and briefing boards, which were updated almost to the hour with figures reflecting the latest adjustment of the IAFEATURE budget and revised listings of all the arms which had been sent to Kinshasa. We were never told exactly how he used the material and it still hadn't entered my mind that Colby might be deceiving the senators in any significant way, while they were distracted by his dramatic disclosures of other historic agency malversations. It probably didn't occur to the senators either.

Potts rarely gossiped, although he would occasionally give us little insights of how the briefings went, if he thought they were important for us to know. One day Kissinger smiled at Colby, Colby returned to tell Potts about it, and Potts repeated it to us in his staff meeting, then instructed me to tell the task force. He also told his secretary to spread it around. It was, Potts felt sure, a favorable judgment of our early efforts that Kissinger had smiled at Colby during a National Security Council meeting. Everyone agreed.

The incident led me to reflect at length, on Kissinger and Colby, who had to be, if anyone was, the master chess players in the game of American intelligence. I often told myself there must be some master plan behind our intelligence policies, someone who saw the effect today's operations would have on tomorrow's world.

As a young officer I had thought of the division chief in those terms, presuming that everything he did, even some inane, drunken instruction that I learn an obscure African dialect, must be part of *The Plan,* rather the way it worked in Le Carre or Fleming's novels.* Now I could see that Potts wasn't "M." And Colby clearly wasn't either—he was only a disciplined, amoral bureaucrat, who fawned over the politicians and game-players on the hill. Kissinger was half-genius perhaps, and half-clown; he appeared to be the master-mind, but consider his Angolan policy. Bobby Fischer would never have blundered the Angolan pawn, even if his mind were focused on the queens and rooks of our rivalry with the Soviets.

Even Shirley Temple Black, the ambassador to Ghana, had some useful thoughts on the subject. In October 1975 she returned to Washington on consultations, and had lunch in the CIA executive dining room, after meeting with the director. Carl attended the luncheon and returned impressed. "That's a lot of woman," he said.

Carl told us she had complained that no one seemed to be coordinating America's overall policy in African affairs, no one was considering what the Angola program might do to our relations with Ghana, or other countries like Nigeria and Tanzania. She pointed

---

*British spy novels represent their intelligence organizations as being directed by a faceless genius who, from an easy chair in his gentlemen's club gives a studied order which launches operations, that move across continents for months until a planned confrontation occurs and the desired objective is achieved, none of which is fully understood by the chain of operatives involved. Only "M" knows from the outset, like Bobby Fischer launching a fifteen-move gambit, what the true objective is and how it will materialize, out of the chaos of the operation itself, in the final drama. This is the unreality, the fiction of British fiction, which separates their novels from the bureaucratic realities of the modern intelligence business. CIA officers escape into *The Spy Who Came in from the Cold* with the same enthusiasm as the average reader. That's the way the intelligence business should be.

However, not all British spy novels are appreciated by the CIA. I was once quietly reprimanded by the senior instructor down at the "Farm" when I recommended that all student case officers be required to read *The Looking-Glass War.* Its story was too close to real life: a pointless little operation, run solely because an army intelligence unit remembered it still had a World War II charter to run agent operations. The agent ignominiously dies, but in the final pages the intelligence chiefs walk away, blithely planning their next operation. After all they still have their charter, don't they?

out that the Soviets' national sport is chess and their foreign policy reflects an effort at long-range planning of coordinated, integrated moves, although they often play the game badly and are given to serious blunders. The Chinese are notorious for planning their foreign policy carefully, with moves designed to reach fruition even years beyond the lifetimes of present leaders. By contrast, Ambassador Black observed, the United States is a poker player. It looks the world over, picks up whatever cards it is dealt, and plays, raising the stakes as more cards are dealt, until the hand is won or lost. Then, after a drag on the cigarette and another sip of whiskey, it looks around for the next hand to be played.

Still, if survival was the name of the game, the CIA was not doing badly in the fall of 1975. Not even the Pike Committee had much effect, as Potts enjoyed reporting after accompanying Colby to a committee hearing. Congressman Pike had proposed to open an investigation of IAFEATURE, only to relent when they told him it would be disastrous to have hearings during an ongoing operation —better not jiggle the hand of the surgeon during an operation, they had said. Potts and Colby had been pleased with themselves, and with the metaphor, "jiggle the hand of the surgeon." Potts went about repeating it for several days.

10

Advisors, Technicians, and Foreign Troops

The Marine Corps major, who had assisted the task force with logistical planning, visited Ambriz (in civilian clothes) and returned to report: "You would have to see it to believe it. I drove around in a jeep with Commandant Lukenge, who is supposed to be the FNLA's best soldier. I picked his M-79 grenade-launcher up one time and tried to open it; you know it breaks open like a single-barrel shotgun. It was rusted shut! He had had it only a few weeks and it was rusted so tight I couldn't force it open. The same thing is happening to their rifles, mortars, and vehicles. They need help!" Of over three hundred Panhard armored cars Zaire had received from France since 1970, less than thirty were still operational at the time of the Angola war in 1975.

The CIA was delivering adequate quantities of arms and ammunition but the "friendly" forces were not able to organize the logistical systems necessary to deploy them or to develop the communications, maintenance, combat leadership, and discipline to organize an effective military effort.

The easiest solution was for the CIA to place its own paramilitary experts with the FNLA and UNITA commands. This was strictly prohibited by the 40 Committee, which wanted no Americans directly involved in the fighting, but we did it anyway. From the outset we were deeply involved in managing the war from Washington, from Kinshasa, and from advance bases inside Angola, and this was reported daily in the flow of cables to and from the field. For cover purposes vis-à-vis the working group we called the advisors we placed inside Angola "intelligence gatherers," although their intelligence effort was always subordinate to their advisory activities.

To cite a few examples: In early August the chief of Special Operations Group (SOG), the marine major, myself, and others met at headquarters to discuss requirements for the battle of Lobito and sabotage operations to be run in Congo (Brazzaville). We relayed our recommendations to the field by cable. CIA communications specialists prepared the tactical communications plan for the battle of Lobito, and then installed the UNITA and FNLA tactical and strategic networks inside Angola. CIA communications officers trained FNLA and UNITA technicians at the Angolan advance bases. Kinshasa cables reported that CIA paramilitary officers were training UNITA forces in Silva Porto and the FNLA in Ambriz in the use of infantry weapons. A retired army colonel was hired on contract and assigned full time to the FNLA command at Ambriz. An infantry training team was sent from headquarters, allegedly to train selected UNITA cadres in Zaire, but the Kinshasa station promptly dispatched the training officers to Ambriz and Silva Porto. On October 31 the COS Kinshasa flew to Ambriz to mediate a quarrel between the CIA senior advisor and Roberto.*

The DDO gave the officers who were working inside Angola authority to go about armed.** In many cases they also wore utility

---

*In *Honorable Men,* Colby states, "no CIA officers were permitted to engage in combat or train there [in Angola]."

**The DDO is under constant pressure from field stations to approve sidearms for case officers. I always argued that case officers should not be armed. Gun laws are stricter in European and African countries than in the United States, and pistols require licenses and permits. Diplomats are among the last to carry guns. How does a case officer explain to the local police he thinks he needs a pistol? Does he say, "Well, I have to go down these dark alleys every night meeting agents . . ."? If he carries one illegally, all of the risks of exposure are magnified. What if he shoots uniforms and in some cases even used the cover story that they were mercenaries.

When the Kinshasa station renewed its request on September 17 for a network of bases inside Angola, I confronted Potts. The proposal amounted to a major escalation of our involvement, a move to be taken seriously and only with full approval.

Potts snapped that I was out of line. St. Martin worked for him, not for me, and his own policy was to avoid second-guessing the man in the field.*

Stymied, I turned to leave the office, as Potts gave me the final word. Actually, he said, there were no American advisors in Angola. Only "intelligence gatherers." That was the party line. That it wasn't true was not important. Habitually, case officers lie to all non-CIA acquaintances as they live their cover stories: they lie to agents they are recruiting; to State Department colleagues and ambassadors

---

someone? Where does he stand trial? And what does the inevitable publicity do to the United States embassy's position in that country? What does it do to his own career? The standard response from many case officers is, "Screw all that! I carry a pistol and shoot my way out of a tight spot, at least I survive. I can always come back to Washington and find another way to make a living."

My own first experience with this problem was in Lubumbashi where bandits were uncontrolled and armed robbery a daily occurence. I carried a pistol for a while but eventually locked it in my safe in the office. What good is a thirty-eight against teams of machine gun–armed bandits? I decided my odds of survival were better without a pistol and instead I carried on my dashboard a carton of giveaway cigarettes and practiced talking my way out of bad situations.

In 1970 I was forced to think my position out further when a young Zairian rebel from across Lake Tanganyika brought a letter to our Burundi embassy, which he claimed to have intercepted. It outlined a plan to kidnap the American ambassador. (This young rebel claimed to be part of the same group which in May 1975 kidnapped four students from the shores of Lake Tanganyika.) I reported by IMMEDIATE cable and headquarters returned an alarmed response instructing me to be extremely wary, to meet the young man only inside the embassy, and to carry a pistol to the next meeting.

I thought about it and drafted my response, agreeing to follow headquarters' advice, but asking if I had headquarters' permission in case of trouble to shoot him: (a) in the head; (b) in the stomach; (c) in the foot. Obviously, no matter what headquarters put in a cable, if I shot someone, especially inside the U.S. embassy, I would be held responsible in the aftermath.

*A chief of station is responsible to the division chief, and above. Other headquarters officers such as a task-force commander, the chief of operations, and the deputy division chief are not strictly in the chain of command.

about controversial operations; and at a certain level to the United States Congress, to cover up those operations. In the Angolan operation we were now lying to each other, even while we read and wrote cables which directly contradicted those lies. In fact, there were several levels of untruth functioning simultaneously, different stories for different aspects of our activities, one for the working group, another for unwitting State Department personnel, yet another for the U.S. Congress. By this point in our careers, after years of role-playing cover stories, we would not falter as we switched from one story to the next. In one conversation we might mention training we were doing inside Angola, remember a working group paper about "intelligence gatherers," and remind ourselves to have State deny to the press that the U.S. was in Angola. Significantly, we did not think of these things in terms of lying—Potts did not think of himself as lying when he was giving the working group a "party line," and Colby might have passed a lie-detector test while he was giving the Senate essentially false briefings.

In fact, the intelligence production of CIA "intelligence gatherers" in Angola was a disappointment and an embarassment to headquarters throughout the program—so bad that the African Bureau of the State Department at one point delivered a formal written complaint to Secretary Kissinger about the CIA's inadequate intelligence coverage. The reasons for this intelligence failure were basic. The men who went into Angola were predominantly paramilitary specialists and technicians, not experienced intelligence officers. And the field managers of the program emphasized the paramilitary aspects at the expense of intelligence. Inside the CIA, we hadn't noticed our intelligence failure, we were accustomed to hustling the easy intelligence targets: African politicians, diplomats, and political parties.

The failure of the CIA to produce adequate intelligence in Angola was more typical than people would realize. The Pike Committee analyzed the agency's intelligence performance and reached emphatically negative conclusions. The committee's final report, January 19, 1976 (suppressed by the House, but published illegally by the *Village Voice,* February 1976), analyzed six illustrative CIA intelligence failures: the Tet offensive in Vietnam in 1968; the Russian invasion of Czechoslovakia (in which the CIA lost track of the Soviet army for two weeks); the 1973 Mideast war (in which the CIA relied on distorted Israeli reporting, causing the United States to misunderstand the situation and skirt the brink of global confrontation with the Soviet Union); the 1974 coup in Portugal (which the CIA failed to predict or analyze correctly, leaving the United States without prepared options for dealing with Portuguese colonies in Africa); the first nuclear explosion in the Third World, in India in 1974; and the overthrow of Archbishop Makarios in Cyprus (an intelligence failure which precipitated a diplomatic failure, which seriously undermined NATO's southern flank, led to a deterioration of our relations with Greece, Turkey, and Cyprus, and got our ambassador, Roger Davis, killed).

One might add the CIA's intelligence failure in Saigon in April 1975, when the CIA station chief chose to believe the communist Hungarian ambassador instead of agency intelligence sources regarding Hanoi's final intentions for Saigon; the agency's failure to cover the developing South African nuclear capability; and its inability to cover the invasion of Zaire by Katangese gendarmes in March 1977. The list of CIA intelligence failures is almost endless. Representative Pike concluded emphatically that CIA intelligence production was lousy.

The Angola program itself was grounded in three substantial intelligence failures. First, the "Tar Baby" report of 1969 (NSSM 39) discounted the tenacity of the black nationalist movements. Second, we failed to predict and prepare for the coup in Portugal. And the options paper which the CIA presented to the 40 Committee on July 14, 1975 stated that a United States program of $40 million would likely match any Soviet increase in aid to Neto—the Soviet Angola program eventually exceeded $400 million.

To correct the Angolan intelligence deficit, headquarters sent endless reminders and warnings to the field, all to no avail. By the end of the war we had little more detailed knowledge of our allies than we had after my trip in late August; no "book" had been made, no lists of FNLA/UNITA commanders, troop units, or advisors. As the war evolved the CIA advisors reported some battles as they occurred, but not all, and were not able to account for allied combat losses. The field stations clamored endlessly for more arms and ammunition, but kept no record of what weapons were issued to which units.* Roberto and Savimbi never cooperated to the point of telling

---

*After the war it was learned that in some cases UNITA had dumped some of our

us about their other allies: the Chinese, Portuguese, and South Africans. The Pretoria and Paris stations were euphoric, having greater access to BOSS and SDECE* representatives than ever in agency history, but the intelligence exchange was entirely one-sided. The South Africans and French accepted voluminous intelligence reports and detailed briefings from those CIA stations but never reciprocated with much information about what they were doing in Angola.

There was little reporting on UNITA and FNLA political organization or diplomatic efforts. In November, when the two established a provisional government in Nova Lisboa (renamed Huambo) and sought international recognition, the CIA had inadequate coverage of its substance, structure, or leadership.

And if the intelligence coverage of our allied forces was disappointing, our knowledge of the MPLA was nil. Almost no information was produced by the clandestine services about MPLA armies, leadership, or objectives.

There was a flow of intelligence reporting from the field—vague, general, and often inaccurate. One important example: in October numerous CIA agents began reporting the presence of MIGS in the Congo (Brazzaville) and Angola. Eventually every CIA agent in those areas reported their presence, and several claimed to have seen them.

If true, this was an ominous development. Coupled with the arrival of large numbers of Cuban troops, MIGs could dominate the Angolan battlefields. The working group stirred uneasily and began to discuss an answer: Redeye missiles. The Redeye was a small, man-packed, ground-to-air missile designed to give infantry units the capability of defending themselves against jet fighter bombers. Traveling at mach 1.5, it homes on an aircraft engine's infra-red emissions and explodes when very near the target. The Redeye was a sensitive, classified weapons system that had been released only to close American allies, including Israel.

---

useless, obsolete carbines into a river. This was reported by Leon Dash, a *Washington Post* reporter who walked into Angola in October 1976 and spent six months with UNITA forces.

*The South African Bureau of State Security and the French Service de Documentation Exterieure et Contre-Espionage.

The agency wanted to put Redeye missiles in Angola. The Defense Department stalled and the 40 Committee was troubled because the Redeye could only come from the United States. Its discovery in Angola would confirm our serious involvement in the war. Was the agency absolutely certain the MIGs were there?

The agency was not. Despite the unanimous confirmation from our human intelligence sources, we were not willing to assure the working group that MIGs were definitely in Angola. This was a subject of hard intelligence. The MIGs either were there or they were not, and the truth would eventually be confirmed. It was not a political subject about which exaggerations and distortions could never be proven right or wrong, and we inside the agency would not endorse our human intelligence to the working group on the subject of MIGs.

Our caution was vindicated. In October, November, December, and January no MIGs appeared on the Angolan battlefields, or were confirmed by American witnesses or by any other irrefutable sources.*

Still, the CIA advisors were not enough for FNLA/UNITA needs. To supplement their efforts we searched the world for allies who could provide qualified advisors to put into the conflict, or better yet, regular army units to crush the MPLA and deliver the country to Roberto and Savimbi. We canvassed moderate friends—Brazil, Morocco, South Korea, Belgium, Great Britain, France, and even Portugal, without success. South Africa eventually came to UNITA's rescue, but the Zairian commando battalions in northern Angola were only slightly better than the FNLA forces they joined.

Mercenaries seemed to be the answer, preferably Europeans with the requisite military skills and perhaps experience in Africa. As long as they were not Americans, the 40 Committee approved. We began an exhaustive search for suitable candidates, a search which brought me in conflict with my bosses and kept me at odds with them even into March 1976, months after the Senate had ordered a halt to the

---

*MIGs eventually appeared in Angola in March 1976, when they destroyed a UNITA supply flight at Gago Catinho in eastern Angola. By then the agency had traded fifty Redeye missiles to Israel for fifty inferior Soviet SA-7 Grail missiles, which we delivered to Angola. These were fired at the MIGs but they all malfunctioned.

Angola program. The conduct of European and South African mercenaries in previous African civil wars had left them with a murderous reputation, and the use of white mercenaries at the crest of the era of black nationalism was a blunder, I felt, which could only damage United States credibility in the Third World. In addition, the mercenaries who have appeared in previous African wars have been a mixed bag, more often self-serving, ineffective, unmilitary. Potts, Bantam, Nelson, St. Martin, Foster—all lacked enough experience in Africa to know that. They tended to idealize mercenaries and exaggerate their capabilities. And they lacked sensitivity for the disgust the word "mercenary" stirs in the hearts of black Africans. Nor did Colby know Africa, although perhaps he was in a class by himself. The mild, likable, church-going, master case officer who had commanded the PHOENIX program in Vietnam would hardly have qualms about a few mercenaries fighting blacks in Africa.

I spoke out in staff meetings and in Potts's office everytime the subject of mercenaries came up. Whenever a memo or buckslip or cable about mercenaries circulated the office I added my own critical comment in the margins, and I did have some effect. After several weeks of my pressure, the word "mercenary" became tabu at headquarters. Potts forbade its use in cables, memoranda, and files, at headquarters and in the field. Thereafter the mercenaries who were hired and sent to Angola were to be called "foreign military advisors."

And so we proceeded to search the world for acceptable "foreign military advisors." We began the search with no leads whatsoever—astonishingly, we found that nowhere in the CIA, not even the Special Operations Group, with all its experiences in Southeast Asia, was there a file, reference list, or computer run of individuals who might be recruited as advisors. Anti-Castro Cubans, such as had been used in the Congo, the Bay of Pigs, and Watergate, were ruled out because they carried United States green resident alien cards and hence would fall under the 40 Committee's restrictions against using Americans. South Vietnamese refugees were approached, but they were busy rebuilding their lives in the new world, and were unanimously wary of a CIA adventure in black Africa. They too carried green cards. The British refused to help. South Koreans were excluded because of language and cultural problems. Biafrans and other Africans were rejected out of political considerations, and because they wouldn't have the impact of whites. Finally, five sources seemed to be available: Portuguese, French, Brazilians, Filipinos, and South Africans.

Portuguese were already being recruited in small numbers by the FNLA, Colonel Castro, Captain Bento, and their men. We decided to expand this effort by recruiting three hundred Portuguese Angolans to support the FNLA. But for UNITA we needed two dozen technicians, and Savimbi wouldn't accept Portuguese.

France would not give us regular army troops, but it had no hesitation concerning mercenaries. The French intelligence service introduced CIA case officers to onetime Congo mercenary Bob Denard, and for $500,000 cash—paid in advance—he agreed to provide twenty French mercenaries who would "advise" UNITA on short-term contracts. Denard was encrypted UNROBIN/1 and this mercenary program was UNHOOD. To the waggish the twenty Frenchmen were "Robin's Hoods" or the "French Hoods" for the duration of the program.

Brazil seemed also to offer a good source of manpower. Savimbi and Roberto both thought they could work comfortably with black Brazilians, who had the advantage of speaking Portuguese. General Walters, the CIA deputy director, felt sure he could influence the Brazilian military command to help us recruit. Walters had served as defense and army attaché in Brazil in the mid-1960s and was still somewhat euphoric about that experience. We sent a cable instructing the chief of station, Brasilia, to query the Brazilians about the general's desire to visit, but the polite answer came back that Brazil could not at that time entertain the (highly visible) CIA deputy director. In Walters's place Dick Sampson, the chief of Latin America Division, went and returned, empty-handed. The Brazilians politely declined to permit the recruitment of mercenaries in their country.

In Vietnam, Filipinos had provided the CIA with extensive help, keeping radios, vehicles, and air conditioners running, managing warehouses and tending bar at cocktail parties—all the things that highly paid CIA staffers could not be expected to do with much enthusiasm. This support had been managed through a Philippine company, ECCOI, and, naturally enough, headquarters remembered and sought the same help for Angola. For five months, beginning in August, we sent repetitive cables to the Manila station asking it to query ECCOI, but the response was so slow as to amount to rejection. Supporting black liberation movements inside Angola on short-term CIA contracts in a controversial, clandestine program was not attractive to the Filipinos. Possibly they remembered the evacuation of Vietnam a few months before: the CIA had left 250 of its Filipino employees behind at the mercy of the communists.

South Africa was a different matter. It came into the conflict cautiously at first, watching the expanding U.S. program and timing their steps to the CIA's. In September the South Africans began to provide arms and training to UNITA and FNLA soldiers at Runtu on the Angolan/South-West African border. First two, then twelve, then forty advisors appeared with UNITA forces near Silva Porto. Eventually the South African armored column—regular soldiers, far better than mercenaries—teamed with UNITA to make the most effective military strike force ever seen in black Africa, exploding through the MPLA/Cuban ranks in a blitzkreig, which in November almost won the war.

South Africa in 1975 was in a dangerously beleaguered position. Its blacks were increasingly restive, its whites emigrating, the white buffer states of Rhodesia, Mozambique, and Angola were threatened, and its economy was sagging. The Arab states' oil embargo had pushed up the cost of fuel despite continued supplies from Iran. South Africa's policies of sharing economic and technical resources with its northern neighbors, had seemed enlightened and effective. By 1975, however, it was clear they had not stemmed the tide of resentment against the white redoubt's apartheid policies.*

The 1974 coup in Portugal had exposed South Africa to fresh, chill winds of black nationalism, as Mozambique and Angola threatened to succumb to Soviet-sponsored, radical, black movements, which promised increased pressure on Rhodesia, Namibia, and South Africa itself. The white buffer concept was no longer viable. The South African fall-back position was to attempt to create in Mozambique and Angola moderate states which, like Malawi and Botswana, would be friendly or at least not hostile to South Africa.

The South African government attacked the threat in Mozambique with impeccably correct diplomacy and generous economic

*See "South Africa: Up against the World," by John de St. Jorre, *Foreign Policy,* No. 28 (Fall 1977).

concessions. In Angola, however, it felt there were sound reasons for military intervention. There were masses of Angolan refugees to succor. The million-dollar hydroelectric plant it was building at Cunene in southern Angola required protection. SWAPO (South West African People's Organization) guerrilla bases in Angola could be destroyed. Most important, of course, was the temptation to influence the outcome of the Angolan civil war in favor of Savimbi, who was considered the most likely to establish a government in Luanda which would cooperate with South Africa.

The South Africans had some encouragement to go into Angola. Savimbi invited them, after conferring with Mobutu, Kaunda, Felix Houphouet-Boigny of the Ivory Coast, and Leopold Senghor of Senegal, all of whom favored a moderate, pro-West government in Angola. I saw no evidence that the United States formally encouraged them to join the conflict.

The South Africans hoped to gain sympathy from the West by supporting the same side as the Zairians, Zambians, and United States in the Angolan conflict. They felt that their troops, even though white, would be more acceptable to most African leaders than the non-African Cubans. They also expected to be successful, understanding that the Ford administration would obtain U.S congressional support for an effective Angola program. On all three points they were disastrously wrong.

Eschewing hawkish plans for a decisive military strike, South African Prime Minister John Vorster opted for a small, covert task force. Only light armor and artillery would be used; there would be no tanks, infantry, or fighter bomber aircraft. Posing as mercenaries and remaining behind the UNITA troops, the soldiers would remain invisible. A curtain of silence in Pretoria would further protect them. The task force would do the job and withdraw quickly, before the November 11 independence date.

The South African government was playing a dangerous game. With scarcely a friend in the world, it was inviting further condemnation by intervening in a black African country. And it was forced to run its program covertly, like the CIA, concealing it from its own people. Only recently, in March 1975, had it withdrawn its forces from Rhodesia, and racist whites would question why their sons were now fighting for black freedom in Angola. Still, South Africa entered the war, watching the United States program closely and hoping for an overt nod of recognition and camaraderie.

To the CIA, the South Africans were the ideal solution for central Angola. Potts, St. Martin, and the COS's of Pretoria and Lusaka welcomed their arrival in the war. Especially in the field, CIA officers liked the South Africans, who tended to be bluff, aggressive men without guile. They admired South African efficiency. Quietly South African planes and trucks turned up throughout Angola with just the gasoline or ammunition needed for an impending operation. On October 20, after a flurry of cables between headquarters and Kinshasa, two South African C-130 airplanes, similar to those used by the Israelis in their raid on Entebbe, feathered into Ndjili Airport at night to meet a CIA C-141 flight and whisk its load of arms down to Silva Porto. CIA officers and BOSS representatives met the planes at Ndjili and jointly supervised the transloading. At the same time St. Martin requested and received headquarters' permission to meet BOSS representatives on a regular basis in Kinshasa. Other CIA officers clamored for permission to visit South African bases in South-West Africa. On two occasions the BOSS director visited Washington and held secret meetings with Jim Potts. On another, he met with the CIA station chief in Paris. The COS, Pretoria, was ordered to brief BOSS about IAFEATURE, and nearly all CIA intelligence reports on the subject were relayed to Pretoria so his briefings would be accurate and up to date.*

The CIA has traditionally sympathized with South Africa and enjoyed its close liaison with BOSS.** The two organizations share a violent antipathy toward communism and in the early sixties the

---

*On p. 440 of *Honorable Men,* Colby states, falsely, ". . . thanks in part also to support to UNITA from South Africa, *which the CIA stayed well away from* . . ." (emphasis mine).

**On p. 115 of *Uncertain Greatness* (New York: Harper & Row, 1977), Roger Morris reports of an NSC meeting December 17, 1969: "The real client at hand appeared next in the standard CIA intelligence brief on the area, read with occasional mispronunciations and fractured syntax by Director Helms. So transparently pro-white was the CIA presentation, so disdainful of black African opposition, so reflective of the views of the white security services on whose reports CIA analysis was based, that at one point even the customarily cynical Kissinger passed a puzzled note to an aide, 'Why is he doing this?' At the one-word reply, 'Clients,' he gave a knowing scowl . . ."

South Africans had facilitated the agency's development of a mercenary army to suppress the Congo rebellion. BOSS, however, tolerates little clandestine nonsense inside the country and the CIA had always restricted its Pretoria station's activity to maintaining the liaison with BOSS. That is, until 1974, when it yielded to intense pressures in Washington and expanded the Pretoria station's responsibilities to include covert operations to gather intelligence about the South African nuclear project. In the summer of 1975 BOSS rolled up this effort and quietly expelled those CIA personnel directly involved. The agency did not complain, as the effort was acknowledged to have been clumsy and obvious. The agency continued its cordial relationship with BOSS.

Thus, without any memos being written at CIA headquarters saying "Let's coordinate with the South Africans," coordination was effected at all CIA levels and the South Africans escalated their involvement in step with our own.

The South African question led me into another confrontation with Potts. South African racial policies had of course become a hated symbol to blacks, civil libertarians, and world minorities—the focal point of centuries-old resentment of racism, colonialism, and white domination. Did Potts not see that the South Africans were attempting to draw closer to the United States, in preparation for future confrontations with the blacks in southern Africa? If he did, he was not troubled by the prospect. Potts viewed South Africa pragmatically, as a friend of the CIA and a potential ally of the United States. After all, twenty major American companies have interests in South Africa and the United States maintains a valuable NASA tracking station not far from Pretoria. Eventually Potts concluded, in one of our conversations, that blacks were "irrational" on the subject of South Africa. This term caught on. It even crept into the cable traffic when the South African presence became known and the Nigerians, Tanzanians, and Ugandans reacted vigorously.

Escalation was a game the CIA and South Africa played very well together. In October the South Africans requested, through the CIA station chief in Pretoria, ammunition for their 155 mm. howitzers. It was not clear whether they intended to use this ammunition in Angola. At about the same time the CIA was seeking funds for another shipload of arms and worrying about how to get those arms into Angola efficiently. Our experience with the *American Champion* had us all dreading the thought of working another shipload of arms through the congested Matadi port and attempting to fly them into Angola with our ragtag little air force. The thought of putting the next shipload of arms into Walvis Bay in South-West Africa, where South African efficiency would rush them by C-130 to the fighting fronts, was irresistible to Jim Potts.

At the same time, Savimbi and Roberto were both running short of petrol. The South Africans had delivered small amounts in their C-130s, but they could not be expected to fuel the entire war, not with an Arab boycott on the sale of oil to South Africa. The MPLA's fuel problems had been solved when a tanker put into Luanda in September, and Potts, in frustration, began to consider having a tanker follow the second arms shipload to Walvis Bay.

When Potts proposed this to the working group, he met firm opposition: He was told by Ambassador Mulcahy that the sale or delivery of arms to South Africa was prohibited by a long-standing U.S. law. Never easily discouraged, Potts sent one of his aides to the CIA library, and in the next working group meeting triumphantly read to the working group the text of the thirteen-year-old "law."

"You see, gentlemen," he concluded with obvious satisfaction. "It isn't a *law*. It's a policy decision made under the Kennedy administration. Times have now changed and, given our present problems, we should have no difficulty modifying this policy." He meant that a few technical strings could be pulled on the hill, Kissinger could wave his hand over a piece of paper, and a planeload of arms could leave for South Africa the next day.

Ambassador Mulcahy continued his phlegmatic pipe puffing for a long moment, always fully awake when something important was being said. Then he spoke calmly but firmly.

"There is one problem." he said.

"What's that?" Potts leaned forward.

"If you do ship any arms to South Africa, I will resign in protest." Mulcahy might have stated his preference for coffee over tea with more inflection. But there was no question of his sincerity and the unsaid words were, "resign and *go public* in protest." He and Potts sat looking at each other for two long minutes. Mulcahy had nothing more to say and Potts was speechless. No one in the room was drowsy at that moment. Even General Fish was silent. Eventually Potts began to fumble for his papers, at first with his eyes still locked on Mulcahy, until he tore them away and focused on the next item on the agenda.

Potts remained silent on the subject of formal involvement with South Africa *for the next six months;* at least I never heard him mention it again. Mulcahy had not even leaned forward, and before long he seemed to drowse again, his eyes drooping heavily and his pipe sagging on his chin. CIA case officers continued to coordinate with the South Africans in Angola, Pretoria, and Kinshasa, with tacit approval from Jim Potts, but the CIA stopped trying to expand that cooperation at the policy level. I have wondered since if Potts finally at that moment, understood the negative importance of South Africa in our foreign policy, or if he merely concluded that Mulcahy was also "irrational" on the subject.

11

Propaganda and Politics

Politically the war was complicated, with a strange conglomeration of bedfellows. The FNLA and UNITA were supported at one time by the United States, China, Rumania, North Korea, France, Israel, West Germany, Senegal, Uganda, Zaire, Zambia, Tanzania, and South Africa. The MPLA was supported by the Soviet Union, Cuba, East Germany, Algeria, Guinea, and several Eastern European countries. Throughout the war there was a constant sorting out and dozens of countries eventually shifted their support to the MPLA. On October 24, the Chinese withdrew from the Angola war, their advisors packing and leaving, holding a press conference at Ndjili Airport as they left.

France was intrigued by the smell of Angolan oil and Zairian minerals, and predisposed to involvement in Angola by its long history of meddling in the affairs of young African countries.* Like

---

*More than any European power France has remained active in the affairs of newly independent African countries. French army units have been garrisoned in Niger,

the United States, France saw the Angolan war as a chance to ingratiate itself with Mobutu. In August French intelligence directors had met with the CIA's deputy director, Vernon Walters, and obtained his promise that the CIA would give them $250,000 as proof of the United States' good faith in Angola. The money was delivered, although it was clear to no one, possibly not even to General Walters, why the United States had to prove its good faith in Angola to the French. A liaison evolved in which the CIA briefed the French intelligence service in detail about its Angola program, while the French listened carefully but told the CIA nothing about their own activities in Angola and Cabinda. France did provide ENTAC antitank missiles, 120 mm. mortar rounds, and ammunition for Mobutu's Panhard armored cars, which it asked the CIA to haul from Istres, France, to Kinshasa. In December, France donated four missile-firing helicopters, which were delivered to Kinshasa by the CIA without pilots or ground crews.

Black African leaders watched the birthing of the new nation in their midst with sympathy and jealous interest. By 1975 they had learned painful lessons about the competition of West and East in Africa. Almost to a country they had been exploited in civil wars, coups, arms races, and competitive aid programs by the Soviet Union, United States, and various European, Asian, and Latin American countries. They had of course encouraged the Angolan liberation movements in their struggles against Portuguese colonialism, and when civil war erupted in July 1975, most had supported an embargo on the delivery of additional arms to the Angolan factions. Most were predisposed to resent outside interference in what they regarded as a purely African matter. The flagrant Soviet arms program was at first greeted with noisy indignation. All but the staunchest Soviet allies protested the Soviet interference in Angola. The new government of Nigeria expressed its concern. President Nyerere of Tanzania made public speeches criticizing the Soviet arms program. Idi Amin of Uganda castigated the Soviet Union and

contended with rebels in Chad, and been on call for crises in other areas. French diplomats and technical advisors have been correspondingly influential in the new governments, while the French intelligence service has maintained agents throughout and sent mercenary squads into various situations, the Comoro Islands, Cabinda, and elsewhere.

stormily threatened to sever relations. Egypt and the Sudan denied them overflight clearances for their arms flights to the MPLA.

The United States launched a major political effort to embroil and entrap as many countries as it could into opposition of the MPLA. Secret agents were sent to third world conferences, including the Non-Aligned Nations summit in Sri Lanka, and the Organization of African Unity in Addis Ababa. United States ambassadors throughout Africa were "brought onboard" in varying degrees, receiving carefully tailored messages which were formulated by the CIA and delivered to the State Department through the working group, ordering them to use whatever leverage they could manage with their host governments to prejudice them against the MPLA.

Savimbi caused the United States a minor embarassment in September, when he sent feelers to the MPLA for a negotiated solution. The CIA learned of this move through an article in the world press, and a Kinshasa station officer promptly interrogated Savimbi. We wanted no "soft" allies in our war against the MPLA. Similarly, on October 22, when an MPLA delegation arrived in Washington to plead the MPLA's potential friendliness towards the United States, it was received by a low-level State Department officer who reported perfunctorily to the working group.

President Kaunda was a potential problem. While he sympathized with Savimbi, he was primarily concerned with getting his copper to the sea, and with the Benguela railroad closed his only alternative was the expensive and humiliating route through Rhodesia and South Africa. On September 10 he gave Savimbi sixty days, until Angolan independence, to get the Benguela railroad open. Otherwise he could not guarantee continued support.

To the CIA, Kaunda's ultimatum was a challenge. How could we get him so involved he could never defect? The key seemed to be the transshipment of arms through Zambia. Kaunda had publicly supported the international embargo against the shipment of arms to Angola, and it was felt that if one planeload of arms could be introduced through Zambia, with Kaunda's permission, he would be irreversibly committed to UNITA's support—"pregnant" we said in CIA headquarters.

At first the African leaders did not know about the United States arms program thanks to our ruse of working through Kinshasa. Similarly, the Soviets tried to hide their shipments through the

Congo (Brazzaville), but the size of their program made it impossible to conceal. And of course, the CIA launched a major propaganda effort to expose the Soviet arms shipments.

Propaganda experts in the CIA station in Kinshasa busily planted articles in the Kinshasa newspapers, *Elimo* and *Salongo*. These were recopied into agency cables and sent on to European, Asian, and South American stations, where they were secretly passed to recruited journalists representing major news services who saw to it that many were replayed in the world press. Similarly, the Lusaka station placed a steady flow of stories in Zambian newspapers and then relayed them to major European newspapers.

In Kinshasa, Ray Chiles's prolific pen and fertile imagination produced a stream of punchy articles and clever operations to spearhead the agency's propaganda effort. For example, he procured a mimeograph machine for FNLA headquarters in Kinshasa and produced leaflets, which were dropped from airplanes over Luanda itself. The first such leaflet was unaccountably read verbatim over the MPLA's Radio Luanda the next morning, provoking a ripple of laughter in CIA stations throughout Europe and Africa, when they heard of it.

The propaganda output from Lusaka was voluminous and imaginative, if occasionally beyond credibility. In late September, Lusaka news stories began to charge that Soviets were advising MPLA forces inside Angola. This was at first a plausible line and Lusaka kept it going. Certainly Soviet advisors might have been inside Angola, although we had no evidence to that effect. The world press dutifully picked up Lusaka's stories of Soviet advisors, while we at headquarters watched nervously, preferring that propaganda ploys have at least some basis in fact. Then, two months later, Lusaka reported that twenty Soviet advisors and thirty-five Cubans had been captured when UNITA took Malanje. UNITA spokesmen gave this information to David Ottoway, who was visiting Lusaka, and it was published in the November 22 edition of the *Washington Post*. The *Post* also printed the TASS denial the same day, carrying stories from the world's two largest intelligence services in the same issue; unwitting that the first story came from the CIA and that it was false; aware that TASS was the Soviet's propaganda arm, but not sure that this time it was telling the truth.

UNITA had captured no Soviet advisors nor had it taken Malanje.

World interest in the story put UNITA under uncomfortable pressure and the CIA Lusaka station abashedly let the story die a quiet death.

Another Lusaka fabrication accused Cuban soldiers of committing atrocities in Angola. It mentioned rape and pillage. Then its stories became more specific, "reporting" a (totally fictitious) incident in which Cuban soldiers had raped some Ovimbundu girls. Subsequently it wrote that some of those same soldiers had been captured and tried before a tribunal of Ovimbundu women. Lusaka kept this story going endlessly throughout the program.

Later, Caryle Murphy, a *Washington Post* stringer who had covered Luanda, told me the Cuban soldiers had universally fallen in love with Angola and were singularly well behaved.* The only atrocity we were able to document had Cubans as victims rather than criminals. Sixteen Cuban soldiers captured in October were executed by UNITA soldiers at the end of the war.

Young Cuban soldier, captured and later executed by UNITA.

*Ms. Murphy had no relationship whatsoever with the CIA. Our conversation occurred in late 1976, after I had decided to leave the CIA.

Bubba Sanders returned to headquarters shortly after I did and began to work on a "white paper" which the FNLA could present to the United Nations General Assembly. A white paper is one in which the source and therefore the potential bias is not concealed; the FNLA would readily admit their sponsorship of the document. The CIA's role would be concealed. Bubba collected information from agency intelligence reports about Soviet arms shipments and included photographs of Russian ships and weapons taken by journalists who were on the CIA payroll and had visited Luanda on the basis of their press credentials. One of Africa Division's translators put the text of Bubba's message into African-sounding French, i.e., with idioms and expressions which would be used by a literate man in Kinshasa but not in Paris.

Potts enjoyed this sort of thing. He supervised Bubba closely, questioning him in detail during each staff meeting, stubbornly insisting that no corners be cut, that the document meet rigorous standards. The two of them argued about paper and type, as well as text and layout. The end product was assembled in a small folder, printed on rough paper identical to that used by one of the Kinshasa printing offices and even printed with machines similar to those used in Kinshasa. The cover bore the picture of a dead soldier on the Caxito battlefield.

The white paper was barely off the press when FNLA representatives arrived in New York in late September to lobby at the United Nations General Assembly. They were broke. Bubba Sanders set up a small task force in a Manhattan hotel room to direct our United Nations propaganda operation. In daily meetings the New York officers secretly funded the FNLA delegation and plotted strategy as they made contacts at the United Nations and with the New York newspapers. They distributed the white paper in the UN and to the U.S. press. They also toured Africa with it, and distributed copies to the Chinese.

The UNITA representatives also arrived broke, and although we did not have a paper for them to distribute, the New York officers provided funds and guidance. Far more capable than the FNLA, UNITA representatives began to establish useful contacts. Both delegations were supplied with up-to-date intelligence. News and propaganda releases were cabled directly from the African stations to the permanent CIA offices in the Pan Am building and two nearby skyscrapers on Third Avenue, and East Forty-second Street. The MPLA and Soviets were active too, but defensively so. Although they managed to prevent an open debate of Angola on the floor of the General Assembly, they could not check the momentum of sympathy which UNITA and the FNLA began to enjoy. Secretary General Waldheim expressed his concern, and announced that the United Nations would send a fact-finding mission into Angola.

During a staff meeting I voiced my concern to Potts—were we on safe ground, paying agents to propagandize the New York press? The agency had recently been warned against running operations inside the United States and propagandizing the American public. Potts seemed unconcerned. We were safe enough, he said, as long as we could plausibly claim that our intent was to propagandize foreigners at the United Nations.

I wasn't satisfied with Potts's attitude toward the situation in New York. It seemed to me that our propaganda operation was leading us onto explosively dangerous ground.

On October 2 the New York base telephoned headquarters, advising us that it was sending the two UNITA representatives down to Washington for the weekend for some medical treatment and to talk to members of the black caucus in Washington, seeking introductions to key senators and administration officials. The New York base requested that I meet them and give them whatever support they needed. I refused. After the call I went in to see Carl, then Potts. They both agreed that the UNITA representatives had to be reined in. We sent a cable to the New York base reminding them that lobbying in the United States by CIA agents was not permitted.

On Monday, an officer from New York arrived at headquarters, and I learned with a jolt that it was I who was out of step. To begin with, the two UNITA reps had spent the weekend in Washington after all. The officer cheerfully admitted that he had given them money for the trip because, he claimed, they were coming anyway, with or without his approval, and besides, they were damned effective. He described their progress in New York with infectious enthusiasm.

Potts bought the whole show. He and the officer devised a neat solution to our little CIA charter problem. In order to keep the two delegations doing their "good work" in New York and in Washington and still protect the CIA from any blow-back, funds would be channeled to them via overseas banks. The officer at first resisted, on the grounds that this was cumbersome, that he or one of his assistants could just slip them some money when they needed it, say $500 every few days. But Potts insisted, and after the officer went back to New York the task force worked out the details by cabling New York, Lusaka, Kinshasa, and key European stations. Each delegation opened a bank account in Europe to which European-based CIA finance officers could make regular deposits. Thereafter the CIA could plausibly deny that it had funded anyone's propagandists in the United States. It would be extremely difficult for any investigators to prove differently.

This arrangement continued throughout the duration of the program, long after the UN General Assembly closed. The UNITA delegates in New York and Washington were increasingly effective. They managed to see State Department officials, White House representatives, and congressmen, as well as American journalists. Care was taken by their CIA case officers not to record their visits to Washington, although some visits were reported in official memos written by unwitting State Department officers and White House staffers, who did not know they had been visited by CIA agents. UNITA's "news" from Angola continued to be drawn from CIA propaganda, fed to them by their case officers in New York.

In January 1976 Director Colby testified before the House Select Committee on Intelligence, saying: "We have taken particular caution to ensure that our operations are focused abroad and not at the United States to influence the opinion of the American people about things from the CIA point of view."* A remarkable statement in view of what we had been doing in the task force.**

It was impossible to measure the full impact in America of the FNLA and UNITA propagandists, except, perhaps by the response of American citizens who were inspired to enlist to fight communists in Angola. The news services reported that Roy Ennis of the Congress on Racial Equality was seeking one thousand volunteers to join the FNLA in Angola. Another group began training in jungle tactics on a farm in North Carolina. Adventurers, self-styled mercenaries,

*Final Report of the Senate Select Committee to Study Governmental Operations with Respect to Intelligence Activities, April 26, 1976, p. 129.
**Director Colby received copies of all IAFEATURE cables and memoranda.

and restless American citizens began to contact the FNLA, and eventually a few made it to the FNLA fighting front in northern Angola where several met tragic deaths.

We had other lines into the American media. For example, a European film crew was sent to Silva Porto to make a film about the war. Featuring Cuban soldiers Savimbi had captured, the documentary it produced was quite successful on European television. It came to the attention of the Voice of America, which proposed to show it in the United States. After discussing the pros and cons, the working group decided to let it happen—subsequently parts of the film appeared on an American television show.

Another time, a European CIA station cabled headquarters, advising that a journalist was enroute to Washington with an FNLA story. When he arrived, the task force deputy chief, Paul Foster, met him secretly in Washington, then brought an article he had written back to CIA headquarters, where a task-force linguist translated it into passable English. The next day Foster returned it to the reporter, who sold it to the *Washington Post,* which printed it.

The article covered several columns, reading in part:

> A stern countenance, mustachioed and goateed, a stocky frame in a Mao tunic, a sternness in his bearing and in his remarks, often belied by great bursts of truly African laughter—Holden Roberto is a strange blend of war chief and Alabama Baptist preacher, but a man who obviously inspires a quasi-mystical fervor in his men . . .
>
> Question: But you have South Africans on your side?
>
> Roberto strikes the table in his Headquarters violently and sends the general staff maps flying. He seems gripped by a cold rage and starts to walk back and forth across the room, his hands behind his back. "You saw the South Africans, did you see them? I say, in the zones which we control, we, the FNLA? Go and see at Savimbi's headquarters . . . I am telling you that we have no South Africans or Rhodesians among us!"

At first we were successful in keeping our hand in the war hidden, while exposing the Soviet arms program. However, cracks began to appear in our cover facade in early September and the working group discussed ploys to cope. When State Department representatives reported the department was receiving inquiries from the press about Angola, the CIA presented them with working group paper #18 which suggested lines to be used in formal press statements: We could refuse to comment. We could categorically deny U.S. involvement. Or we could state that the United States had supported the Alvor Accord, which permitted the three liberation movements to participate equally in preparing Angola for independence, but the Soviet Union had delivered arms to the MPLA, producing heavy fighting. Angola's neighbors were concerned that the Soviet Union was attempting to carve out a dominant position in Angola. We would add that we were sympathetic but we had not supplied U.S. arms to any of the liberation movements. Whichever, we should emphasize the Soviet Union, so it would not look as though we were attacking a minor liberation movement.

The State Department a few days later reported it had issued a statement refusing to substantiate press inquiries and denying United States involvement:

> We have not been in the business of providing arms to the Angolan movements. However, we have received reports that one of the movements, the MPLA, has for some time been receiving large shipments of weapons from the Soviet Union. It is understandable if African governments are concerned about this development and we are sympathetic to those concerns.

In the field our security was fairly good. We and our allies had control over the only transportation into the fighting areas, especially into Silva Porto, and could restrict those areas from all but a few selected reporters or the extremely hardy individuals who were willing to go in overland. However, one European reporter, whom we knew only as Germani, began focusing on Kinshasa itself and was scurrying about town with a good instinct for where we were hiding the stories. The Kinshasa station reported his presence and the working group discussed the threat he posed. It would be easy to have Mobutu throw him out of the country. Could we get by with asking Mobutu to do it? Germani wasn't American. Did we dare have cables on record ordering the station to pull strings and have a legitimate European reporter thrown out of Kinshasa? The press would be extremely angry if it ever found out. The working group stalled, wondering why the field hadn't thought of this solution without headquarters' guidance. They were in daily contact with Roberto and his deputies and could easily plant the idea. They could see Mobutu. There would be no record. Chiefs of station are supposed to have an instinct for such things.

Like magic, Germani was expelled from Kinshasa on November 22. Without any cables or memoranda being written at headquarters, the string was pulled, the problem solved, and there was nothing in CIA records prove how it had happened.*

Increasingly, the propaganda war became uphill work. On September 10, when the FNLA retreated from Caxito the second time, it left behind crates of munitions which bore fresh U.S. Air Force

---

*This is the way the ouster of Nkrumah was handled in Ghana, 1966. The 40 Committee had met and rejected an agency proposal to oust Nkrumah. The Accra station was nevertheless encouraged by headquarters to maintain contact with dissidents of the Ghanian army for the purpose of gathering intelligence on their activities. It was given a generous budget, and maintained intimate contact with the plotters as a coup was hatched. So close was the station's involvement that it was able to coordinate the recovery of some classified Soviet military equipment by the United States as the coup took place. The station even proposed to headquarters through back channels that a squad be on hand at the moment of the coup to storm the Chinese embassy, kill everyone inside, steal their secret records, and blow up the building to cover the fact. This proposal was quashed, but inside CIA headquarters the Accra station was given full, if unofficial credit for the eventual coup, in which eight Soviet advisors were killed. None of this was adequately reflected in the agency's written records.

This technique has worked for the agency in many other situations. Perhaps an irritating politician in a far corner of the world is magically eliminated, while the CIA records show no evidence of involvement in the crime. When done skillfully it is also the key to the individual case officer's rationalization of his conduct, his "plausible denial" to his own conscience, as though he were not responsible. He can say, "We talked about the problem Germani was causing (or Lumumba, Trujillo, Schneider, et al.), but it never even occurred to me to suggest that anything be done about it." This is my own theory of what really happened in the assassination of Lumumba. The CIA plotted to poison him, but lost its nerve. The now-public record shows that CIA officers discussed the Lumumba threat with other Congolese politicians. They did the rest.

But of course the case officers are responsible; the things wouldn't have been done if they had not been there, setting the stage. For example, in Vietnam I inherited an operational relationship with a sadistic police officer, who occasionally mutilated prisoners in a CIA safehouse called the "Pink House." The police officer was heavily funded by the CIA, which vouched for him to his superiors in Saigon—without this support he would not have held his post. But a succession of CIA case officers had absolved themselves of responsibility for his sadistic orgies by rationalizing that they were only supporting him for his intelligence activities and were not responsible for his other actions.

shipping labels. The MPLA displayed these trophies to western journalists and the press picked up our scent. Nor were the newspapers idle. In Washington and New York IAFEATURE was increasingly exposed with accurate reports of our program, our budget, even the amounts of money in our budget. The *New York Times* seemed to have a particularly direct line to the working group, and the thought that we might have a "Deep Throat" in our midst added some desperately needed excitement to the working group sessions.

While IAFEATURE was being described in the *New York Times,* the presence of South African soldiers in Angola became known. On November 22, a journalist, Ken Bridgefield, filed a story in the *Washington Post,* from Lusaka, reporting that South African soldiers were fighting in Angola. The propaganda and political war was lost in that stroke. There was nothing the Lusaka station could invent that would be as damaging to the other side as our alliance with the hated South Africans was to our cause.

Nigeria, the economic giant of black Africa and the United States' second most important source of petroleum, emphatically shifted its support to the MPLA, providing it with $20 million in aid. A crowd of Nigerians demonstrated before the American embassy in Lagos. Tanzania announced plans to train MPLA soldiers in Tanzania in a joint program with the Soviets. Idi Amin reversed his decision to expel the Soviets from Uganda, and when the Soviets publicly defended their program in late December, Amin supported them. Other countries began to recognize the MPLA as the legitimate rulers of Angola.

12

Business and Money

What role does international business play in operations like Cuba, and wars like the Congo, Vietnam, and Angola?

In Angola several transnational giants, including Gulf, Boeing, DeBeers, Mobil, and numerous smaller companies had interests in the outcome. Before the war Gulf Oil had exclusive access to the Cabindan oil fields. Boeing had contracted to sell two of its 737 jetliners to TAAG, the Angolan national airline, and to install commercial radar control systems at the principal Angolan airports. In September 1975, a New York financier interviewed me for employment as his company's Angolan representative. The offer was fun but it was contingent on a quick and satisfactory resolution of the war, at which time the financier was poised to exploit Angolan diamonds and other mineral resources.

Since 1968 Gulf had been pumping 150,000 barrels a day from 120 wells off the coast of Cabinda. It was paying $500 million per year in royalties to the Angolan colonial government for this oil. All that was interrupted in the fall of 1975. Gulf did make the September payment of $116 million to the Bank of Angola. The next payments due were $100 million on December 11, and $102 million on January 15, 1976. On November 11, the MPLA took control of the Bank of Angola and the dossier of contracts with Gulf and by defeating Mobutu's November 6 invasion of Cabinda it maintained physical control of the Cabindan oil fields.

The war created serious problems for Gulf. Not only was the flow of oil threatened, there were also the lives of its 420 technicians to be considered; 17 of them were Americans. In early November 1975, because of the fighting Gulf was obliged to suspend operations and evacuate its employees from Cabinda. The MPLA urged Gulf to resume operations and guaranteed its technicians' safety. Gulf would gladly have taken the MPLA deal. There was no threat of nationalization, as the MPLA needed Gulf's assistance indefinitely to keep the vital revenues coming in.

The working group was exasperated. Our total budget for IAFEA-TURE was only $31.7 million. Within two months Gulf would yield $200 million cash to the MPLA. CIA and State Department attorneys repeatedly discussed means of blocking Gulf's payments to the MPLA, and pressure was brought to bear. The FNLA and UNITA were jointly attempting to establish a provisional government, but were unable to gain recognition and Gulf could not be persuaded to deliver the money to Roberto or Savimbi unless they controlled Cabinda. On December 23 Gulf compromised and put $125 million in an escrow bank account.

At the same time Boeing wanted very much to consummate its deal and deliver the two 737s to TAAG. The MPLA wanted the planes; the money, $30 million, had already been paid. Twelve TAAG pilots were in Seattle training to fly them. TAAG was also planning to buy four shortened airbuses at $5 million each. Boeing was eager to place its crews in Luanda to begin working on the radar systems. American technicians and businessmen were still welcome despite the war, the Cubans, and the antagonism between the United States and the MPLA. Realists thought the war should have been over by mid-November. The business interests were eager to bury the hatchet and get on with commerce.

But the CIA, the working group, and Henry Kissinger were not about to permit the delivery of new American jet airliners to Luanda. Why provide the means for the MPLA to fly their delegations around the world, drumming up support? In November the State

Department withdrew the export licenses for the planes.

A TAAG delegation promptly flew to Washington to lobby for the release of the 737s. They were joined in Washington by George Wilson, the president of Boeing. The TAAG delegation consisted of two contacts of the Luanda station, encrypted IAMOFFET/1 and IAPORKY/1, who were cordial to the CIA but unrecruited, unshakably loyal to the MPLA. They were accompanied from Lisbon to Washington by Bob Temmons, the chief of the Luanda station, who had evacuated Luanda on November 3. In three months in Luanda, Temmons had come to share GPSWISH's view that the MPLA was best qualified to run the country, that it was not demonstrably hostile to the United States, and that the United States should make peace with it as quickly as possible.

In Washington Temmons made his views known inside CIA headquarters while Wilson and the Angolans separately petitioned the State Department. But the momentum of war was too great. Temmons and Wilson were told that a program affecting the United States national security was at stake.

Then Ambassador Mulcahy had a bright idea—why not ask Wilson, the president of Boeing, to convey to the MPLA an official but very discreet statement of our country's official position vis-à-vis Angola. The State Department drafted the message and I sent someone from the task force to rent a room at Washington's Statler Hilton for a meeting between Wilson, IAPORKY/1, and IAMOFFET/1. Temmons made the introductions and left before Wilson delivered the message. It read:

> THE UNITED STATES CANNOT STANDBY FOR A SOVIET POWER PLAY IN AFRICA.
>
> IF THE MPLA IS WILLING TO WORK FOR A POLITICAL SOLUTION AND COMPROMISE WITH ITS RIVALS, THE UNITED STATES IS WILLING TO BACK A PEACEFUL SETTLEMENT.
>
> THE MPLA WOULD DO WELL TO HEED OUR ADVICE THAT NO GOVERNMENT CAN PLAN THE RECONSTRUCTION IN POSTWAR ANGOLA WITHOUT UNITED STATES AND WESTERN HELP. NO GOVERNMENT CAN OBTAIN THE TECHNICAL AND FINANCIAL RESOURCES TO STIMULATE ECONOMIC DEVELOPMENT WITHOUT AMERICAN CONSENT. IN FACT, THE UNITED STATES WOULD BE QUITE RESPONSIVE AND HELPFUL TO A COALITION GOVERNMENT THAT WAS NOT DEPENDENT ON THE SOVIET UNION.
>
> THE UNITED STATES GOVERNMENT IS PREPARED TO THINK FUR-

THER ABOUT THE SUPPLY OF BOEING AIRCRAFT TO ANGOLA AND IS
WILLING TO UNDERTAKE FURTHER DISCUSSIONS DEPENDING ON
THE COURSES OF EVENTS IN ANGOLA. THIS MESSAGE SHOULD BE
GIVEN TO LUANDAN AUTHORITIES. AS THE MPLA IS AWARE, ACCESS
TO SOPHISTICATED TECHNOLOGY IS A PRIVILEGE; THE PRESENT BOE-
ING CASE IS JUST ONE, BUT A GOOD EXAMPLE OF THE ADVANTAGES
OF HAVING ACCESS TO AMERICAN TECHNOLOGY.

This logic seems to have left the MPLA unmoved, for the war
went on as before.

Almost daily the IAFEATURE officers would meet to worry about
money, to count what had been spent and reprogram the remainder.
In general terms here is how the money went.

Of the original $6 million, $2,750,000 was given to Mobutu in cash
to encourage him to send more arms to the FNLA and UNITA.
Roberto and Savimbi were allotted $2 million for the general opera-
tion of their movements, each to receive $200,000 per month for five
months. The chiefs of station Kinshasa and Lusaka insisted on controlling these funds, and specified that Roberto and Savimbi should
not be told how much they were to receive. Each COS claimed one
of the movements, Roberto belonged to Kinshasa and Savimbi to
Lusaka. Each COS wanted to dole money to his leader, or to be able
to make cash purchases on his leader's behalf.

The next $8 million, released on July 27, was allocated primarily
for the shipload of arms and for the procurement of airplanes to haul
material from Kinshasa into Angola.

On August 20, an additional $10.7 million was authorized for more
arms, aircraft, mercenaries, and maintenance of the liberation forces.
The thousand-man arms package for the invasion of Cabinda came
from these funds.

On November 27, President Ford approved the final $7 million,
which was intended for yet more arms, the recruitment of mercenaries, and the lease of a C-130 aircraft for use in Angola.

The total budget of $31.7 million was applied only to the procure-
ment of arms and for IAFEATURE operations. The salaries and operational expenses of the hundreds of CIA staff employees and the CIA
facilities involved in the program, certainly totaling several million
dollars, were charged to the CIA's FY76 personnel and support
budget, and were not included in the $31.7 million.

The $31.7 million was drawn from the CIA FY75 Contingency Reserve Fund.* With each incremental increase, the process of approval began with a recommendation drawn up by Africa Division and presented to the 40 Committee. The 40 Committee tentatively approved the expenditure, pending presidential endorsement. President Ford approved the expenditure and the Office of Management and Budget (OMB), a separate office in the executive branch, then approached the CIA to supervise the expenditure of the money. OMB had no authority to comment on the operational justification of any expenditures, but as auditor was responsible to ensure the money was spent as intended.

When the CIA FY75 Contingency Reserve Fund was exhausted on November 27, 1975, by the allocation of the last $7 million dollars, the Angola program was stymied. An effort to obtain an additional $28 million from the Department of Defense budget was blocked. Additional funds could only be provided by the Congress, and it refused to cooperate.

Throughout the war, we in Africa Division at CIA headquarters, were careful—to the extent our catch-as-catch-can accounting system permitted—to provide OMB with accurate information of what we were doing with our IAFEATURE funds. We were all highly sensitive to the scrutiny the CIA was receiving and fearful that there would be an investigation which would, if irregularities were discovered, hold us individually responsible à la Watergate.

Only in the CIA's Fiscal Annex to the IAFEATURE Project Outline, dated January 26, 1976, did I detect a thread of fraud. The Fiscal Annex perpetuated the "Big Lie" of the original 40 Committee options paper by stating that the purpose of IAFEATURE activity was to provide assistance to the FNLA and UNITA, to enable them to repulse attacks by the MPLA, thereby creating a sufficiently stable situation to allow for a political settlement.

*The Constitution clearly provides that the Congress has the responsibility to declare war and to supervise the budget, and that the budget will be open for public inspection. These provisions of the Constitution have never been amended, and the CIA's covert wars are literally unconstitutional. Through the CIA and its secret contingency funds the president is able to wage a small war, without congressional approval, and without its budget being published. In Vietnam a president's limited war took on global significance. See *President Kennedy Wages a Secret War,* by Ralph Stavins (New York: Random House, 1971).

Typically, CIA field commanders had an independent perspective. They were concerned with the guns, bullets, and personalities of war, more than with Washington's bureaucratic and political problems. The three principals—the chiefs of the Kinshasa, Lusaka, and Pretoria stations—were unapologetic hawks, openly determined to defeat the "Soviet-backed" MPLA.

The CIA station in Kinshasa was the focal point of the logistical support provided both to Mobutu and to the Angolan liberation movements. All of our arms flights went to Kinshasa, and then directly through the military side of Ndjili Airport and into Angola. When the *American Champion* deposited its cargo in Matadi on the lower Congo River, 144 railroad cars hauled the arms into Kinshasa. There they were warehoused until they could be flown into Angola. The experience was maddening because of Zairian inefficiency and indifference. With paramilitary, logistics, and air experts cajoling, bribing, and bullying the Zairians into getting the arms to the airport on time, in some cases Americans driving the forklifts themselves, the near impossible was accomplished. The *American Champion* docked in Matadi on September 12, and on October 7 IAFEATURE airplanes began lifting ten tons a day into Angola.

The Lusaka station ran intelligence-gathering teams into Silva Porto, coordinated with President Kaunda of Zambia and with Savimbi, and contributed to the propaganda campaign. Pretoria maintained close liaison with the South African government.

The weakest link in the arms flow was between Kinshasa and the Angolan bases. Initially Mobutu's C-130's and DC-4 did the hauling, but this involved an intolerable liability for the CIA. Mobutu's attachment to his C-130's was fabled, and the Zaire economy was nearly bankrupt. If one of his C-130's were lost in Angola, Mobutu would demand that it be replaced, and at $10 to $15 million dollars each, the CIA's Angola program could not underwrite such a loss.

The obvious solution of using U.S. Air Force tactical air transports was constantly sought by the agency, but here the magic phone calls didn't work; they inevitably reached the desk of the secretary of defense, James Schlesinger, who steadfastly said no. Ours was a controversial, covert, CIA program, and Schlesinger wouldn't let traceable U.S. Air Force planes and crews enter the Angolan airspace.

From August 1975 through January 1976 we sought to lease a

commercial C-130, without success. Such planes are expensive—one million dollars rent for three months without pilots—and of course impossible to insure commercially for use in an Angolan bush war. They also require specially trained crews, which we were unable to locate for "mercenary" service.

But from August on, the airspace between Kinshasa and the FNLA/UNITA bases was busy with smaller planes flown by Portuguese Angolan pilots. These planes, belonging to businesses which had operated in Angola (DeBeers among others), were simply comandeered by the CIA in the FNLA's name, and put into service flying arms into Angola. This unorthodox source of air cargo was so economical the CIA encouraged its extension. Word went out to Portuguese still in Luanda that the beneficent Americans would pay $30,000 to any pilot who managed to skyjack a planeload of MPLA arms and bring it to Kinshasa. Eventually the CIA's little air force controlled nine stolen aircraft, including one Aztec, one Cessna 172, one Cessna 180, one Cessna 310, a Rockwell Turbocommander, one Mooney, two Fokker F-27s, and one Allouette III helicopter. Another F-27 was leased from Mobutu's commercial air wing, and the Lusaka station managed to hire a Viscount for $106,000 plus operating costs. These eight planes hauled much of the 1,500 tons of material from Kinshasa into Angola, with a periodic assist from Mobutu's C-130s and South African C-130s.

In Kinshasa, efforts to assemble a navy capable of interdicting shipping between Luanda and Cabinda and supporting coastal infantry action were equally ingenious but much less effective. The two high-performance Swifts were offloaded from the *American Champion* directly onto the Congo River at Matadi and CIA maritime experts turned them over to Zairians who, it was thought, had had experience with similar craft on Lake Tanganyika. The CIA maritime team included only one French-speaker, an officer who had graduated from the agency's French language school in July 1975 with an elementary rating. The turnover was effected, at least in the sense that the agency officers returned to Kinshasa and the Zairians headed the Swifts downriver at full throttle. Six weeks later both boats were inoperative from abuse and sloppy maintenance, and the maritime officers returned to Matadi in a vain attempt to get them back in shape.

Bypassing CIA bureaucracy, the Kinshasa station managed to

obtain a large fishing boat, the *Christina,* and hired a Portuguese crew to man it. It also obtained a lovely twenty-six–foot pleasure yacht, the *Sagittarius,* with twin inboards, long-range tanks, and a wooden hull. The *Sagittarius* was purchased by the Luanda Station and smuggled out of the Luanda harbor in a high-seas adventure. Taken to Ambriz, it was intended for use against unarmed vessels which were supporting the MPLA. However, as no operations were mounted against coastal shipping, the *Sagittarius* contributed little. Eventually it was moved up the coast in concert with the FNLA retreat and at the end of the war, was maintained for outings on the Congo River by individuals who had aided the program in Kinshasa.

Twenty-four rubber assault craft with outboard motors, shipped from the United States into Angola for commando raids, were misplaced in Kinshasa and could not be located when they were needed.

Kinshasa station was indeed active, with St. Martin taking his role as the resident warlord seriously. He continuously proposed extraneous operations involving station support assets, including an agent called IAMOLDY/1 who was a Portuguese Angolan businessman with operations in Luanda and Kinshasa.

First the Kinshasa and Luanda stations cooperated in pouching the personal effects of a non-American agent in the U.S. State Department unclassified diplomatic pouch, arguing that they included printing materials which could be used in the Kinshasa propaganda effort (other printing materials were abundantly available in Kinshasa).

Then we discovered in the Kinshasa station accountings that $50,-000 of the money which was allocated for Roberto had been spent to purchase an ice plant on the lower Congo River for IAMOLDY/1. There had been no discussion of this purchase and we were flabbergasted.

Agency regulations permit a chief of station to spend $500 without prior headquarters approval, if documentation and justification are submitted in the next monthly accountings. Normally a $50,000 expenditure would require staff work at headquarters and at least the DDO's signature. But the Fiscal Annex of the IAFEATURE Project Outline simply waived the usual controls. Over $5 million was delivered in cash to Mobutu, Roberto, and Savimbi by the chiefs of station in Kinshasa and Lusaka, accounted for only by signatures from the liberation leaders and their representatives. Other money was deposited in European bank accounts over which the CIA had no control.

This arrangement placed enormous faith in the honesty of everyone involved. No one on the task force raised any question about it; it was approved by Colby and his comptrollers. All case officers live in glass houses, being required to pass funds to agents in all kinds of situations. The only difference in IAFEATURE was that case officers were disbursing millions rather than hundreds of dollars.

The justification for the ice plant was baroque: IAMOLDY/1 would produce ice to preserve fish for the FNLA. In discussions with Bantam and Potts, I pointed out that ice was indeed used on the Congo River to preserve fish, for the Europeans and rich Africans in the cities. The African population in the bush eats dried fish, which has the virtue of not spoiling quickly even in the tropical sun and humidity. There was no way of carrying ice-packed fish to Ambriz for distribution to the fighting fronts.

My arguments against the ice plant were brushed aside. The money was already expended and it would be unpleasant to bring the matter up for review. In staff meeting Potts said at least twice that one shouldn't try to second-guess the man in the field. Carl Bantam recalled that in Laos the CIA had bought a lumber mill which turned out to be a gold mine, making a profit and providing cover for operational activities. The ice plant wasn't mentioned again.

But the fishing boat, the *Christina,* also involved IAMOLDY/1. Kinshasa station wanted to buy it, for $150,000, in IAMOLDY/1's name, allegedly for use in patroling the coast and hauling supplies to the FNLA.

I argued that $150,000 was too much money for our budget. The *Christina* was an old tub, too slow and cumbersome for coastal patrol or to interdict the flow of anything, much less arms between the Congo (Brazzaville) and Luanda. Any supplies it hauled for us would have to go through the congested Matadi port, where even priority shipments were delayed for weeks. We could deliver supplies from Kinshasa to Ambriz by trucks in less time, with a smaller investment.

Potts listened, politely, as always, then noted that of course we could not approve the purchase of ships without more detailed information, including an insurance underwriter's appraisal of the ship's condition and value, and the station's justification for its use. I took notes and we sent a cable to Kinshasa asking for this information.

When Kinshasa did not respond directly the matter was dropped at headquarters. However, the Kinshasa station nevertheless managed to acquire the ship—presumably they passed Roberto the cash to buy it for them—and manned it with a Portuguese crew. Then they requested that headquarters provide naval mortars to arm it.

St. Martin also proposed to mine the Luanda harbor. But with this he did not get far. Special Operations Group reacted vigorously, pointing out that mine-laying operations are complicated and require a small navy of specialized ships and planes. St. Martin was proposing to fly an F-27 over the harbor of Luanda, shoving a few mines out the door and thereby rendering the harbor unsafe for shipping. That these mines would float around in the South Atlantic, menacing all shipping, was not taken into account. Nor could such mines come from the FNLA alone; they would obviously be American. There would be no plausible denial. As cables went back and forth St. Martin tried to resolve the technical arguments with a second scheme in which he would order a nocturnal raid on Luanda harbor which would feint a mine-laying operation and perhaps blow a small hole in a selected ship. The world might then think the harbor was mined and ships would avoid it. This was discussed in the working group and quickly shuddered out of consideration, but Kinshasa station brought it up two or three times more as the tide of fighting turned against the FNLA forces near Luanda.

And firecrackers. Unable to motivate the FNLA soldiers, the Zairians, or the Portuguese commandos to patrol or raid a mile beyond the front lines, Kinshasa repeatedly cabled to headquarters requests for firefight simulators—firecrackers rigged to sound like small-arms fire—to be dropped in the Luanda suburbs by one of our stolen airplanes.

13

Disaster

On November 11, 1975, the day of Angolan independence, a small force of fifteen hundred men altogether—FNLA, the Zairian Seventh and Fourth Battalions, and a hundred Portuguese Angolan commandos—moved cautiously across the wide, flat Quifangondo valley, twenty kilometers from Luanda. The advancing column was supported by a dozen small armored cars and half as many jeep-mounted 106 recoilless rifles. The four South African 5.5-inch artillery pieces were emplaced on the ridge behind, manned by South African artillerymen. A few kilometers back, the two North Korean 130 mm. long-barrel cannon were located where they could place their devastating shells at any point on the road from Quifangondo to Luanda itself. CIA and South African advisors watched the column's movement across the valley.

Morale was high. The soldiers had confidence in their officers and in each other, for they had recently met and routed the MPLA in several small encounters. From the ridge behind they had seen the fuel storage tanks on the outskirts of Luanda. Every soldier thought hungrily of the city, which lay almost within his grasp. Roberto, a man obsessed with his place in history, saw the goal of a lifetime's struggle just beyond the next ridge, beyond a few MPLA soldiers and some Cubans.

In Luanda, the Portuguese high commissioner had fled without ceremony and frightened MPLA leaders peremptorily celebrated Angolan independence, declaring the People's Republic of Angola. Conspicuously absent were the representatives of forty African nations who should have been present to celebrate the end of five hundred years of Portuguese tyranny in Africa.

A hundred miles southeast of Luanda, the South African armored column was having a field day, covering vast distances so rapidly the Cuban/MPLA forces had difficulty retreating ahead of them.

At CIA headquarters in Langley, the Angolan Task Force celebrated Angolan Independence Day with a late afternoon party, decorating its offices with crepe paper and serving wine and cheese. People came from all over the building, from the Portuguese Task Force, the French Desk, and the Special Operations Group, to drink to the program's continued success.

Then the Cubans' 122 mm. rockets began to land in the Quifangondo valley, not like single claps of thunder, but in salvos, twenty at a time. The first salvo went long, screaming over the heads of bewildered FNLA soldiers and shattering the valley with a horrendous, ear-splitting sound. The next salvo was short, and the little army was bracketed, exposed in an open valley, without cover. Soldiers' hearts burst with a clutching terror as they dived to the ground or stood helplessly mesmerized, watching the next salvo land in their midst. And the next. And the next.

CIA observers on a ridge behind estimated that two thousand rockets rained on the task force as it broke and fled in panic, scattering across the valley in aimless flight, abandoning weapons, vehicles, and wounded comrades alike. Survivors would call it *Nshila wa Lufu* —Death Road.

As for the artillery, one of the North Korean 130 mm. cannon exploded the first time it was fired, killing its Zairian crew. The second misfired, injuring its crew. Both guns were permanently out of action.

The obsolete South African cannon pounded away, but their firepower was a fraction of the rocket salvos and their range scarcely over half that of the 122. If they did bring the truck-mounted 122 mm. rocket-launchers under fire, the latter quickly displaced, resuming their fire from prepared positions nearby.

There was no pursuit and no engagement of troops units by the MPLA, but for the FNLA and Zairians the war was virtually over. Thereafter whenever the MPLA/Cuban force got close enough to lob a few 122 mm. rockets into their ranks, a panicky retreat took place to the next town or port. Disciplined troops can of course cope with such shelling, as the Viet Cong did with American bombing throughout years of war, by means of foxholes and tunnels, controlled withdrawals, and counterattacks. But the FNLA guerrillas and Mobutu's commandos were not diggers. By the second week after Quifangondo they were a demoralized, undisciplined rabble, out of control of their officers. The rate of their retreat was governed solely by the MPLA/Cuban advance, which was slow and methodical. Kinshasa station described Ambriz, the FNLA logistics base seventy miles from Luanda, as in "a stable state of panic." A month later, in mid-December, the MPLA closed on Ambriz and the FNLA fled north, relocating its headquarters in the ancient Kongo capital of São Salvadore, near the Zairian border.

The Zairian troops, Mobutu's finest, vented their frustration on the villages and towns in the path of their flight, in a tidal wave of terrorism, rape, and pillage, until the Kongo tribesmen of northern Angola prayed for the early arrival of the MPLA and Cuban liberators.

Meanwhile in November and December the South African/ UNITA armies continued to sweep north toward Luanda and east along the railroad. On November 14 the primary South African column captured Porto Amboim one hundred miles down the coast from Luanda. A second South African column began to move toward Malange, encountering Cuban regular army troops with more sophisticated weapons, including missile-firing helicopters, T-34 tanks, and 122mm. cannon, which had a twenty-six kilometer range and were considerably more accurate than the 122 mm. rocket. In a battle at Cela on December 17, the South Africans outmaneuvered the cannon, knocked out the tanks and killed scores of MPLA soldiers. A huge store of captured Russian arms was displayed to journalists in Luso, while the third South African column pressed eastward, still attempting to open the railroad to Zaire.

The rout of the FNLA and Zairians at Quifangondo was a disappointment but not a shock to the working group. By then the managers of IAFEATURE were realizing the scope of the Soviet/Cuban commitment in Angola: Soviet expenditures were estimated as high as $225 million by late November. Ours had not yet reached $25 million. The Soviets had sent seven shiploads to our one, a hundred planeloads to our nine.* Thousands of Cuban soldiers were arriving, and we had photographic evidence that they had the larger T-54 tanks. In a penny-ante war, the Soviets had opened their wallets and put real money on the table.

Competitive juices stirred in Washington and the no-win rationale was dropped at all levels. Ambassador Mulcahy flew to Kinshasa to reassure Mobutu of our determination and full support. The National Security Council ordered the CIA to outline a program which could *win* the war. Sophisticated weapons were now discussed freely: Redeye ground-to-air missiles, antitank missiles, heavy artillery, tactical air support, C-47 gun platforms. The working group considered major escalations: the formal introduction of American advisors, the use of American army units, a show of the fleet off Luanda, and the feasibility of making an overt military feint at Cuba itself to force Castro to recall his troops and defend the home island.

There was a thread of unreality, of wishful thinking in these discussions. The gap between Henry Kissinger's egotistical desire to win and the limits of his power in the real world became apparent. In July 1975, Director Colby had warned that it would take a $100 million program to be sure of winning. This was probably high—in August my trip had revealed that a sophisticated weapons system, such as a C-47 gunship costing $200,000, would have shattered the MPLA forces. By December, however, because of the massive Soviet/Cuban build-up, we would be coming from behind, even with a $100 million effort.

On the task force we labored through several nights to produce a new options paper which offered a choice of $30-, $60-, or $100-million programs. They included armor, artillery, tactical aircraft, a C-130 aircraft, and one thousand mercenaries. But the National Security Council was stymied. The CIA Contingency Reserve Fund

*Eventually we mounted a total of twenty-nine C-141 flights, the last one arriving in Kinshasa January 29, 1976.

was depleted, and no more secret funds were available. Further escalations could be financed only with congressional approval, and the Congress was not cooperative.

The administration attempted unsuccessfully to "borrow" $28 million from the Department of Defense budget. The CIA's last $7 million reserves were committed, to keep our effort alive while desperate measures were considered.

These combined circumstances, the lack of funds and an uncooperative Congress, may have saved our nation from a tragic escalation in Angola—another Vietnam. The $30-60-100-million options would have plunged us in deeper, without reversing the situation. We did not have a thousand mercenaries to send to Angola, and even if we had, a thousand undisciplined adventurers would have accomplished little against ten thousand organized Cuban regular army troops.

Under great pressure to pull a magic ace out of a losing hand, the CIA decided to use part of the $7 million to recruit the twenty Frenchmen and three hundred Portuguese mercenaries. It was a senseless gesture, but something, at least, to report to the 40 Committee. And we requested approval to place American advisors in Angola.* Incredibly, Henry Kissinger, having ordered us to assure our allies of our full support, having ordered us to seek every means to escalate the Angolan conflict, could not be bothered to focus on the situation. He grunted and went to China.

Inside the CIA, in November and December, we buckled down and worked ever harder, as though the speed with which we answered cables and produced memos for the working group could vindicate our ineptness on the battlefield. Potts became obsessed with the program, swinging in to work on his crutches in the grey chill of the autumn predawn, his mind brimming with desperate plans for the program. His safes were finally locked hours after dark, when he would slowly make his way down the southwest steps, his face still locked in concentration. His secretary would remain another two hours at her desk, sorting, typing, and filing his paperwork. The task force kept the same pace. Saturdays, Sundays, and holidays blended into Mondays and Fridays.

Case officers in the field responded with a comparable effort. Kinshasa continued a barage of suggestions to headquarters to escalate

*See Prologue, above.

the war: mine Luanda harbor, use United States submarines to inter-
dict shipping, introduce American personnel, air drop firecrackers.
Every CIA station involved in the conflict urged official cooperation
with the South Africans and devised joint operations which would
tempt headquarters into escalating CIA involvement with them. The
Kinshasa station, especially, promoted joint South African activities,
and its officers flew to South Africa to discuss the possibilities. The
Kinshasa station urgently recommended that a U.S. Air Force C-141
be provided to fly six additional twenty-five–pounder cannon with
crews from South Africa to Kinshasa for use in northern Angola,
stating that it was "very much in favor of retaining to the fullest
extent possible South African involvement." It received a frustrated
turndown from headquarters. Undaunted, Kinshasa relayed urgent
South African requests for fuel, for more sophisticated weapons, air
support, and trucks. Then it reported a South African plan to fly a
task force into southern Zaire to attack Texeira da Sousa from the
border. Kinshasa station was encouraged in its policy toward the
South Africans by cables from the CIA stations in Lusaka and
Pretoria.

The French contributed more ammunition and four Allouette
missile-firing helicopters, which U.S. Air Force C-141 airplanes
hauled to Kinshasa in early January. Without pilots or ground crews
they were useless, and the CIA desperately sought mercenaries who
might fly them. We also negotiated with the U.S. Air Force for a
C-130 to support the helicopters at the Angolan battlefronts. The
CIA actually intended to deliver these helicopters and the USAF
C-130 to the South Africans, despite United States policy against
such military collaboration. The French were to be mere intermedi-
aries. But time ran out, and the South Africans withdrew before
pilots and crews could be located.

In November, a security officer hand-carried a report from Kinshasa to headquarters, charging that the immoral personal conduct
and the insecure operations of CIA personnel in Kinshasa were an
embarassment to the United States chargé d'affaires. Such a report
from a security officer would normally carry some weight, but once
again the agency's lack of an effective inspector general was exposed,
as the DDO and director took no disciplinary action.

The program was four months old and TDY officers began rotat-
ing back from the field, bringing with them anecdotes and personal
accounts of the things that don't get written into official cables, the

human side of IAFEATURE. There was one marriage, between a records officer and a reports officer. Other returnees never spoke to each other again. One young officer was eager to get back to Angola, having decided that he would smuggle home a handful of diamonds on the next mission.

About this time St. Martin requested approval to put his wife on a contract to help Ray Chiles write propaganda articles for the newspapers. Mrs. St. Martin, it was said, was bored, and her low morale was becoming a problem. Agency regulations strictly forbade such nepotism, and station chiefs, especially supergrades, are prohibited from putting their families on the government payroll. However, a contract was approved for St. Martin's wife to write for the Kinshasa station, on the basis of a special dispensation from Colby himself.

Carl Bantam, the Africa Division deputy chief, took his first orientation trip to Africa in December, visiting Kinshasa, Pretoria, and Lusaka. He left determined to perform his historic role as enforcer, to bring St. Martin down to earth. He returned strangely silent about the trip. Later I learned that St. Martin had hosted a dinner in his house for Carl and selected personnel of the IAFEATURE program. This group, under St. Martin's leadership, had literally shouted Bantam down when he attempted to bring them into line and explain the limitations of our charter in Angola. Now St. Martin was the chief of station, on his own turf, reporting to Potts. Carl Bantam, although a GS 17, was only a staff officer, not in the chain of command.

Paul Foster came back from his second TDY to Kinshasa just before Christmas. His natural confidence was buoyed even higher, because he now could pronounce the names and knew where places were on the map. He briefed the working group and gave a fascinating account of the battle of Quifangondo which apparently he had watched from the ridge. "We taught them how to build bunkers and *advised* them to spread out. It did no good." he said. At the word "advised" the working group members looked at each other knowingly. The National Security Council had said there should be no American advisors in Angola, but they had nevertheless suspected that the CIA was cheating on that caveat. Now they knew.*

---

*By this time, of course, the National Security Council was urgently seeking the means for escalation and was scarcely inclined to reprimand the CIA for its aggressiveness.

With all else failing, the CIA turned to its mercenary recruitment programs with renewed determination. Already underway, the recruitment of the French Hoods was proceeding slowly. The CIA station in Paris had fine rapport but little influence with the French service, and could not seem to expedite that program. The French service insisted that the CIA work directly with Bob Denard, who was doing the recruiting.

Denard was himself a famous mercenary. He had fought for Mobutu in the Congo (in a program financed by the CIA) and had later defied Mobutu, been wounded, and convalesced in Rhodesia in 1967. In November 1967 he had brought sixteen mercenaries on bicycles across the Angolan border into the Katanga province of the Congo and bluffed his way three hundred kilometers against Mobutu's commandos, to the outskirts of the huge Kolwezi copper mines, apparently hoping that the Katangese gendarmes would rise up under his leadership. At Kolwezi, however, Mobutu's commandos made a stand which checked Denard's advance and forced his withdrawal back across the border. Since that time Denard had lived in France, performing useful services for any intelligence service or government that paid cash, playing all ends against his bank account. The CIA had reports that in the fall of 1975 Denard, now back in Mobutu's good graces, had recruited mercenaries to support Mobutu's invasion of Cabinda and to run an operation in the Comoro Islands.

I was opposed to all mercenary operations, but this one was at least more palatable than the others. The Frenchmen would be white neocolonials, but not as offensive to Africans as the Portuguese. And the sponsorship of the French service reduced the likelihood of psychopaths and sadists. The contract called for technicians and skilled military veterans.

Bob Denard was to handle all the recruiting activities, and only he would meet with a CIA representative. The French service would facilitate passports and visas. UNITA representatives would house the men as they staged through Kinshasa, and Savimbi would supervise their activities in Angola. This arrangement gave the CIA plausible denial of involvement in the operation and protected the United States government from claims that might be lodged by the families of any mercenaries killed in Angola.

A paramilitary officer, who was a lieutenant colonel in the Marine

Corps Reserves and had for years managed an air proprietary company in Africa, was sent to Paris. I was satisfied with his selection, although I wondered if he would be a match for Denard in working out the terms of the contract. At the outset of the program the French intelligence crowd had taken General Walters for $250,000, and our station in Paris had consistently been outmaneuvered by the French. I expected Denard would manage to obtain very favorable terms for himself and his men.

Even my cynical projections did not steel me for the demands that came by cable from the Paris station on November 24. Denard agreed to field twenty men for five months for $350,000 cash and would deliver them to Kinshasa ten to thirty days *after* the entire $350,000 was deposited to his Luxembourg bank account! He expected us to give him the entire sum *before* he began his recruiting efforts.

I read the Paris cable in the morning but made little comment at staff meeting. No doubt Denard would eventually get the full $350,-000. The agency never bargains hard in dealing with agents and Potts was desperate to place the mercenaries in action. It never entered my mind that we would agree to pay the mercenaries *in advance*. Other things involved me during the day and only late that evening did I find on my desk a cable written by the support office, authorizing immediate payment of the $350,000. Potts wasn't in. I took it across the hall to Carl Bantam's office and confronted him with it.

"Carl," I said. "Possibly you don't understand about mercenaries. Their code is money and their only loyalty is to money. There aren't half a dozen in the world who can be paid in advance and still fulfill their contracts when it's hot and dirty and the rockets start landing on the battlefield. With mercenaries you pay as they perform, not before."

He argued that this situation was different because the French had recommended Denard.

"So? We know Denard as well as they do." I said. "But that is beside the point. This is business and it doesn't make sense. It's unthinkable for the CIA to pay him in advance."

I held my ground and personally tore up the cable. Instead, we sent out a reply suggesting that we should make a lesser deposit against Denard's recruiting expenses and pay the remainder in increments as the operation developed.

A cable shot right back from Paris, energetically relaying De-nard's arguments that he had been burned once before, when Mobutu had diverted CIA funds and failed to meet his payrolls. Now he would only work with cash in advance. Once again I balked—this time Denard was working directly with a CIA case officer and we could crack the whip at him by asking the French to intervene. Nevertheless Potts, making reference to mercenary "honor" and "professional codes," authorized payment of 50 percent immediately and the remainder when the first mercenaries boarded planes in Paris bound for Kinshasa. The total had been increased to $425,000 to include life insurance for the twenty men. Eventually it would be increased again, to $500,000.

The first eleven "Hoods" arrived in Kinshasa January 10, and for two days were trained by CIA weapons experts in the use of the SA-7 ground-to-air missile. Then they were flown to Silva Porto in IAFEA-TURE airplanes. The remainder went into Angola on January 27. One of them was obviously a French agent.

Our Portuguese mercenary program received even less enthusias-tic support from me. The black Angolans had just won a bloody, fifteen-year struggle against the Portuguese. To ally ourselves with the same Portuguese losers, especially when the Soviets were repre-sented in Angola by popular Cuban revolutionaries, was the height of foolishness. Nor could we expect our Portuguese force to stand against the Cuban juggernaut that was forming.

The Portuguese recruitment program nevertheless moved for-ward. A CIA case officer met Colonel Castro in Madrid in early December and with the help of an interpreter, working in hotel rooms, began to hammer out a program for the recruitment of three-hundred men. First, Colonel Castro opened a bank account to which the CIA finance office in Berne deposited $55,000 for operating expenses; and then Avery gave him another $55,000 in untraceable cash. They signed an agreement, approved by head-quarters, in which Colonel Castro agreed to recruit, pay, and di-rect the three-hundred Angolan (refugee) Portuguese commandos to fight alongside the FNLA in Angola. Colonel Castro would be reimbursed for all recruiting expenses, three-hundred round-trip plane tickets to Kinshasa, salaries and bonuses, maintenance in Angola, and medical expenses up to a grand total of $1.5 million. The contract obliged the men to fight in Angola for five months.

The salary scale was:

Rank	Number of men	Monthly Salary in U.S. Dollars
Private	198	$ 500
Sargeant	80	650
Second Lieutenant	15	800
First Lieutenant	3	1000
Captain	3	1400
Major	1	2500

The gross monthly salary would be $172,700, or $863,500 for five months.

An additional monthly separation allowance would be paid at the rate of $100 per wife and $50 for each child, grossing $60,000 per month, or $300,000 for five months.

Travel was estimated at $200,000; medical costs, $50,000; bonuses, $100,000; and subsistence, $75,000.

Colonel Castro himself would receive a commission of $25,000 (plus whatever other benefits he squeezed out of the rest of the budget).

The recruiting began slowly, too slowly it seemed to CIA officers who were watching the FNLA fleeing in northern Angola. We had believed Castro's early claims that he had six hundred men waiting for his call. As weeks went by he explained with some embarrassment that it was difficult to work effectively over the Christmas holidays. And he had to develop the infrastructure to put together the small army.

When Castro wanted additional funds we balked, demanding to see a list of names of the recruits and an accounting of how the $110,000 had been expended. Castro argued that he had been promised a free hand and was obligated by the contract only to deliver three-hundred men to Kinshasa. We backed down about the accounting, and Castro eventually provided the names of a few dozen recruits. The first man, a sergeant, arrived in Kinshasa January 1, 1976, followed by twelve others on January 28. By then the FNLA was collapsing across the border and Castro was told to suspend the recruiting. The thirteen men were returned to Europe without seeing Angola.

Simultaneously a third mercenary force of about 150 British and Americans was being assembled by Roberto himself. No memos were written about this program at CIA headquarters and no cables went out approving it. Since it overlapped extensively with our other activities, however, we became increasingly concerned at headquarters. IAFEATURE airplanes were carrying these fighters into Angola. They were being armed with IAFEATURE weapons. Their leaders met with CIA officers at IAFEATURE safehouses in Kinshasa to discuss strategy and receive aerial photographs and briefings. It seemed likely Roberto was using CIA funds to hire them. Two Englishmen, Nick Hall and a Doctor Bedford, had been recruiting for Roberto in England as early as October 1975. By late December their mercenaries were trickling into Kinshasa and Angola. In January, over one hundred Englishmen were fighting for the FNLA in northern Angola. Their quality was exceptionally low, some had no previous military training. In two cases London street sweepers were recruited directly from their jobs and dispatched to Angola.

In New York, Florida, and California adventurers and publicity seekers began grandstanding. One American named Bufkin appeared on American television claiming to be a CIA agent and to have fought in Korea and Vietnam. He contacted Roberto and then flew to Kinshasa, where he paraded about the Continental Hotel in a paracommando uniform with empty holsters on each hip. A half-dozen Americans joined the British mercenaries in Angola. Among them were some serious, though misguided, individuals. A young father of four, Daniel F. Gearhart, from Kensington, Maryland, answered the call. A highly respected former CIA paramilitary officer, George Bacon III, joined him. Neither would return alive.

Our nervousness about the publicity and exposure these mercenaries were getting led to requests that Kinshasa station provide an accounting of how IAFEATURE funds were being used by Roberto. Were the mercenaries on the CIA payroll? Kinshasa replied that it was difficult to get an accounting from Roberto. In fact, we had written the IAFEATURE project so accountings would not be required. However, it was confirmed that the Englishmen were being paid new hundred-dollar bills, just like those we were using to fund Roberto.

Beginning in December 1976, headquarters began to get, we thought, a better feeling for these mercenaries through operational cables from Kinshasa. Agency officers flying in and out of northern Angola took note of an Englishman named George Cullen, also known as Costa Georgiu, who had somehow become Roberto's field

Mercenary George Cullen.

general in Angola. Kinshasa, reporting favorably on his activities, wanted to recruit him as an in-place observer of the fighting. He was fit and aggressive, it was reported. Almost singlehandedly he had ambushed and routed a small MPLA column near Negage. Cullen, a native of Leeds, England, had been a British paracommando, then a mercenary in Oman; he spoke Greek, Arabic, English, and some Portuguese. Altogether, a good man, it seemed.

Only days later Cullen seemed much less of a good thing. Incredible tales concerning him began filtering out of the war zone. Cullen was beating up blacks; Cullen was murdering blacks; Cullen had stripped, beaten, and humiliated Zairian officers; Cullen was a psychopath.

On February 1, 1976, a mobile patrol of twenty-five mercenaries went on a reconaissance operation near São Salvadore. On the way back they attacked a forward defense post of their own men, mistaking their colleagues for Cubans and a little Panhard armored car for a T-34 tank. Then they fled to São Salvadore.

Two days later Cullen, having tracked them down, lined fourteen of the malefactors beside the road, and gunned the whole lot down. Stripping their bodies, he left them in the sun as an example to others and disappeared into the bush.

Two days after that Roberto went to São Salvadore with three mercenaries, including a Brit named Peter MacLeese and an unidentified American, to deal with Cullen. They were met at the airstrip by two mercenaries, one of them Cullen's sidekick. MacLeese smashed one with a rifle butt, then stripped them both to the waist and marched them into town, their hands over their heads. After a summary court marital, the sidekick was found guilty of participating in the execution of the fourteen. On the spot he was dealt the same fate.

A few days later, fifteen other mercenaries commandeered a plane and flew to Kinshasa, armed and angry, not at their comrade's execution, but because they had not been paid. They were seeking Roberto to take what they could by force. Fortunately they were met at the airport by a CIA officer who reasoned with them and gave reassurances, until they relinquished their weapons and calmed down. Mobutu, always concerned for his own safety, kept aggressive police and paracommando battalions in Kinshasa. He was particularly sensitive about mercenaries, who, on previous occasions, had not only rebelled against him but also had occupied the eastern provincial capital of Bukavu. Whites are generally welcome in Kinshasa, but they do not wisely go about brandishing weapons. Had this band of mutineers blustered into downtown Kinshasa with a show of arms, almost certainly a slaughter would have ensued.

As for George Cullen, he was captured by the MPLA. Three months later he was tried and executed in Luanda.

14

CIA v. Congress

It was back in September, while I was writing a cable requesting more information about Senator Clark's tour of southern Africa, that I first began to understand the agency's manipulative attitude towards Congress. Clark, the chairman of the Subcommittee on African Affairs of the Senate Foreign Relations Committee, was touring southern Africa from Tanzania south and back up to Zaire, meeting African chiefs of state and our ambassadors, seeking to understand the issues in Angola.

Before his departure, on August 4, 1975, Senator Clark had been briefed by Director Colby about the Angola program. Colby had explained our objectives in terms of the original 40 Committee charter, i.e., that we were sending arms to replenish Mobutu's arsenal as he sent weapons into Angola. No American arms would be sent into Angola. No Americans would be involved in the conflict. The objective was to encourage Mobutu to prop up the FNLA and UNITA so they could resist the MPLA until elections could be held in October. As Senator Clark traveled this IAFEATURE cover story was

being thoroughly tested. Insisting on consulting every principal involved, Clark was visiting Luanda, Kinshasa, and even Ambriz and
Silva Porto, and talking to Neto, Roberto, Savimbi, and Mobutu.
Ominous rumors were trickling back about his reaction. What if he
chose to expose our program to the public or go on record against
it within the Senate? At headquarters we wanted detailed reporting
from the field about Clark's reactions.

As I drafted the cable I read through a soft file* on Senator Clark,
and found a cable from headquarters to Kinshasa instructing the
chief of station to see Mobutu and Holden Roberto and prep them
for their meeting with Senator Clark. The COS should advise
Mobutu and Roberto that Senator Clark had been briefed in very
general terms about our program to help the Angolan liberation
front leaders and to resupply Zaire, to make up for the aid it had
given the Angolans. The cable stated that Senator Clark had agreed
not to discuss the program in Zaire. Therefore the two African
politicians should be encouraged to promote their interests in Angola, confident that Senator Clark could not turn the conversation
to the CIA program.

After a staff meeting, as we walked back to the Africa Division
offices, I asked my colleagues if we could get by with that sort of
thing.

What sort of thing? someone asked.

"Coaching African politicians before they meet with one of our
own senators."

No one seemed to grasp my point, so I tried again.

"Senator Clark was sent by the Senate Foreign Relations Committee to get the facts on Angola. Can we tell Africans he wants to meet
what they should and should not tell him?"

A chorus of sharp voices pounded me. Clark shouldn't waste the
taxpayers' money on such a trip. It was the agency's job to gather
intelligence. We had already told Clark everything he needed to
know about Angola. Besides, you couldn't trust senators any further
than you could throw them, someone added, recalling an incident in

*Since the Freedom of Information Act, the agency increasingly uses a system of
"soft," "unofficial," or "convenience" files for sensitive subjects, especially any
involving surveillance of Americans. Such files are not registered in the agency's
official records system, and hence can never be disclosed under the FOIA.

Southeast Asia, when a prominent senator had been briefed on the CIA program in detail and even shown upcountry installations, and later publicly denied any knowledge of the program. If Clark was going to mess around our program, talking to Africans, then we damn well better see that our own agents put their best feet forward.

Someone admitted that it wasn't very smart having a cable like that in the files.* Eventually we could expect the Senate to close the program down and investigate it. They just might get their hands on such a cable and kick up a fuss.

Senator Clark returned from his trip skeptical of his CIA briefings and of the Angola program. He was concerned that we were secretly dragging the United States into a broad conflict with dangerous, global implications. Specifically, he was concerned *(a)* that we were in fact sending arms directly into Angola; *(b)* that Americans were involved in the conflict; and *(c)* that the CIA was illegally collaborating with South Africa. However, Clark could not disprove our cover story and he had few moves to make against us. He could not precipitate a public debate because he was now muzzled by the CIA —in receiving the CIA's briefing about IAFEATURE, he had given his tacit oath not to expose the information he received. The atmosphere in Congress was such that he would be highly discredited with his colleagues, jeopardizing his effectiveness on the Senate Foreign Relations Committee, if he spoke out. Dozens of other legislators were similarly entrapped, as Colby methodically continued his briefings throughout the program—thirty-five briefings altogether between January 1975 and January 1976. Systematically, he misled congressmen about what we were doing in Angola, but nevertheless deprived them of the option of going public.** This was the flaw of the Hughes-Ryan Amendment, aside from the fact that it did not specify

*Although the file on Senator Clark was "soft," and therefore safe from Freedom of Information Act demands, the cable also appeared in the IAFEATURE chronological files and in the computer which records every agency cable.

**In *Honorable Men,* Colby claims, in a thesis that recurs throughout the book, that he worked with determination to make the CIA "an integral part of our democratic system of checks and balances among the Executive and Congress and the Judiciary," by testifying before the congressional committees. And yet, while he was answering their questions about past CIA operations, he was feeding them patently false information about the ongoing Angolan operation, depriving them of the full information which they needed to perform their constitutional role.

that CIA briefings of congressional committees must be complete or accurate.

Quietly, Clark continued to watch the Angola program, trying to discern the truth through our shields of secrecy and falsehood. In early November he queried the State Department about the Angolan conflict and was told that Mobutu was not using United States aid to support the Angolan factions. On November 8 Colby defended the Angola program to the Senate Foreign Relations Committee, repeating the party line that we were delivering arms to Mobutu, who was supplying the two Angolan factions, etc. On December 12 Colby reassured the House Intelligence Committee that there were no Americans involved in Angola.*

The only weapon left to Senator Clark was the Senate's indirect control of the CIA budget. On December 5 Clark recommended to the Senate Foreign Relations Committee that it vote to terminate American involvement in Angola. The committee agreed, stirred to anger when a spokesman of the working group was exposed flagrantly lying to the committee. Bill Nelson, the CIA deputy director of operations, and Ed Mulcahy, the deputy assistant secretary of state for African affairs, had been summoned to testify. Before Mulcahy arrived, Nelson was questioned and admitted the truth, that the CIA *was* sending arms directly into Angola.** Minutes later Mulcahy arrived and testified, adhering to the working group line that arms were *not* being sent into Angola. Senator Clark confronted Mulcahy with Nelson's contradictory testimony and asked him to explain his apparent "lie.". Beneath the angry stares of committee members Mulcahy kept his poise, and calmly reversed himself, admitting that arms *were* being sent into Angola. Senator Case angrily denounced the lying. The committee unanimously endorsed Senator Clark's bill.

---

*See above, p. 177.

**On November 3, Colby had been fired impetuously by President Ford, who then had been obliged to reverse himself and ask Colby to stay on until the congressional hearings were completed and a successor could be named. Thus, on December 5, Bill Nelson, who was a Colby protegé, knew that his own days of power were numbered. Only he could tell if this influenced him to betray Colby's IAFEATURE cover story and tell the Senate the truth. Certainly, it must have been a difficult decision for Nelson to make. Richard Helms, a former director, was under investigation of perjury for lying to the Senate, and by December 5, it was a safe conclusion that any false testimony about the Angola program might eventually be exposed.

The battle was thus joined. The administration lobbied for support for its proposed escalations in Angola. The CIA intensified its propaganda efforts, its agents focusing on New York and Washington. Our United Nations ambassador, Daniel Patrick Moynihan, noisily accused the Soviets of attempting to colonize Africa. Kissinger huffed publicly, "We have to be extremely tough, even brutal when they [the Soviets] step over the line." The senators could not answer publicly, muzzled as they were by the CIA.

In silence they focused on the CIA budget for the coming year. So far the Angola program had been run from FY75* contingency funds which had been approved by the Senate a year before. But the FY76 Defense Appropriations Bill was then before the Senate, and the CIA budget was buried in it. Senators John Tunney, Alan Cranston, and Dick Clark introduced an amendment which would prevent the use of any FY76 defense funds in Angola, except to gather intelligence. Clark pointed out that in Angola, ". . . we are dangerously close to an open ended confrontation with the Soviet Union in a country that is of no real strategic concern to either country." The Tunney Amendment was approved by the Senate, 54 to 22, on December 19,** and on January 27 the House voted 323 to 99 in its favor. On February 9 President Ford signed it into law.

Simultaneously, overseas, the Angola program fell apart. The Cuban build-up accelerated in December and January. On November 11, there were approximately 2,800 Cuban soldiers in Angola; by February an air bridge they called *Operation Carlotta* had brought

---

*The fiscal year running from July 1, 1974, to June 30, 1975.
**The day before, on December 18, my task force work was interrupted by an awards ceremony in which I was given the CIA's Medal of Merit for my activities in Vietnam. The ceremonies were embarassing to many who received awards, who felt that the agency's conduct had been dishonorable and that the awards ceremony was part of Colby's efforts to whitewash the episode. One young officer came to my office ahead of time, tearfully asking if I thought he should accept his medal. Another mimed that he would wear a paper bag over his head to cover his embarassment. I myself called Colby's office and asked to be taken off the list of "heroes" but was told Colby had decreed no one would be permitted to refuse his medal.

Unwilling to jeopardize my position on the task force at this critical date, I walked across the stage and took the medal from Colby. He began his pat recitation of my "heroism" but faltered as he looked me in the eye.

At the door of the auditorium a secretary took the medals back, to hold in our files until our eventual retirement from the agency. In 1977, when I resigned, I quietly refused to take mine with me.

their numbers at least to 12,000. They moved as modern, regular army units, with trucks, helicopters, tanks, armored cars, artillery support, and eventually MIG-21 jet fighter aircraft. In February, the Soviets' Angola program was estimated by the CIA to have reached $400 million.

By mid-January of 1976 it had become clear to the South Africans that they would receive no public support for their Angolan effort, not even from Savimbi, who owed them so much. Realizing that the United States government would itself soon be forced to abandon its Angolan program, and facing a Cuban/MPLA force which was no longer a pushover, they gave up in disgust and retired back across the border as efficiently and quietly as they had come.

Vorster's plan—putting in a small, covert force—had violated the cardinal rule of military strategy—the clear definition and pursuit of a desired objective. Emphatically, South Africa had been taught a hard lesson: certain black African countries would accept its covert aid, but few sincerely bought its thesis of an African brotherhood which transcended racial issues. Despite the CIA's camaraderie, and despite whatever reassurances the South Africans felt they had received from the Ford administration,* the United States had rejected their bid for overt support. Three months later the United States joined in a critical vote against them in the United Nations Security Council. The South African military was bitter, feeling that it was discredited in the eyes of the world. The campaign had been expensive, costing the South African government $133 million. The damage to its white population's morale, the bitterness over the deaths of its soldiers in a secret, ill-conceived campaign in Angola, the humiliation of having two soldiers paraded before the Organization of African Unity in Addis Ababa, were all impossible to measure. Two months later, in March 1976, the South Africans were obliged to turn the Cunene hydroelectric project over to the victorious MPLA.**

*A U.S. embassy cable from Capetown on February 5, 1976, reported that United party leader Sir De Villiers Graaf and foreign affairs spokesman Japie Basson both noted to the visiting Bartlett congressional delegation ". . . the general belief that South Africa had gone into Angola with some understanding that the United States intended to put up strong resistance to Soviet and Cuban intervention."
**See "South Africa: Up against the World," by John de St. Jorre, Foreign Policy No. 28 (Fall 1977).

In mid-January the French announced their disengagement. The Zairian Seventh and Fourth commandos continued straggling across the border into Zaire.

An OAU summit meeting was scheduled for January 11 and 12, 1976, and the United States became almost desperate to avoid censure by a majority of the African leaders. William Schaufele, the under-secretary of state for African affairs, began a hasty tour of Africa, seeking support. President Ford sent personal letters to thirty-two African chiefs of state. Ambassador Moynihan continued to attack the Soviet program in the UN. The CIA marshaled every agent it could muster and sent them to Addis Ababa. A task force officer flew from Washington to Addis Ababa to bolster the CIA station's be-hind-the-scenes efforts to influence the outcome. Even then the agency was greatly relieved to achieve a 22–22 deadlock tie in the voting on the Angolan issue. The relief was only temporary. Within six weeks, forty-one of the forty-six OAU members had recognized the MPLA government in Luanda.

The military situation turned from bad to disastrous. Without South African armor and leadership, UNITA could not stand in the face of the Cuban/MPLA advances. Savimbi reported one engage-ment east of Luso which left him stoically incredulous at the Cubans' use of helicopters in a vertical envelopment. At night the UNITA force had been facing several hundred Katangese troops, he said, and the next morning they found a full battalion suddenly behind them, attacking from the rear and blocking their retreat. UNITA's position crumbled rapidly throughout central Angola. By February 1, Savimbi was pushed back to Huambo and Silva Porto, not sure how long he could hold those.

In Washington the intent of the Senate was clear enough, it wanted to halt the Angola program. Technically, however, the Tunney Amendment only restricted future funds, and we still had $5 million of the original $31.7 million. The CIA urgently tried to use that money for more arms flights, while the administration sought to squeeze another $9 million out of the CIA's FY75 budget. The administration continued exhorting the CIA; in a 40 Committee meeting in the White House situation room on January 6, Bill Hy-land, the deputy to the national security advisor to the president, instructed the CIA to concentrate on *winning* the war, and urged the recruitment of mercenaries and the shipment of weapons like the

C-47 gunships and 105 mm. howitzers to reverse the FNLA defeats. Five more C-141 arms flights went from Washington and France to Kinshasa, destined for Angola, between December 19, 1975 and January 29, 1976. On January 9 we were desperately seeking to repaint a U.S. Air Force C-130 to deliver to the South Africans, along with the French helicopters, to encourage them to remain in Angola.

Sensing our defiance, the Senate responded angrily. Senator Tunney wrote President Ford, threatening to review the budget if the Angolan activities did not cease. Senator Clark summoned Colby and Kissinger to answer blunt questions: Were Americans involved in the conflict? What was our relationship with South Africa? Kissinger said, among other things, "The Soviet Union must not be given any opportunity to use military forces for aggressive purposes without running the risk of conflict with us." His testimony included several misleading and inaccurate statements. Even in mid-January the senators did not have complete enough information—the whole truth—to refute his testimony.

Only after February 9, when the president's signature legalized the Tunney Amendment, did the CIA acknowledge defeat and begin to withdraw. The Portuguese commando force was terminated and some of the IAFEATURE temporary duty officers were ordered home from the field. But even then, after February 9, the CIA continued making arms shipments into Angola, sending twenty-two additional flights from Kinshasa to the air strip in Gago Coutinho in eastern Angola, delivering an additional 145,490 pounds of arms and ammunition.

By early February the FNLA had ceased to exist as a viable fighting force and UNITA was crushed back to Huambo and Silva Porto. Savimbi came to the COS, Kinshasa, and asked for a clarification of United States policy and intentions. Should he attempt to fight for the cities? Or should he revert to guerrilla warfare?

St. Martin asked Savimbi if UNITA might not attempt to reach an understanding with the MPLA. St. Martin had participated in the CIA's effort to bring Savimbi back into line in September, when he had first attempted to open negotiations with the MPLA. Savimbi replied that he doubted the MPLA would be receptive under the present circumstances.

St. Martin then relayed Savimbi's query to headquarters. No answer was available for two full weeks—in February, even after Ford had signed the Tunney Amendment into law, the White House and Kissinger were still seeking a miracle to reverse the tide of defeats, and they were casting about for public support for a major, overt escalation of the war. While discussions were being held in Washington, UNITA lost six hundred soldiers in a crushing defeat at Huambo.

When Washington finally answered, it encouraged Savimbi to continue fighting. On February 11 the CIA spokesman promised Savimbi another million dollars in arms and money. On February 18, 1976, Secretary Kissinger sent the American chargé in Kinshasa a cable, instructing him to tell UNITA leaders that the United States would continue to support UNITA as long as it demonstrated the capacity for effective resistance to the MPLA. By that late date Kissinger knew full well that we could provide no more support to UNITA. His message was perhaps an example of being "tough, even brutal . . ." As he had said in Senate testimony about his callous misuse of the Kurds: "One must not confuse the intelligence business with missionary work."*

While Kissinger was drafting his cable, Savimbi was sending a message of quite another kind to President Kenneth Kaunda of Zambia:

> UNITA lost 600 men in the battle for Huambo. The machine of war that Cuba and the Soviet Union have assembled in Angola is beyond the imagination. To prevent the total destruction of our forces we have decided to revert immediately to guerrilla warfare. The friends (the CIA and United States) that have promised to help us did not fulfill their promises and we must face our own fate with courage and determination.
>
> I have two requests for Your Excellency: *(1)* No one is responsible for this disaster but the big powers. This is why with my humble and limited understanding I beg your excellency that my brother for years, Zambian Minister for Foreign Affairs, Rupiah Banda, be spared so that UNITA can be sacrificed (i.e., at UNITA's expense). Rupiah is

---

*In 1974 and 1975, the CIA, under orders from Kissinger, had mounted a program to arm and encourage the Kurdish people to revolt against the Iraqi government. This was done at the request of the shah of Iran, who was contending with the Iraqis. When the shah had reached a satisfactory understanding with the Iraqis, the CIA was called off and it abruptly abandoned the Kurds, leaving them helpless, unable to defend themselves against bloody reprisals from the Iraqi army. Explaining this to the Church Committee, Kissinger made his now-famous statement.

a big African, though very young. *(2)* I am sending with this my mother who is seventy-one years old so that she will be able to die in Zambia. My sister and three children and my two children are with my mother. Accompanying them are the wife of our Secretary General with two children and the wife of our Commanding General with four children.

The Political Bureau of Central Committee of UNITA joins me to thank you once more for everything. Whatever stand your government takes on Angola, we will accept with resignation. It is paramount that Zambia survives and the love and admiration we have shared with my colleagues for your leadership and wisdom will be sufficient to comfort us in the dark days of our country.

I would like to end this letter by asking Your Excellency to convey my greetings to Mwalimu [Tanzanian president] Julius Nyerere. I have read his interview concerning me. It is a pity that President Nyerere did not believe and know me. I have always tried to the best of my ability and courage to serve the interests of Angola and Africa. I am not a traitor to Africa and the hard days that we expect ahead will prove to the world that I stand for my principles. In Angola might has made right but I will remain in the bush to cry for justice.

God bless your beloved country,
God bless you.
Savimbi Jonas.

In his last meeting with a CIA officer, on February 1, 1976, Savimbi vowed never to leave the Angolan bush alive.

Clearly, the administration, Henry Kissinger, and the CIA had been checked by a stubborn Congress. But how was the CIA doing with the Church and Pike Committees and their devastating exposures? There seemed no end to the sordid tales coming to light about the agency.

In late November 1975 more dramatic details of CIA assassination programs were leaked to the press by the Senate investigators. The CIA had been directly involved with the killers of Rafael Trujillo of the Dominican Republic, Ngo Diem of South Vietnam, and General Schneider of Chile. It had plotted the deaths of Fidel Castro and Patrice Lumumba.

In the Lumumba assassination plot the CIA was particularly diligent in its planning. Sid Gottlieb, chief of Technical Services Division, and courier of the poison, had no sooner reached Kinshasa than headquarters had followed him with cables urging that the poison be given to Lumumba promptly, before its power diminsihed. An agent was located who agreed to administer the fatal dose. A CIA staff officer on the one hand refused to do the killing, but on the other did agree to lure Lumumba into a situation where he could be poisoned. The poison was not used, apparently because of difficulties in staging the killing, but a month later, on January 17, 1961, Lumumba was beaten to death by henchmen of Congolese politicians who had close relationships with the CIA.

On December 19, 1975, while the Senate voted on Angola, the Olsson family accepted $1.25 million in restitution for the death of Dr. Olsson in CIA drug experiments. The money came from the U.S. taxpayer. The perpetrators of the crime, the directors of the CIA, the chief of the Technical Services Division, and the scientists involved, were never punished. They served out their careers, receiving promotions and awards until they retired. After retirement they continued to draw government pensions of up to $20,000 per year.

On December 23, 1975, fate intervened on the behalf of the CIA. The CIA station chief in Greece, Richard S. Welch, was killed by terrorists in front of his villa in a luxurious suburb eight kilometers from Athens. Three days before, his name and CIA identity had been published in a local newspaper. No conceivable action or incident could have been more beneficial to the CIA at that time. Colby bitterly denounced the enemies of the CIA who were exposing it. A reaction set in on Capitol Hill and in the press community. Doors began to close on the congressional investigators in the rush of sympathy and support for CIA officers who were thought to be living hazardous lives in the service of their country. When Church Committee members traveled abroad to investigate CIA stations, they were berated by case officers' wives, who claimed that even their children were endangered by the committee's disclosures.

The CIA officers' martyr role was only another CIA ploy. CIA case officering is certainly far less dangerous than other branches of the foreign service. During my twelve years of service I knew of no other CIA case officer murdered, although at least twenty State Department, USIS, and AID officers had been killed, kidnaped, or suffered harrowing experiences during that period. This was despite the publication of hundreds of officers' names in recent years by enemies of the CIA. The reason is simple enough. Eighty-five percent of all CIA field case officers already are well known in their local communities because of their liaison relationships with foreign police, their own open admissions of CIA identities, their free-wheeling, high-profile life-styles, and the gossip and conspicuous clannishness of their wives. In Abidjan, my first post, all CIA station personnel were listed in the embassy's unclassified, public telephone book as the "Political II Section." "Political I" was legitimate State Department personnel.

No one has been killing CIA case officers because no one cares to. The Soviets, Chinese, and even the North Koreans, like the CIA, do not want the intelligence world to be complicated by James Bond–type behavior. It isn't done. If a CIA case officer has a flat tire in the dark of night on a lonely road, he will not hesitate to accept a ride from a KGB officer—likely the two would detour to some bar for a drink together.* Terrorists are not going to waste suicidal missions on U.S. embassy second secretaries, even if they are CIA. Terrorism requires dramatic targets: an Israeli Olympic team, an OPEC minister, a 747 jetliner, or at least an ambassador or consul general.

In Athens the CIA station was huge, and most of its personnel were well known in the local community. Its case officers, especially Welch and his predecessors, had separate offices in the embassy and passed the same residences to generations of successive case officers. Athens's chiefs of station had always been identified to a procession of changing Greek officials, and they had meddled in the violent crises of Cyprus, the Arab-Israeli conflicts, and in Greece itself. The significant point is not that Welch died as he did, but that other case officers before him and since were never hurt in any of these wars and coups.

After Welch's death the Church Committee ran out of support. It published its final report in April 1976, but the CIA was permitted to edit that report before it was released. The Pike Committee report on the CIA was completely suppressed. (Although subsequently leaked to Daniel Schorr who had it conveyed to the *Village Voice* in New York.)

In July 1977, when the House of Representatives established an oversight committee to help keep the CIA in line, the agency im-

---

*In fact CIA and KGB officers entertain each other frequently in their homes. The CIA's files are full of mention of such relationships in almost every African station.

mediately put the congressmen on the defensive by charging they
could not be trusted with its information. The representatives clamored publicly to reassure the CIA they could keep secrets. Not one
legislator promised to tell the American people if the CIA again
abuses their rights or attempts to drag the nation into foolish wars.*
And while the oversight committees are preoccupied with proving to
the CIA that they can keep a secret, the clandestine service continues
to do its thing in most corners of the world.

*See "Intelligence: The Constitution Betrayed," by Henry Steele Commager, *New
York Review,* January 1976.

15

Disengagement

On February 12, Jonas Savimbi withdrew his forces from Silva Porto and fled two hundred miles south to Villa Serpa Pinto, where he planned to set up a temporary headquarters and prepare his forces for protracted guerrilla warfare. At Serpa Pinto he hoped to receive a final resupply of CIA arms and funds. The CIA intended that the French Hoods, who still had three months remaining on their contracts, would provide leadership and technical assistance to the guerrilla army. The Hoods were joined by a young European couple—a husband wife photographic team—who would keep the CIA apprised of UNITA's adventures.* But neither Savimbi nor the CIA had yet grasped the speed with which the Cuban juggernaut would crash through UNITA's puny defenses. In three days the Cubans

---

*CIA headquarters had foreseen that it would soon be too dangerous to risk one of its own officers in Savimbi's company in the Angolan hinterlands. Hence, the European couple was enticed away from their plantation in another region and sent to Savimbi's headquarters.

blasted UNITA out of Serpa Pinto and Savimbi fled east.

Two weeks after that, on March 1, 1976, Savimbi appeared at Gago Coutinho at the far eastern border of Angola. The CIA immediately began to airlift arms and food from Kinshasa.

The FNLA was faring no better than UNITA. On March 2 the last FNLA contingent fled north across the Congo River into Zaire. Roberto's mercenaries traveled overland to Kinshasa and disbanded. The 150 Brits returned to England and the thirty Portuguese who had gone the whole distance with Roberto in Angola dispersed to South Africa and Europe. Captain Bento made his way to South Africa, where he examined the possibilities of developing a guerrilla force from FNLA remnants in southern Angola. Eventually he gave up and emigrated to Brazil.

In March 1976, Boeing was given permission to deliver the 737 jetliners to the MPLA. Boeing technicians went to Angola to install the radar systems in the airports. Gulf delivered $125 million to the MPLA and resumed pumping Cabindan oil.

William E. Colby retired, perhaps more troubled by two years of fending off congressional committees than by the unfortunate paramilitary operations, PHOENIX and IAFEATURE, which he had run. With him into retirement went William Nelson, the deputy director of operations.

Ed Mulcahy was designated as ambassador to Tunisia. In a previous tour there he had been ordered to supervise the expenditure of an accumulation of blocked local currency on the construction of a palatial ambassador's residence. Now fate had decreed that he should return to enjoy its splendor as his retirement post. Larry Devlin appeared at Mulcahy's swearing-in reception on the seventh floor of the State Department, only to be reminded by Mulcahy that he had not been invited.

Sheldon Vance retired to open a consulting office in Washington, advising clients about Zairian investment opportunities.

Jim Potts took leave for some much-needed rest, then departed on a tour of African stations, leaving Carl Bantam to sort out the problems of disengagement.

The new director, George Bush, inherited the burden of extricating the CIA from Angola while dealing with a furious Congress. Congress knew all too well the CIA had ignored the intentions of the Tunney Amendment and was still trying to send military support to the liberation forces in Angola. Bluntly threatening to review the agency's overall budget, it subjected Director Bush to a series of hostile committee hearings, in which it demanded to be given, for once, full and accurate information. To make sure the CIA hadn't secretly used other funds in addition to the $31.7 million, the House Appropriations Committee placed a team of auditors in CIA headquarters to review IAFEATURE accountings.

The new director's first problem was to rein in the free-spending chiefs of station in the field, until he could placate the Senate and coordinate an orderly disengagement. On March 12 he sent a cable to all stations, ordering that no funds *whatsoever* be expended under the IAFEATURE program. Abruptly, the chiefs of station in Kinshasa and Lusaka were cut off from all funds—not even St. Martin would defy such an edict from a new director. High-living UNITA and FNLA cadres, mercenaries, agents, collaborators, landlords, hotel managers, and businessmen were suddenly denied further CIA money, even for previously incurred bills. And St. Martin could only bombard headquarters with a series of cables pleading his dilemma. "Our situation is barely short of intolerable," one said.

Even so, St. Martin managed the unthinkable. To feed Savimbi's forces, St. Martin had proposed in late February to have IAMOLDY/1 purchase $220,000 worth of combat rations in Rhodesia to be flown from Salisbury to Gago Coutinho. Headquarters had nervously approved this operation, stipulating in repeated cables that, other than passing funds to the UNITA representatives, CIA personnel should have no involvement whatsoever with the foodlift. UNITA alone should contract with IAMOLDY/1 and make all the arrangements for transportation. Six headquarters cables underscored the importance of the Kinshasa station staying out of it. With Congress closing in, responsibility for a rogue airplane was the last gaffe anybody at Langley wanted.

On March 14 and 15, a mere three days after Bush's ultimatum, we began receiving reports of a downed F-27 at Gago Coutinho. The details were not immediately clear, but it seemed very likely that the CIA was liable for the uninsured plane. And so it was. St. Martin had not only ignored headquarters' instructions and managed the foodlift himself, he had used Mobutu's precious F-27—the one we had leased—to haul the rations.

Fate had intervened in the form of two MIG-21s. On March 13, while the F-27 was on the ground at Gago Coutinho, having offloaded food and other supplies, the MIGs arrived. Each fired one rocket on the first pass; one of them exploded under the right wing of the F-27, and the other a few meters in front. The pilot and copilot, who were in the plane, received minor wounds. As the MIGs made their second pass, one of the French Hoods armed and fired an SA-7 rocket. It malfunctioned and plunged back to earth. A second rocket spiraled into the sky, missing the jet. Direct hits destroyed the F-27.

After several more passes at the airport of Gago Coutinho, the MIGs turned to attack the small column of vehicles fleeing to Ninda, forty-five kilometers to the south. A rescue operation was quickly mounted and the pilots were evacuated from Ninda to Runtu, South-West Africa. The French Hoods went with them and made their way back to France; twenty-two had eventually been sent into Angola at a cost of over $500,000; two had been killed in action. Savimbi disappeared into the Angolan bush. The CIA could have no further contact with him because the European couple had also panicked and fled with the French Hoods.

On the task force, the consensus was that St. Martin might be disciplined for disobeying orders and losing the plane. The CIA was now liable for a great deal more money than he could include in his monthly accountings, and Congress was angrily examining IAFEA-TURE. Worse yet, Jim Potts, St. Martin's tolerant supervisor at head-quarters, was away on a trip. Nelson and Colby had retired. The new director was not a member of the club. St. Martin seemed to be in a bit of a jam. Carl Bantam could not conceal his satisfaction as he drafted the first of a series of cables which would bring his escapades to a halt.

Betting began. Would St. Martin find a way out? I hedged. Certainly he seemed to be completely boxed in, skewered by his own fine hand, but in every previous confrontation he had proven more than a match for headquarters. Even without Potts's presence you could not rule out the possibility that he would find some way to wriggle off the hook.

He made it look easy. A cable from Kinshasa advised us that Mobutu was extremely upset about the loss of his plane and was demanding $2 million dollars in restitution, or that the F-27 be replaced by a Boeing 737 jetliner (costing approximately $15 million). St. Martin, headquarters, and Mobutu knew a replacement for the

F-27 could be purchased for less than $500,000 in the United States.

The working group panicked at the thought of Mobutu's anger. He was notoriously temperamental about large airplanes, which he viewed as symbols of wealth and prestige. He probably knew the MPLA was getting two 737s from the United States, at exactly the time he was suffering the humiliation of defeat at their hands. Morale throughout the Zairian army was low, and his regime was seriously threatened from within. He could easily decide to make the United States into a scapegoat for getting him into the war, for leading him on, and for letting him down. He might sever relations and turn completely to the East for support. A 737 jetliner or even a $2 million restitution could not be written off by the administration without congressional approval, and the Congress was looking for such an issue to attack the program and expose it to public scrutiny. The CIA would be held to blame for everything.

A frantic exchange of cables ensued. Headquarters was only quibbling about the price. Then St. Martin reported that he had managed to see Mobutu and talk him into accepting a $600,000 settlement for the lost plane. Headquarters' reaction was enormous relief and gratitude that St. Martin had gotten the CIA off the hook so lightly. Congress just might approve $600,000. Nothing more was said about St. Martin's sending the F-27 into Angola in the first place.

Shortly thereafter St. Martin was promoted to GS 17. He was recommended for an award for his "outstanding" participation in the Angola program.*

In February the CIA began making generous payoffs to anyone who had been associated with our side of the Angolan war. The original Portuguese Angolan commandos, who had fought with Bento in northern Angola were compensated as though they had been on contract as CIA mercenaries throughout the war. Then pilots, boat crews, and propaganda specialists began to line up for bonuses and plane tickets to leave the country.

Colonel Castro, of course, received special consideration. He had delivered only 13 men of the 300, but in February he made the novel claim that 126 men had *all* quit their jobs in preparation for their

---

*A year later St. Martin was designated for assignment as chief of station of an important Middle-Eastern capital, where the United States spends large sums of money on arms, drug controls, and intrigue.

departures to Angola and that they all must be paid *as though they had fought in Angola for the full five months.* There was no proof these men even existed, and it was known that Castro had been recruiting among the ranks of desperate, unemployed Portuguese Angolan exiles. But the CIA acquiesed and on February 25 Colonel Castro was given $243,600. Including a $110,000 advance in January, this made $353,600 Colonel Castro had received in secret payments in two months time.* There was of course no assurance Castro would share the money with anyone, but it was argued that the agency's reputation was at stake; it would be unseemly for us to quibble about it.

Eventually, when Director Bush persuaded the congressional committees that all aggressive IAFEATURE activities had ceased, they agreed to a final budget, to dispose of $4.8 million which remained of the $31.7 million:

UNITA	$2,000,000
FNLA	900,000
Final Carrier Claims (unpaid transportation bills)	700,000
Wind up Administrative Costs	250,000
Return to Agency Reserve	1,031,000
	$4,881,000

The $2,000,000 for UNITA was to include such as the following: final payment to Pearl Air for the Viscount, $146,390; relocation of seventy-six UNITA cadres, $104,000; IAMOLDY/1 settlement, $120,000; Rhodesian rations, $120,000; transportation for Rhodesian rations, $96,000; compensation for the downed F-27, $600,000; funds for continuing UNITA activities, $540,700.**

Of the FNLA's $900,000, Roberto would receive $836,000, and $64,000 would pay off the fishing boat *Christina*'s crew.

In late April a case officer hand-carried $2,500,000 to Kinshasa, but there were technical problems. How does one give $836,000 in cash to a fifty-year-old liberation leader, at the nadir of his activities, without tempting him to retire? And how do you deliver $540,000 cash to another leader who has buried himself in the Angolan hinter-

---

*The total bill for the abortive Portuguese mercenary program came to $569,805.
**The wording which satisfied Congress was to the effect that these funds would be used by Savimbi to resist the total annihilation of his forces by the MPLA.

lands? The disbursements had to be made promptly, as Congress had decreed there would be *absolutely* no lingering involvements with Angolan personalities.

For a week we considered having a case officer walk into Angola from Zambia and deliver the money to Savimbi. Case officers, myself included, began to scramble for the assignment, wanting to see Savimbi one last time in his guerrilla redoubt. But the program directors abandoned the idea, fearing the capture of a case officer by the Cubans, and we sought other solutions.

Eventually, on April 28, 1976, the money, $1,986,700, was delivered to Mobutu. Of that, $600,000 would be for his lost plane. The rest he could dole to Roberto and Savimbi's representatives in appropriate increments. Conveniently ignored was the fact that Mobutu was as eager as we were to be rid of the liberation movements.

It was only a matter of days before UNITA and FNLA leaders were hounding the Kinshasa station, desperate, hungry, their debts still unpaid. Roberto wailed that thousands of displaced FNLA tribesmen in lower Zaire were starving. And Mobutu refused to receive anyone. He was pocketing their $1,376,700.*

The Kinshasa station made a feeble effort to obtain another million dollars from headquarters, but it was over. There was no more money. We were not in the missionary business and our involvement with the Angolan revolutionaries was ended.

On March 24, 1976, a CIA intelligence source with contacts among the Portuguese exiles in Spain reported that Colonel Castro was claiming the CIA had welched and refused to provide any funds for him to terminate the PAC force.

One of the French Hoods angrily claimed that he had not been paid by Bob Denard. Denard denied this, and the two blustered, threatening each other.

---

*Jim Potts and crew were aware of this potentiality when they ordered the money delivered to Mobutu. They rationalized that it would mollify him, bribe him not to retaliate against the CIA.

It is an interesting paradox that the Securities and Exchange Commission has since 1971 investigated, and the Justice Department has prosecuted, several large U.S. corporations for using bribery to facilitate their overseas operations. At the same time, the U.S. government, through the CIA, disburses tens of millions of dollars each year in cash bribes. Bribery is a standard operating technique of the U.S. goverment, via the CIA, but it is a criminal offense for U.S. business.

The IAMASKs were given a generous bonus and returned to their plantation.

Others were not so fortunate. It was of course impossible to count the total numbers of Africans who lost their lives during the program. The figures doubtless ran into the thousands. No CIA staffers were killed or suffered any discomfort worse than malaria, but this is normal, as the CIA always operates behind the scenes, letting others run the serious risks.

The thirteen mercenaries who were captured in northern Angola in February included three Americans. Gustavo Grillo, Daniel Gearhardt, and Gary Akers were tried as war criminals, and sentenced by an international tribunal in Luanda, in June 1976. President Ford sent personal messages to President Neto pleading for clemency, to no avail. Gearhardt was executed in Luanda on July 10, 1976, and the Italian embassy shipped his body back to his widow and four children in the United States for burial. Akers was sentenced to thirty years in prison. Grillo received a lesser sentence.

George Bacon III had been killed in an ambush in February.

At headquarters, the task force was disbanded, its people moving to other assignments. A nucleus of five was retained for nine long weeks, in case there was an investigation or follow-up activity. With little to do, I began jogging at noontime, running out the back gate and down the George Washington Parkway to Turkey Run Park. There was too much time to reflect on the program and its appalling mediocrity.

Nothing had worked. We had delivered into Angola thirty thousand sidearms for ten thousand troops, but nothing equal to the enemy's 122 mm. rocket. The Swift patrol craft never saw action, disintegrating in short weeks of the Zairians' pounding misuse. The twenty-four rubber boats had been lost. The *Sagittarius* contributed nothing. Money was wasted on ice plants and fishing boats. Captain Bento's commandos never could be persuaded to raid and patrol. Bob Denard and Colonel Castro had made our case officers look silly in bargaining sessions. The French Hoods had fled, months short of contract, at exactly the moment UNITA needed their skills the most. The European couple fled after a week in Angola, depriving us of follow-up intelligence from Savimbi's headquarters. The PAC force never materialized. The SA-7 rockets misfired, without downing a plane. The French helicopters were delivered without pilots or ground crews. The British/American mercenaries had drawn world attention to the program with shocking, psychopathic killings. And the agency's performance of its primary mission of intelligence gathering was conspicuously inadequate. The little stolen air force seemed to have done the job, but the air operations officer returned from Kinshasa to write a trip report of bungled air operations and bitter conflict with the Zairians. And, finally, the disengagement payoffs were clumsy and wasteful; while certain individuals pocketed almost $2 million, our former allies were left starving.

Most serious of all, the United States was exposed, dishonored, and discredited in the eyes of the world. We had lost and fifteen thousand Cubans were installed in Angola with all the adulation accruing to a young David who has slain the American Goliath.

When Potts returned from his tour of African stations, his secretary staged a surprise early morning coffee and donuts party to welcome him back. She assembled the Africa Division staff, and as Potts walked through the door everyone began singing "for he's a jolly good fellow, for he's a jolly good fellow . . . ," to his obvious embarassment.

I stood to one side, sipping my coffee and watching. "For he's a jolly good fellow!" Potts was a gentleman, correct and polite in his dealings with his staff. He and I were on cordial terms despite our profound disagreements. But I wondered if Mrs. Gearhardt, or the other widows and victims of our program, would think of us as jolly good fellows.

Our last task-force function was to produce recommendations for awards for everyone who had been involved, over one hundred people altogether. The rationale was that, although things hadn't gone very well, we had worked hard and the defeat was not our fault. Medals and awards would bolster morale. Writing these commendations was the ultimate challenge of my "professionalism," for I was in no mood to invent flowery platitudes about the things we had done. But the new director, a consummate politician, had suggested it, and Potts worked out a list of those to be commended: 26 medals and certificates, 140 letters of appreciation, and 1 meritorious salary increase. It took us weeks.

St. Martin, Potts, Colby, and Kissinger. The Jolly Good Fellows. And Stockwell. In another few years he'll be one too, if he gets his head straight.

Postscript

I knew I should resign. My illusions about the intelligence business were dead, but it was difficult to make the move. The CIA was the only world I knew. It provided close friends, financial security, and protection. I came in a way to appreciate Hamlet's dilemma. True, his choices were harder—suicide or murder—while I merely sought the courage to abandon my career and struggled to decide if I should also expose the agency.

For months I procrastinated. In the cynical post-Watergate times, why should I be the one to abandon a lucrative and comfortable career, and the friends and security that were part of it? Why not just take a cushy field assignment and run off the years until retirement. My jogging increased to ten miles a day, then twenty one Sunday, down the towpath further and further, and back again.

While I vacillated, the Horn and Central Branch was reorganized into a group and I was appointed the central branch chief, responsible for seven countries. Angola was one of those countries, and we handled it with a small desk staffed by two young officers. Branch chief was a good job for a GS 14 but I could not get interested either in the work or the prestige.

In September we were summoned to brief the new deputy director of operations, Bill Welles. A colleague made some introductory remarks about the Horn of Africa. Then Brenda MacElhinney, the new Ethiopia/Somalia section chief, took the floor and began to describe the situation in her countries. Ethiopia and Somalia were nearly at war. The Soviets had been arming Somalia with modern weapons; jets; tanks; rockets that would fire from the Somali coast to the capital of Ethiopia; and Soviet as well as Cuban advisors.

The United States was almost forcing its arms on the not too friendly Ethiopian leaders, as it sought to confront the Soviet Union. A senior State Department officer at the post had written a letter protesting the expanding U.S. involvement but it had been suppressed.

Welles commented that we should stay on top of the situation. The CIA might well be asked to launch a covert program in the Horn of Africa.

When he said that, I spoke out. The Horn wasn't my area of responsibility but I could not resist.

"Sir," I said, "are we really going to do it again? I mean, this war hasn't started yet, and we still have time to get ourselves out of it."

He looked at me and laughed outright.

"You'd like to win for once, wouldn't you? I know what you mean." He paused and then continued. "But remember, we're professionals. We might well be called on to harass the Soviets while they are making a move in Somalia, just so it won't be easy for them."*

The CIA was casting about for the next war, amoral, ruthless, eager to do its thing. Its thing being covert little games where the action was secret and no one kept score.

But history increasingly keeps score, and the CIA's operations are

*As the world turned, a year later, in the fall of 1977, the Soviets were expelled from Somalia and began to arm Ethiopia. The United States promptly leaped to the Somali side, threatening in February 1978 to arm Somalia if Ethiopia mounted hostile action across the border. This time, however, the State Department prevailed over the CIA option. The United States launched an effort through diplomatic channels to force a cessation of hostilities.

never secret for long. Inevitably they are exposed, by our press, by whistleblowers in our government, by our healthy compulsion to know the truth. Covert operations are incompatible with our system of government and we do them badly. Nevertheless, a succession of presidents and Henry Kissingers have been lured into questionable adventures for which, they are promised by the CIA, they will never be held accountable. Generally they are not, they move on to sinecures before the operations are fully exposed. Our country is left to face the consequences.

Claiming to be our Horatio at the shadowy bridges of the international underworld, the CIA maintains three thousand staff operatives overseas. Approximately equal to the State Department in numbers of staff employees overseas, the CIA extends its influence by hiring dozens of thousands of paid agents. Operationally its case officers "publish or perish"—an officer who does not generate operations does not get promoted. The officers energetically go about seeking opportunities to defend our national security.

The CIA's function is to provide the aggressive option in foreign affairs. The 40 Committee papers for the Angolan operation, written by the CIA did not list a peaceful option, although the State Department African Affairs Bureau and the U.S. consul general in Luanda had firmly recommended noninvolvement. In 1959 the CIA did not recommend to President Eisenhower that we befriend Fidel Castro and learn to live with him in Cuba. No, it presented the violent option, noting that it had the essential ingredients for a covert action: angry Cuban exiles, a haven in Guatemala, a beach in the Bay of Pigs, intelligence (later proven inaccurate) that the people of Cuba would rise up in support of an invasion. Presidents Eisenhower and Kennedy were persuaded. The operation was run, and it was bungled. Today we are still haunted by it.

At the end of World War II, we were militarily dominant, economically dominant, and we enjoyed a remarkable international credibility. With a modicum of restraint and self-confidence we could have laid the foundations of lasting world peace. Instead, we panicked, exaggerating the challenge of a Soviet Union which had just lost 70,000 villages, 1,710 towns, 4.7 million houses, and 20 million people in the war.*We set its dread KGB as a model for our own

*Daniel Yergin, *Shattered Peace* (Boston: Houghton Mifflin, 1977) p. 64.

alter ego in foreign affairs. In the words of the Hoover Commission report of 1954:

> There are no rules in such a game. Hitherto acceptable norms of human conduct do not apply. If the U.S. is to survive, long-standing American concepts of "fair play" must be reconsidered. We must develop effective espionage and counterespionage services. We must learn to subvert, sabotage and destroy our enemies by more clever, more sophisticated and more effective methods than those used against us. It may become necessary that the American people be acquainted with, understand and support this fundamentally repugnant philosophy.

It was a tragic, fallacious thesis. Our survival as a free people has obviously not been dependent on the fumbling activities of the clandestine services of the CIA, but on the dynamism of our economic system and the competitive energies of our people. Nor was Hoover's philosophy "fundamentally repugnant." Rather, it was *irresistible*, for it created an exhilarating new game where all social and legal restraints were dissolved. Cast as superpatriots, there were no rules, no controls, no laws, no moral restraints, and no civil rights for the CIA game-players. No individual in the world would be immune to their depradations, friends could be shafted and enemies destroyed, without compunction. It was an experiment in amorality, a real-life fantasy island, to which presidents, legislators, and the American people could escape, vicariously.

Not surprisingly, the mortals of the CIA were unable to cope with such responsibility. Over the years, a profound, arrogant, moral corruption set in. Incompetence became the rule. The clandestine services, established a solid record of failure: failure to produce good intelligence; failure to run successful covert operations; and failure to keep its operatives covert. And its directors also failed to respect the sacred responsibility they were given of extraconstitutional, covert license. Eventually, like any secret police, they became abusive of the people: they drugged American citizens; opened private mail; infiltrated the media with secret propaganda and disinformation; lied to our elected representatives; and set themselves above the law and the Constitution.

But our attachment to the CIA's clandestine services nevertheless seems to be unshaken. We still argue that, no matter what it does, the CIA is essential to our national security.

Where is the ancient American skepticism, the "show-me" attitude for which our pioneer forefathers were famous? We only need the CIA if it contributes positively to our national interests. Obviously, our nation needs broad intelligence coverage, and we have been getting it. It comes through the Directorate of Information of the CIA, the central intelligence office which collates, analyses, and disseminates information from all sources. Our presidents receive the DDI reports and briefings and, with some misgivings about their quality,* insist that they are essential to the wise functioning of that office. But even presidents forget to distinguish between the Directorate of Information and the clandestine services, quite possibly not realizing how little of the DDI's information actually comes from the covert human agents of its shadowy alter ego. The bulk of all raw intelligence, including vital strategic information, comes from overt sources and from the enormously expensive technical collection systems. The human agents, the spies, contribute less than 10 percent, a trivial part of the information which is reliable and of national security importance. Good agent penetrations of the "hard targets," individual spies who have confirmed access to strategic information, who are reliable, and who manage to report on a timely basis, are extremely rare. It is a shocking truth that the clandestine services have failed to recruit good agents in Moscow (Pentkovsky and Popov walked in on the British service which shared them with the CIA). It has failed completely in China—not even a walk-in. In Pyongyang, North Korea—not one Korean agent. And CIA case officers are literally afraid of the Mafia, the Chinese Tongs, and the international drug runners. They have recruited scores of thousands of Third World politicians, rebels, and European businessmen, whose voluminous reporting scarcely justifies the clandestine services' existence.

In March 1976 President Ford reorganized the National Security Council, renaming the 40 Committee, calling it the Operations Advisory Group. At that time he expanded the CIA charter, authorizing it to intervene even in countries which are friendly to the United States, and in those which are not threatened by internal subversion.

In January 1977, at the crest of two years of exposure of its short-

*See *Armies of Ignorance,* William Corson (New York: Dial, 1977).

comings, misdeeds, and depraved behavior, President Carter announced a reorganization of the intelligence community, which was based on the hypothesis that the clandestine services are essential to our national security. He elevated the position of the director of central intelligence and increased its powers. The offices that have traditionally been responsible for supervising the CIA were renamed. The Congress was reassured that it will receive briefings on CIA activities. Director Turner initiated a housecleaning, dismissing four hundred people, so the Directorate of Operations will be "lean and efficient."

The scope of CIA operations is not being reduced, and its overall effectiveness, including the cover of its operatives overseas is only being upgraded to a slight degree. The clandestine services still have their charter to do covert action. Only thirteen overseas positions are being cut; forty stations and bases will still function in Africa alone, from Nairobi to Ouagadougou, with case officers energetically seeking opportunities to protect our national security.

Not Horatio. The clandestine service is an unfortunate relic of the Cold War, entrenched in our government, protected by our self-indulgent, nostalgic commitment to its existence. The CIA presence in American foreign affairs will be judged by history as a surrender to the darker side of human nature.

Already we are paying dearly for indulging ourselves. As we have succeeded in making ourselves more like our enemies, more like the KGB, the world has taken note. Throughout Africa, Latin America, and Asia, at least, every legitimate American businessman, teacher, and official is suspiciously viewed as a probable CIA operative, capable of dangerous betrayals. The world knows that, in fact, numbers of actual CIA case officers are posing as just such people, while they recruit agents, bribe officials, and support covert adventures. The positive contribution of such activity to our national security is dubious. But mounting numbers of victims, the millions of people whose lives have been trampled or splattered by CIA operations are increasingly cynical of America. Because of the CIA the world is a more dangerous place. Americans have reduced credibility. Worst of all, by retaining the CIA we are accepting ourselves as a harsh and ruthless people. It's the wrong game for a great nation. And the players we've got are losers.

Appendixes

APPENDIX I: *An Angolan Chronology*

1483	Portugal explores along Angolan coast.
1575	Portugal begins slave raids.
1900–1932	Three major tribes conquered, but all resist consolidation of Portuguese rule.

Bakongo	*Mbundu*	*Ovimbundu*
Northern Angola	North Central Angola (Luanda)	Central Angola (50 percent total population of Angola)

Modern nationalist movements of Angola

Holden Roberto, president FNLA or National Front—1961, most warlike. Based in Zaire; initiated bloody revolt of 1961. Sporadic contact with CIA.	Agostinho Neto, Marxist intellectual, president MPLA— Popular Movement; best political organization. Guerrillas fought from Zambian base and Congo (Brazzaville). Sporadic help from Russia.	Jonas Savimbi, president UNITA— 1966. Based in Zambia. Personally led guerrilla fighting from 1967–present. Twelve officers trained by North Koreans.

1961	Protracted guerrilla warfare begins, waged separately by all three movements, opposed by Portuguese army using NATO arms supplied by the United States.
1969	NSSM 39 ("Tar Baby" Report).
April 1974	The Portuguese army, tired of colonial wars, seizes government of Portugal.
1973–1974	FNLA accepts large arms deliveries and advisors from China and UNITA receives arms from China.
May 1974	112 Chinese advisors join FNLA in Zaire. China ships 450 tons of arms for FNLA.

July 7, 1974

CIA begins covert funding of Roberto (not approved by 40 Committee) and lobbies in Washington for support for FNLA.

August 1974

Soviets react to Chinese and United States initiatives by announcing moral support of MPLA.

Fall 1974

Soviets begin filtering small amounts of arms to MPLA via Congo (Brazzaville).

January 15, 1975

In the Alvor Accord all three liberation movements agree to peaceful competition, under Portuguese supervision, for elections and independence scheduled for November 11, 1975.

January 26, 1975

40 Committee approves $300,000 for Roberto.

February 1975

FNLA destroys prospect for peaceful solution by attacking MPLA in Luanda and northern Angola.

March 1975

Soviets respond by escalating their arms shipments to the MPLA. Soviet and Cuban advisors go to Angola.

July 1975

40 Committee approves $14 million paramilitary program to support FNLA and UNITA against MPLA.

MPLA evicts FNLA and UNITA from Luanda.

United States ignores Senegal's appeals for United Nations or Organization of African Unity mediation.

CIA arms deliveries begin going into Angola via the Kinshasa airport.

Zairian army armored units join FNLA and UNITA in Angola.

August 1975   FNLA force threatens Luanda.

                                     CIA lying to U.S. Congress about arms
                                     deliveries into Angola and use of
                                     American advisors.

                                     U.S. assistant secretary of state resigns
                                     in protest of U.S. paramilitary
                                     intervention.

Early September 1975   MPLA regains initiative. Holds open
                                     press conference to show captured U.S.
                                     arms which have fresh U.S. Air Force
                                     shipping labels.

Mid–September 1975   Zaire army commits two
                                     paracommando battalians.

September 1975   CIA initiates policy of feeding biased
                                     information to the U.S. press. CIA
                                     discourages UNITA/MPLA discussion
                                     of peaceful solution. State Department
                                     rebuffs MPLA overtures for discussions.

October 1975   Cuba begins introducing regular army
                                     units into Angola.

                                     Secret South African armored column
                                     joins UNITA and sweeps north. South
                                     Africa/CIA collaboration in the field.

November 12, 1975   MPLA/Cubans rout and demoralize
                                     FNLA/Zaire army north of Luanda.

November 1975   CIA begins recruiting mercenaries in
                                     France.

December 1975   CIA begins recruiting 300 Portuguese
                                     mercenaries.

November–December 1975   CIA still lying to Congress about arms
                                     and advisors used in Angola;
                                     administration loses battle for
                                     congressional support.

January 1976   South Africans withdraw.

January–February 1976   Large Cuban/MPLA army, with jets,

	helicopters, and heavy armor crushes FNLA and UNITA.
April 1976	CIA payoffs, $3.85 million given to people who supported the program.
June 1976	CIA begins writing citations and commendations for over one hundred of its people who were in the Angola program.

APPENDIX 2: *Control and Direction of U.S. Foreign Intelligence within the National Security System*

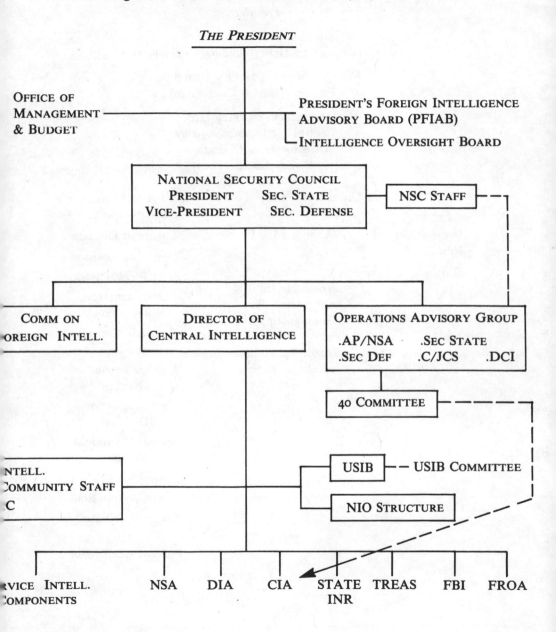

APPENDIX 3: *Organizational Chain of Command of the Angola Program*

President

National Security Council
(Dominated by Henry Kissinger 1969–1976)

Operations Advisory Group
(Formerly the 40 Committee)

Interagency Working Group
Central Intelligence Agency
Directorate of Operations
(Clandestine Services)

Africa Division

East Asia Division
(Vietnam Operations)

Horn & Central
Branch

Angola Task Force

European Division

Kinshasa Station

Near-East Division

(A temporary office
responsible from
headquarters for
planning, supervision
and operation of the
Angola paramilitary
operation, August
1975–June 1976.)

Soviet Block Division

Latin American
Division

Domestic Contacts
Division

Foreign Resources
Division

Technical Services
Division

Special Operations
Group

Division "D"

Covert Action Staff

Counterintelligence
Staff

Foreign Intelligence
Staff

APPENDIX 4: *Summary of* American Champion *Cargo**

I Rifles and Antitank:
   Rifle, M-16   9,000
   Ammunition, M-16   5,000,000 rounds
   LAWS, M-72   6,000

II Supplemental Equipment:
    Swift boats (57 ft. and 55 ft.)   2
    Machine guns, 50 cal. w/tripod, M-6   50
    Mortar, 81 mm.   53
    Mortar, 4.2 inch   18
    Radio, PRC-77   300
    Batteries, BA4386   3,000

III Ammunition:
     Machine gun, 50 cal.   102,000
     HE, 81 mm.   9,630
     Smoke   1,080

IV Vehicles:
    1/4-ton truck, M-151A1   20
    1 1/4-ton truck, M-715   20
    2 1/2-ton truck, M-35A2   20
    1 1/2-ton truck, M-105   20
    Large trucks   60
    Trailers   20

V Tentage and Material:
   GP tents (medium)   500
   Pr. boots   10,000
   Pr. socks   20,000
   Web belts   5,000

VI 30 Cal. Package Plus Excess
    Carbines (28,800); .45 cal. pistols (1,350); .45 cal. machine guns
    (5,379); .30 cal. light machine guns (1,814); 3.5 rocket-launchers
    (380); 60 mm. mortars (999); radio ANPRC-10 (97); radio ANGRC
    9/87 (90); 7.3 million rounds of ammunition.

*Reconstructed by the author from his notes.

VII   7.62 Cal. Package
Rifles (5,810); 9 mm. cal. pistols (350); 9 mm. cal. submachine guns (810); 7.62 cal. light machine guns (460); 40 mm. grenade-launchers (620); 66 mm. rocket-launchers (1,800); 60 mm. mortars (140); radios ANPRC 25/77 (270); radio Racal TRA92 (70); 8.2 million rounds of ammunition.

VIII   Miscellaneous
60 trucks
20 trailers
25 rubber boats with motors

APPENDIX 5: *Total Arms and Materiel Delivered to FNLA and UNITA**

TYPE	QUANTITY/KIND	
Missiles	26	SA-7 "GRAIL" Anti-aircraft, surface-to-air
Heavy Weapons	14	120mm mortars
	14	106mm recoilless rifles
	38	4.2 inch mortars
	90	3.5 inch rocket launchers
	20	82mm mortars
	80	81mm mortars
	319	60mm mortars
	20	.50 cal heavy machine guns
	2	12.7mm heavy machine guns
	25	RPG-7 rocket grenade launchers
Machine Guns, Rifles and Individual Weapons	4,210	66mm M-72 LAW's
	410	40mm M-79 grenade launchers
	240	.30 cal light machine guns
	124	7.62mm light machine guns
	10	.30 cal BAR
	7,771	7.62mm rifles
	12,215	.30 cal carbines
	66	9mm submachine guns
	150	9mm pistols
	1,170	hand grenades
Ammunition	3,430	rds 120mm HE mortar
	1,974	rds 106mm HEAT recoilless rifle
	1,800	rds 106mm HEP recoilless rifle
	2,549	rds 4.2 inch HE mortar
	100	rds 4.2 inch WP mortar
	100	rds 4.2 inch ILLUM mortar
	1,649	rds 3.5 inch rocket launcher
	2,456	rds 90mm HE
	2,032	rds 90mm HEAT
	9,743	rds 81mm HE mortar

*This is an unclassified CIA document.

810	rds 81mm WP mortar
249	rds 81mm ILLUM mortar
19,821	rds 60 mm HE mortar
1,760	rds 60mm WP mortar
490	rds 60mm ILLUM
108,758	rds 40mm (M-79)
5,060	rds .50 cal spot (F/U/W 106mm RR)
17,345	rds .50 cal LINK API
12,700	rds 12.7mm LINK
4,240,420	rds 7.62mm
849,000	rds .30 cal LINK
3,406,400	rds .30 cal carbine
46,080	rds 9mm

Miscellaneous		
	200	radio PRC-25/77
	20	radio ANGRC-9
	10	radio RF-301
	4	radio TAR-244
	49	radio TRA-921
	1,800	lbs medical supplies

(Thirty-six Panhard armored cars and artillery provided by Zaire are not included.)

APPENDIX 6: *Total Arms and Materiel Delivered to Zaire for Angola Program**

TYPE		*QUANTITY/KIND*
Armored Vehicles	12	Armored personnel carriers M-113
Missiles	50	SA-7 "GRAIL" anti-aircraft, surface-to-air
Heavy Weapons	14	106mm recoilless rifles
	38	4.2 inch mortars
	1,272	82mm, 81mm, 60mm mortars
	180	3.5 inch rocket launchers
	64	.50 cal, 12.7mm heavy machine guns
	25	RPG-7 rocket grenade launchers
Machine guns, Rifles and Individual Weapons	9,413	LAW's
	641	40mm M-79 grenade launchers
	2,248	.30 cal, 7.62mm light machine guns
	17,258	7.62mm, 5.56mm rifles
	28,800	.30 cal carbines
	6,121	.45 cal, 9mm sub-machine guns
	1,668	.45 cal, 9mm pistols
	96,300	Hand grenades
Vehicles	60	Trucks, 1/4 ton, 1 1/4 ton, 2 1/2 ton
	20	Trailers, 1 1/2 ton
	2	Swift boats, 58' and 50'
	25	Boats (rubber), with motors
Ammunition	3,140	rds 106mm HEAT and HEP recoilless rifle
	1,000	rds 120mm HE mortar
	4,454	rds 4.2 inch HE, SP, and ILLUM mortar
	1,980	rds 3.5 inch rocket launcher
	16,799	rds 81mm HE, WP, and

*This is an unclassified CIA document.

	ILLUM mortar
64,620	rds 60mm HE, WP, and ILLUM mortar
261,840	rds 40mm (M-79)
17,200	rds .50 cal spot (F/U/W 106mm RR)
112,726	rds .50 cal, 12.7mm link
2,811,947	rds .30 cal, 7.62 × 54mm link
14,255,866	rds 7.62mm, 5.56mm rifle
5,332,386	rds .30 cal carbine
290,400	rds 7.62 × 39mm (F/U/W AK-47)
3,508,807	rds .45, 9mm sub-machine gun

Miscellaneous		
	641	Radio PRC-25, PRC-77, PRC-10
	100	Radio ANGRC-9/87
	12	Radio AN/WRC-46/47
	68	Radio FM-1B, FM-5B
	108	Radio TRA-921
	25	Radio RF-301
	50	Radio HT-2A
	6	Radio TAR-224
	4	Radio BEI-990
		Tentage, Medical supplies, Fieldgear
		Vehicle parts, Aircraft parts, Boat parts
		Demoliton materials, Combat rations

APPENDIX 7

Adm. Stansfield Turner
Director, Central Intelligence Agency
Washington, D.C.

Sir:*

We have not met and will not have the opportunity of working together, as you are coming into the Central Intelligence Agency when I am leaving. Although I am disassociating myself from the Agency, I have read with considerable interest about your appointment and listened to some of your comments.

You have clearly committed yourself to defending the Agency from its detractors and to improving its image, and this has stirred a wave of hope among many of its career officers. However, others are disappointed that you have given no indication of intention, or even awareness of the need, for the internal housecleaning that is so conspicuously overdue the Agency.

You invited Agency officers to write you their suggestions or grievances, and you promised personally to read all such letters. While I no longer have a career interest, having already submitted my resignation, numerous friends in the DDO (Deputy Directorate for Operations) have encouraged me to write you, hoping that it might lead to measures which would upgrade the clandestine services from its present mediocre standards to the elite organization it was once reputed to be.

While I sympathize with their complaints, I have agreed to write this letter more to document the circumstances and conditions which led to my own disillusionment with CIA.

First, let me introduce myself. I was until yesterday a successful GS 14 with 12 years in the Agency, having served seven full tours of duty including Chief of Base, Lubumbashi; Chief of Station, Bujumbura; Officer in Charge of Tay Ninh Province in Vietnam; and Chief, Angola Task Force. My file documents what I was told occasionally, that I could realistically aspire to top managerial positions in the Agency.

I grew up in Zaire, a few miles from the Kapanga Methodist Mission Station, which was recently "liberated" by Katangese invaders, and I speak fluent English and Tshiluba, "High" French and smatterings of Swahili and other dialects.

---

*This letter was published as an open letter in the April 10, 1977 edition of Outlook section of the *Washington Post,* immediately after the author's resignation from the CIA.

My disillusionment was progressive throughout four periods of my career. First, during three successive assignments in Africa from 1966 through 1977 I increasingly questioned the value and justification of the reporting and operations we worked so hard to generate.

In one post, Abidjan, there was no Eastern bloc or Communist presence, no subversion, limited United States interests and a stable government. The three of us competed with State Department officers to report on President Houphouet-Boigny's health and local politics.

I attempted to rationalize that my responsibility was to contribute, and not to evaluate the importance of my contribution which should be done by supergrades in Washington. However, this was increasingly difficult as I looked up through a chain of command which included, step-by-step: a) the Branch Chief, who had never served in Africa and was conspicuously ignorant of Black Africa; b) the Chief of Operations, who was a senior officer although he had never served an operational overseas tour and was correspondingly naive about field operations; and c) the Division Chief, who was a political dilettante who had never served an operational tour in Africa . . . Their leadership continuously reflected their inexperience and ignorance.

Standards of operations were low in the field, considerable energy was devoted to the accumulation of perquisites and living a luxurious life at the taxpayer's expense. When I made Chief of Station, a supergrade took me out for drinks and, after welcoming me to the exclusive inner club of "chiefs," proceeded to brief me on how to supplement my income by an additional $3,000 to $4,000 per year, tax-free, by manipulating my representational and operational funds. This was quite within the regulations. For example, the COS Kinshasa last year legally collected over $9,000 from CIA for the operation of his household.

Most case officers handled 90 per cent of their operations in their own living rooms, in full view of servants, guards and neighbors. And I expect few individuals would accept CIA recruitments if they knew how blithely their cases are discussed over the phone: "Hello, John . . . when you meet your friend after the cocktail party tonight . . . you know, the one with the old Mercedes . . . be sure to get that receipt for $300 . . . and pick up the little Sony, so we can fix the signaling device."

In Burundi we won a round in the game of dirty tricks against the Soviets. Shortly after my arrival we mounted an operation to exploit the Soviets' vulnerabilities of having a disproportionately large embassy staff and a fumbling, obnoxious old ambassador, and discredit them in the eyes of the Barundi. We were apparently successful, as the Barundi requested that the ambassador not return when he went on leave, and they ordered the Soviets to reduce their staff by 50 per cent.

We were proud of the operation, but a few months later the Soviets assigned a competent career diplomat to the post, and he arrived to receive a cordial welcome from the Barundi, who were more than a little nervous at their brashness, and eager to make amends. For the rest of my tour, relations were remarkably better between the two countries than before our operation. The operation won us some accolades, but it left me with profound reservations about the real value of the operational games we play in the field.

Later Africa Division policy shifted its emphasis from reporting on local politics to the attempted recruitments of the so-called hard targets, i.e., the accessible eastern European diplomats who live exposed lives in little African posts. I have listened to the enthusiastic claims of success of this program and its justification in terms of broader national interests, and I have been able to follow some of these operations wherein Agency officers have successfully befriended and allegedly recruited drunken Soviet, Czech, Hungarian, and Polish diplomats by servicing their venal and sexual (homo- and hetero-) weaknesses.

Unfortunately, I observed, and colleagues in the Soviet Division confirmed to me, that none of these recruited individuals has had access to truly vital strategic information. Instead they have reported mostly on their colleagues' private lives in the little posts. Not one has returned to his own country, gained access to strategic information and reported satisfactorily.

Agency operations in Vietnam would have discouraged even the most callous, self-serving of adventurers. It was a veritable Catch-22 of unprofessional conduct. Ninety-eight per cent of the operations were commonly agreed to be fabrications but were papered over and promoted by aware case officers because of the "numbers game" requirements from Headquarters for voluminous reporting . . . At the end, in April 1975, several senior CIA field officers were caught by surprise, fled in hasty panic and otherwise abandoned their responsibilities.

One senior officer left the country five days before the final evacuation, telling subordinates he was going to visit his family and would return. Later it became apparent he never intended to return and was abdicating all responsibility for the people who had worked for him and for the CIA in his area. Almost ninety percent of the Vietnamese employees from his area were abandoned in the evacuation. Numerous middle- and lower-grade officers vigoriously protested this conduct, but all of these senior officers, including the one who fled, have subsequently received responsible assignments with the promise of promotions.

After Vietnam I received the assignment of Chief, Angola Task Force. This was despite the fact that I and many other officers in the CIA and State Department thought the intervention irresponsible and ill-conceived, both in terms of the advancement of United States interests, and the moral question of contributing substantially to the escalation of an already bloody civil war, when there was no possibility that we would make a full commitment and ensure the victory of our allies.

From a chess player's point of view the intervention was a blunder. In July 1975, the MPLA was clearly winning, already controlling 12 of the 15 provinces, and was thought by several responsible American officials and senators to be the best-qualified to run Angola; nor was it hostile to the United States. The CIA committed $31 million to opposing the MPLA victory, but six months later the MPLA had nevertheless decisively won, and 15,000 Cuban regular army troops were entrenched in Angola with the full sympathy of much of the Third World, and the support of several influential African chiefs of state who previously had been critical of any extracontinental intervention in African affairs.

At the same time the United States was solidly discredited, having been exposed for covert military intervention in African affairs, having allied itself with South Africa, and having lost.

This is not Monday-morning quarterbacking. Various people foresaw all this and also predicted that the covert intervention would ultimately be exposed and curtailed by the United States Senate. I myself warned the Interagency Working Group in October 1975, that the Zairian invasion of northern Angola would be answered by the introduction of large numbers of Cuban troops—10,000 to 15,000 I said—and would invite an eventual retaliatory invasion of Zaire from Angola.

Is anyone surprised that a year later the Angolan government has permitted freshly armed Zairian exiles to invade the Shaba Province of Zaire? Is the CIA a good friend? Having encouraged Mobutu to tease the Angolan lion, will it help him repel its retaliatory charge? Can one not argue that our Angolan program provoked the present invasion of Zaire, which may well lead to its loss of the Shaba's rich copper mines?

Yes, I know you are attempting to generate token support to help Zaire meet its crisis; that you are seeking out the same French mercenaries the CIA sent into Angola in early 1976. These are the men who took the CIA money but fled the first time they encountered heavy shelling.

Some of us in the Angolan program were continuously frustrated and disappointed with Headquarters' weak leadership of the field, especially its inability to control the Kinshasa station as it purchased ice plants and ships for local friends, and on one occasion tried to get the CIA to pay Mobutu $2 million for an airplane which was worth only $600,000. All of this and much more, is documented in the cable traffic, if it hasn't been destroyed.

I came away from the Angolan program in the spring of 1976 determined to reassess the CIA and my potential for remaining with it. I read several books with a more objective mind, and began to discuss the present state of the American Intelligence establishment from a less defensive position. I read [Morton] Halperin's book and [Joseph] Smith's and [David] Philips's. I was seriously troubled to discover the extent to which the CIA has in fact violated its charter and begun surveilling and mounting operations against American citizens. I attempted to count the hundreds, thousands of lives that have been taken in thoughtless little CIA adventures.

A major point was made to me when I was recruited in 1964 that the CIA was high-minded and scrupulously kept itself clean of truly dirty skullduggery such as killings and coups, etc. At that exact time the CIA was making preparations for the assassination of certain Latin American politicians and covering its involvement in the assassination of Patrice Lumumba.

Eventually we learned Lumumba was killed, not by our poisons, but beaten to death, apparently by men who were loyal to men who had Agency cryptonyms and received Agency salaries. In death he became an eternal martyr and by installing Mobutu in the Zairian presidency, we committed ourselves to the "other side," the losing side in Central and Southern Africa.

We cast ourselves as the dull-witted Goliath, in a world of eager young Davids. I for one have applauded as Ambassador [Andrew] Young thrashed about trying to break us loose from this role and I keenly hope President Carter will continue to support him in some new thinking about Africa.

But, one asks, has the CIA learned its lesson and mended its ways since the revelations of Watergate and the subsequent investigations? Is it now, with the help of oversight committees, policed and self-policing?

While I was still serving as the Central Branch Chief in Africa Division last fall, a young officer in my branch was delegated away from my supervision to write a series of memos discussing with the Justice Department the possibilities for prosecution of an American mercenary named David Bufkin.

Bufkin had been involved in the Angola conflict, apparently receiving monies from Holden Roberto, quite possibly from funds he received from the CIA. In anticipation of the possibility that during a trial of Bufkin the defense might demand to see his CIA file under the Freedom of Information Act, it was carefully purged.

Certain documents containing information about him were placed in other files where they could easily be retrieved but would not be exposed if he demanded and gained access to his own file. I heard of this and remonstrated, but was told by the young officer that in his previous Agency assignment he had served on a staff which was responding to Senate investigations, and that such tactics were common—"We did it all the time"— as the Agency attempted to protect incriminating information from investigators.

None of this has addressed the conditions which my former colleagues have begged me to expose. They are more frustrated by the constipation that exists at the top and middle levels of the DDO, where an ingrown clique of senior officers has for a quarter of a century controlled and exploited their power and prestige under the security of clandestinity and safe from exposure, so that no matter how drunken, inept, or corrupt their management of a station might be, they are protected, promoted and reassigned.

The organization currently belongs to the old, to the burned out. Young officers, and there are some very good ones, must wait until generations retire before they can move up. Mediocre performances are guaranteed by a promotion system wherein time in grade and being a "good ole boy" are top criteria, i.e., there are no exceptional promotions and the outstanding individual gets his promotions at the same time as the "only-good" and even some of the "not-really-so-good" officers, and he must wait behind a line of tired old men for the truly challenging field assignments.

These young officers are generally supervised by unpromotable middle-grade officers, who for many years have been unable to go overseas and participate personally in operational activity. These conditions are obviously discouraging to dynamic young people, demoralizingly so, and several have told me they are also seeking opportunities outside the Agency.

With each new Director they hope there will be a housecleaning and reform, but each Director comes and goes, seven in my time, preoccupied with broader matters of state, uttering meaningless and inaccurate platitudes about conditions and standards inside the DDO. The only exception was James Schlesinger, who initiated a housecleaning but was transferred to the Department of Defense before it had much effect.

You, sir, have been so bold as to state your intention to abrogate American constitutional rights, those of freedom of speech, in order to defend and protect the American intelligence establishment. This strikes me as presumptuous of you, especially before you have even had a good look inside the CIA to see if it is worth sacrificing constitutional rights for.

If you get the criminal penalties you are seeking for the disclosure of classified information, or even the civil penalties which President Carter and Vice-President Mondale have said they favor, then Americans who work for the CIA could not, when they find themselves embroiled in criminal and immoral activity which is commonplace in the Agency, expose that activity without risking jail or poverty as punishment for speaking out. Cynical men, such as those who gravitate to the top of the CIA, could then by classifying a document or two protect and cover up illegal actions with relative impunity.

I predict that the American people will never surrender to you the right of any individual to stand in public and say whatever is in his heart and mind. That right is our last line of defense against the tyrannies and invasions of privacy which events of recent years have demonstrated are more than paranoiac fantasies. I am enthusiastic about the nation's prospects under the new administration, and I am certain President Carter will reconsider his position on this issue.

And you, sir, may well decide to address yourself to the more appropriate task of setting the Agency straight from the inside out.

Sincerely,
John Stockwell

Index